AF541774

BANKER AND CUSTOMER RELATIONSHIP

BANKER AND CUSTOMER RELATIONSHIP

By

Dr. Penumarthi Veera Venkat Satyanarayana

Director & Associate Professor
VS Lakshmi MBA Colleges for Women
Kakinada (Andhra Pradesh)
(India)

DISCOVERY PUBLISHING HOUSE PVT. LTD.
NEW DELHI-110 002

Published by:
Tilak Wasan
DISCOVERY PUBLISHING HOUSE PVT. LTD.
4383/4B, Ansari Road, Darya Ganj
New Delhi-110 002 (India)
Phone : +91-11-23279245, 43596064-65
Fax : +91-11-23253475
E-mail : discoverypublishinghouse@gmail.com
sales@discoverypublishinggroup.com
parul.wasan@gmail.com
web : www.discoverypublishinggroup.com

***First Edition:* 2013**

ISBN: 978-93-5056-237-6

Banker and Customer Relationship

Printed at:
Dynamic Printers
Delhi

Dedicated

to

HOLY LORD JESUS CHRIST

Preface

The relationship between a banker and a customer depends on the activities; products or services provided by bank to its customers or availed by the customer. Thus the relationship between a banker and customer is the transactional relationship. Bank's business depends much on the strong bondage with the customer. "Trust" plays an important role in building healthy relationship between a banker and customer.

The subject of customer experience in retail banking has never been more important, never been timelier, and never been more essential to achieving and maintaining business success. Banks win by getting, keeping, and growing customers. How to get more customers, how to keep them longer, and how to increase the value of each individual customer—that is the critical challenge that must be met in order to grow organically. Overcoming that challenge starts with the realization that the quality of customers' experiences is key.

Today, more than ever before, the ability to maximize customer loyalty through close and durable relationships is critical to retail banks' ability to grow their businesses. As banks strive to create and manage customer relationships, several emerging trends affect the approach and tools banks employ to achieve sustainable growth. These trends reflect a fundamental change in the way banks interact with the customers they have " and those they want to acquire.

Customers create value for a bank in two ways. First, customers buy more (or less) products and services today and thereby increase (or decrease) the bank's current-period cash flows. Second, customers change their intention to buy products and services tomorrow and thereby impact the bank's future cash flows. What influences both of these factors? When a customer of a bank has a poor experience and decides to reduce future purchases as a consequence, the bank has lost value at that very instant.

The book is divided into eight chapters. The first chapter of this book seeks to explain the historical perspective of banking sector in India, Banking System and banking business. The second chapter discusses literature review and research design. Chapter three explains selected banks profile and growth. The growth of banking services in India, the competition scenario, the policies and organization system for the development of Indian banking sector are discussed in Chapter IV.

Chapter V converse the nature of the Banker-Customer relationship. Here the book seeks to determine the relationship by explaining the possible areas of the relationship based on the usual customs. The findings of the employees' opinion survey are presented in detail in Chapter VI, while the findings of consumers' opinion survey are shown in Chapter VII. The conclusions and suggestions are presented in Chapter VIII.

Author

Acknowledgement

The making of the Book ***Banker and Customer Relationship*** included help, support, guidance and directions of more than many of my teachers, well wishers, colleagues and friends. It is my duty to acknowledge each and every one of these for the same. It may not be possible to thank all of them in person here. However, I express my deepest sense of gratitude to one and all involved.

In the first place, I sincerely thank Prof. G .N. Brahmanandam, my Guide, Principal, Dean, Faculty in Commerce and Management Studies, Acharya Nagarjuna University, Guntur for his guidance and valuable suggestions that lead to bringing this work into the present textbook form. I Specially thank Prof. Belverd E. Needles, Jr., Ph.D. CPA Professor of Accounting, School of Accountancy, Vice-President-Education American Accounting Association, DePaul University, USA for his continuous related interactions during the preparation of the Book. Many thanks to Prof.B.Parvathiswara Rao Rector, Andhra University, Visakhapatnam for his constant support. I also express my respectful thanks to Prof. DJPN Reddy, Director, and Dr.V. Sitaramaraju, Chairman, VSL Group of Institutions, Kakinada for providing the necessary encouragement. I owe my gratitude to the interest shown and help rendered towards the completion of the work by Prof. P. Rajendra Karmarkar, Special Officer and Prof. B.Kuberudu, Head, Department of Management studies, AUMSN PG Centre, Kakinada. I am immensely grateful to Dr. S.G. Rama Rao, Associate Professor, V. S. Lakshmi Institute of Computer Applications and Management Studies for Women, Kakinada who helped me during the preparation of manuscript.

Last but not the least; I extended my thanks to the Publisher, Discovery Publishing House for bringing out this work in print form. Mention must be made of the moral support from my wife Kopparthi ChantiAmmai and my son P.Narayana Pratap that has motivated me to complete this book.

Dr. P.V.V. Satyanarayana

Contents

CHAPTER

Introduction

The new communication focused on how its services have changed keeping in mind the changing needs of today's consumers. Over the past couple of years, made a concerted bid to don a new persona that is more in sync with the times. Most of them have made aggressive efforts in last few years to set up core banking networks, internet and mobile banking. While they continue to have large branch networks, their ATM count has also increased considerably. Thanks to the regulatory compulsion of compliance with the Basel II frame work, they have invested big bucks in improving risk management capabilities, especially credit scoring modes and databases top manage operational risk. Economic liberalization. Globalization, information technology revolution, changing customer requirements and increasing competition have posed a lot of challenges to the existing banking sector in India. With E-banking, the brick and mortar structure of the traditional banking gets converted into a click and portal model thereby giving real shape to the concept of virtual banking. The new generation banks and foreign banks have expanded banking services through ATMs, Internet banking, Mobile banking, Home banking etc.,

Now the major objective of both private and public sector

Indian banks is to attract a large customer base by offering more delivery channels, giving more importance to customer relationships. The success of new service like Internet banking, mobile banking, ATM facility, home banking, priority Banking insurance products, investment and financial advisory services, de-mat Account, 24 hour tele-banking, etc., is highly depends upon its usage by the customers. The Present study is an attempt to examine how far the banks in Costal Andhra Pradesh have succeeded in popularizing their new banking services. The study also tries to find out the reasons for low level of awareness of customers on various services and products. The findings may help the banks to widen their customer base and to detect the deficiencies in their present services and can be of useful for policy formulation in this sphere.

The banking sector in India has undergone tremendous change during the past quarter century. Gone are the days when commercial banks were only "purveyor of credit", now they serve in catalytic agents in the economic progress of the nation. There was a period when only city dwellers alone were able to access and enjoy their services. Till the nationalization of 14 major commercial banks in 1969, the banks in India strictly adhered to traditional commercial banking principles. After nationalization banks have introduced umpteen diversification's and innovations in their services and business. Now banks extend their services even to common people and their activities touch even unbanked areas.

The Indian banking industry has undergone major changes after liberalization and globalization reforms in the 1990's. In order to improve the functioning of the financial sector, particularly the banking sector, in India, Narashimham Committee (1991), Goiporia Committee (1990), Rangarajan Committee (1993) and Saraf Committee (1994) have proposed wide-ranging measures. The Narashimham Committee (I & II) made several recommendations to improve the productivity, efficiency and profitability of the banking and financial systems. In September 1990 RBI setup another committee on customer services, under the chairmanship of Sri M.N. Goiporia, Chairman, State Banks of India to examine the problems of customer services in banks and suggested measures to improve the situation. The Rangarajan Committee (1993) had highlighted that computerization must be looked upon as a means to improve the quality of customer services and enhance its efficiency. The Saraf Committee (1994) on technology issues advocated the system of Electronic Fund Transfer. Accordingly, the RBI started EFT system in 1996.

In 1993 the RBI through its announcement approved the entry of foreign banks. The economic reforms envisaged by the Government of India allowed establishing of new private sector banks. UTI Bank promoted by the UTI, LIC, GIC and its four associates was the first of the new generation bank to have begun operations in 1994. The Housing and Development Finance Corporation Ltd, was amongst the first to receive an approval from the RBI (1994) to set up a bank (HDFC Bank Ltd.) in the private sector. ICICI bank, India's second largest bank was formed in 1995 at the initiative of World Bank and Government of India. Global Trust Bank, Centurion Bank, IDBI Bank and Kotak Mahindra Bank also came into operation. ING Vysya Bank Ltd. Is an entity formed with the merger of erstwhile Vysya Bank Ltd. with ING of Dutch during 2002. The Oriental Bank of Commerce took over Global Trust Bank in 2005 when it collapsed. In 2005 IDBI Bank merged into IDBI Ltd. with the sanction of the RBI. Centurion Bank and Bank of Punjab were merged and formed Centurion Bank of Punjab in 2005. The new generation banks rapidly expanded their network by way of opening branches in cities and towns. The policy makers are now striving hard to down size the public sector banks and to consolidate them into a few model and giant Global Corporate entities through mergers and amalgamations.

New generation and foreign banks are operating in a highly sophisticated environment by offering up-to-date products and services. Improved customer service has become very important for public sector and old private banks to survive and to grow in the emerging deregulated financial markets. Consequently, banks are under increasing pressure to offer today what customer would expect tomorrow. The banks now compete with one another to offer value-added services to customers to widen their client bases. Up-to-date products and services are offered to the customers by Indian banks viz. ATM, Any Where Banking, International Debit cum ATM Card, One window Service, Mobile Phone Recharge Facility, Priority Banking Insurance Products, Investment and Financial Advisory Services, Demat Account, 24 Hour Tele-Banking, At Par Cheque Facility, Electronic Fund Transfer Clearing Service, MICR Cheque Processing, Banking Ombudsmen Scheme, Computerized Statements, Payment of Insurance Premium, Utility Bills etc.

Services Introduced as A Result of Financial Sector Reforms

For measuring the awareness level of customers about new services, ten important banking services/products were identified. The variables are identified by the researcher on the basis of available literature and discussions with banks officials. All questions in the schedule are qualitative in nature. The following are the variables identified by the researchers for the study.

Automated Teller Machine (ATM)

This is a modern technology introduced by the banks to enable the customers to have access to money round the clock and also throughout the year. The ATM enables a customer to withdraw and deposit cash and cheque, check balance in account, print mini account statement, transfer funds between own accounts, payment of utility bills, recharge prepaid mobile card etc., By the end of 1990, Indian private and public sector banks have come up with their own ATM networks under the initiative of the Indian Bank Association in Mumbai. The Bank of India is the first nationalized bank to provide ATM have brought about a great change in the quality of service and gaining popularity among customers. It is against this background the researcher identified that it is an important variable to study the awareness level of customers.

Any Where Banking

Any where banking is a modern technology introduced by connecting all branches of a bank through a net work to enable the customers to carry on banking transactions across the country. Earlier banking operations of a customer were restricted to the particular branch in which the account was maintained. With the introduction of this facility by banks customers can operate their account in any branch of the bank across the country during banking hours. This facility is also becoming immensely popular among customers and has been giv en due importance in this study.

Internet Banking

With the Internet banking facility the customer of the bank is just a click away from the bank. The customer can check their account status, fund transfer, make bill payment, place online requests for new cheque books, review term deposits etc. In addition, it enables the customers to conduct online trading, mutual fund purchases, online shopping, and payments to services such as insurance, electricity, telephone and mobile services across the country. Banking products and services such as deposits, remittances, credit card etc. as well as all-important banking information's can be made available with easy access to customers on Internet. Customers can make use of these services with out being restricted by office hours, queues, tellers, and waiting. In view of the above facts, Internet banking facility is considered as an important variable.

Credit Cards

Credit care or plastic money is a convenient medium of exchange. It enables its holder to purchase goods and services form the member establishments with out using hard money. Credit cards are made of plastic material and are designed to avoid the use of either cash or cheque. They can use them in all those establishments, which have agreed to accept them. The credit card organizer makes payment to the concerned establishment once in a month and sends an invoice to the credit card holder for all his purchases of the previous month. Banks issue different types of credit cards and credit limit of each card varies. Credit cards have found widespread acceptance in the metros and cities but are not popular in small towns and villages. This facility has become immensely popular since 1990 among all the customers and has been given due importance in this study.

Mobile Banking

In traditional banking, customers have to visit the branch of the bank in person to carry on the basic banking transactions. E – banking is of great convenience to the customer. With Mobile banking, the concept of anytime, anywhere banking is literally at the fingertips of the customer. Mobile alerts such as debits and credits to the account, registered bill payment, inquiries like balance inquiry, last few transaction statements, de-mat account details, mobile banking password change etc. are made available to the customers through mobile phone at a nominal charge by the bank. It is against this background that mobile banking facility is taken as an important variable for measuring the level of awareness of customers.

E-Bills Payment

E-Banking opens new vistas of banking by way of providing enlarged, efficient, economic and quality service to the customers. With electronic banking, clients are able to deal with banks and get a lot of requests serviced through their desktop computers or through telephone. It facilitate the immediate payment of utility bills of customers such as electricity, water, telephone, mobile bills, payment of insurance premium, tuition fees, hostel fees of wards etc. Payment of utility bill is a novel technique adopted by banks since 1994 to attract customers. Hence it is considered as an important variable to assess the awareness level of customers.

Banking Ombudsmen

Banking Ombudsmen Scheme was announced in June 1995 to protect the interest of customers and to redress their grievances. It is a quick and inexpensive facility. The main objective of this institution is to settle the complaints of customers with regard to banking services and to the satisfaction of customers. This scheme is applicable to all commercial and scheduled co-operative banks operating in India. Any person with a grievance against a bank can forward a complaint in writing to the Banking Ombudsmen either by himself or through his authorized agent. On receipt of the complaint as well as the information from the bank concerned, the Banking Ombudsmen will try to settle the complaint through an agreement between the complainant and the bank by way of conciliation or mediation. The concept of Ombudsmen is gaining importance and it is indeed a land mark institution in the history of Indian banking. Against this background the researchers take Ombudsmen scheme as an important variable.

Insurance Products

Customers are being provided with additional delivery channels, which are more convenient to customers and are cost effective to the banks. Commercial Banks in association with insurance companies offer insurance products to its customers. It provides for coverage of insurance of personal accident, household articles, jewelry, cash and other valuables against fire, robbery, flood, riots etc. and medical insurance product with cash less hospitalization and cash payment to meet incidental expenses, travel etc. This facility is also becoming very popular among the customers and has been given due importance in this study.

Investment and Financial Advisory Services

Financial advisory services or personal fiancé solutions are provided by commercial banks to its customers. Through financial advisory services banks try to understand the investment requirements of their customers and prepare appropriate tailor-made financial solutions. Beyond merely advising the customers, the banks also help the customers to invest in a variety of instruments including mutual funds, RBI bonds, bonds of financial institutions, fixed deposits, insurance products, capital gain tax saving bonds etc. The banks also supply daily and weekly market roundups and quarterly newsletters to its customers. This is an innovative scheme introduced by commercial banks and the researchers considered it an important variable for study.

Electronic Fund Transfer

RBI started Electronic Fund Transfer (EFT) system in 1996. The system facilitated transfer of funds from one center to another across banks. The advantage of this system is that it facilitates transfer of funds on the same day. This is also considered an important variable for study by the researchers.

The ongoing economic reforms initiated in India during 1990s have led to relaxation of controls and increased customer service in terms of quality and quantity. This is due to the process of economic liberalisation, privatisation and globalisation. Further, information technology, changing customer expectations and increasing competition have posed a challenge to the existing banking scenario.[1] As such banks need to adopt new strategies and suitable work culture for their sustenance in tune with the changing demand of the customers. The present study, therefore, attempts to measure customer satisfaction on the basis of primary data collected at random from bank customers selected for the study in Andhra Pradesh. The focus of the study is on groups of bank customers classified into five categories.

Banking is essentially a service-oriented industry. Its existence is due to its quality of service to the society.[2] The survival and growth of a bank depend not only on its size of fund but also on its ability to provide qualitative services to its customers on a sustainable basis. In order to compete, the bankers need to understand the various needs of different customers so as to provide customised services which will not only satisfy the customers but also enlighten them. Despite six decades of economic planning, India continues to exhibit the basic characteristics of an underdeveloped country.[3] Its central problem is mass poverty indicated by a low level of per capita income. An underdeveloped economy can have good potential prospects for using material and human resources towards achieving a higher rate of economic growth in terms of per capita income. The economy also exhibits lack of suitable economic organisation which is necessary for adequate capital formation. Landlords, moneylenders, and indigenous bankers acted as parasites and appropriated a major share of production which was spent in extravagance[4]. Hence, the need for a better financial institutional infrastructure of credit is felt.

Banking System Vis-à-vis Economic Development

Banking is a multifaceted concept. It indicates the integration of financial transitions of credit and borrowings of the industries which include small-scale, business, micro-credit agriculture, household and other sectors of the economy[5]. Banking system occupies an important place in a nation's economy as it is one of the critical factors of infrastructures. A banking institution is indispensable in a modern society, as it plays a pivotal role in the economic development and forms the core of the money market in any county. Further, the expansion of banking system depends on the relationship of banker and customers of the various sectors.

In India, the money market is still characterised by the existence of both the organised and unorganised segments. Institutions in organised money market have grown significantly and are playing an increasingly important role. The unorganised sector, comprising the moneylenders and the indigenous bankers caters to the credit needs of a large number of persons especially in the countryside.[6]

Before the establishment of banks, the majority of rural population depended more on money lenders to meet their daily business and commercial transactions, and agricultural activities including agro-based industry. Consequently, these people were very much exploited with high interest rates imposed by the moneylenders. Owing to irregular monsoons, farmers have been facing uncertainty from the beginning of cropping to harvesting. At the same time, the allied sectors of the agriculture like agro-based industries are affected by the structural changes which have been taking in agriculture. If the climate is unfavourable, the entire agriculture and the agro-based industries face adverse results, and ultimately farmers may fall in debt. On the other hand, if the monsoons are favourable, output in agriculture may increase consequent on which the price of agriculture commodity may fall down. In both the situations, agriculture farmers get losses and fall into the cob-webs of debts. It implies that the farmers born in debt, grow with debt and die in debt. Therefore, the government has recognised the significance of service motive and the need to protect the farmers. The banking system has been making great efforts in this regard. Bank credit has a dynamic role to play in regions and sectors, for the millions of self-employed productions units, small farmers and small-scale enterprises alike. They depend on the Bank credit for survival and growth.[7]

For financing agriculture and allied activities in the rural areas, along with co-operative credit societies and central co-operative banks, commercial banks had begun their active participation after the nationalisation of major banks in 1969.[8] Long and medium-term credit to the farmers is provided by another specialised institution, namely, the land development banks, which have a two-tier structure such as primary land development banks at the state and national level. The National bank for Agriculture and Rural Development (NABARD) is the full-fledged apex institution in the field of agriculture and rural development.[9]

In the field of industrial finance, the government has made drastic efforts and established many financial institutions like Industrial Development Bank of India (IDBI), State Financial Corporation (SFC), Small-Scale Industrial Development Corporation(SIDC), Industrial Credit Investment Corporation of India (ICICI), Industrial Re-construction Bank of India (IRBI) etc., They are established with a view to meeting the financial requirements of the industries. Some other financial institutions like the Life Insurance Corporation of India (LIC), General Insurance corporation of India (GIC), Unit Trust of India (UTI) etc., are carrying on their business investing in the corporate, Government and Semi-Government sectors.[10] All these banks are concentrating mainly on medium and long term loans although, in the process they have neglected the small business to a large extent.

The commercial banks are the oldest institutions among the banking institutions in the organised sector, having a wide network of branches, commanding utmost public confidence and having a lion's share in the total banking operations by attracting the customers through various deposits, savings and other schemes.

The contribution of banking sector towards the process of economic development can be described as under.

Development of Financial Infrastructure

Commercial Banks, a major part of the financial infrastructure, provide both "saving intermediation' and 'money-market intermediation'. This process brings about consistency among the assets preferences of the households, the ultimate savings units, the liability preferences of business firms and the fundamental investing units. This is being facilitated by the ability of these banks and the size of the money market to emit liabilities with risk attributes that households' prefer to absorb, while absorbing assets instruments with risk attributes that business firms prefer to produce.

The development of commercial banking also helps the money market to grow, for its progress would be the progress and expansion of the money market[11]. Thus, these banks are important as they provide the basic financial infrastructure, which facilitates uninterrupted functioning of the economic system.

Capital Formation

Capital formation has been one of the important requirements for economic development. It requires the real savings of the community to be invested in the production of capital goods. It is here that commercial banks can play a pivotal role as intermediaries by bridging the gap between savings and investments. Banks, as "repositories of peoples' savings" mobilise small and scattered savings of the community, and as 'surveyors of credit', channelise the savings so mobilised into the production of capital goods and, thereby, facilitate capital-formation.[12] In other words, funds lying idle with savers and small funds scattered far and wide with marginal savers are mobilised and potential savers are encouraged to save with commercial banks. Besides, they transfer funds from the savers to the investors for more profitable use by providing mobility to capital funds through its savings and money market intermediations. Thus, commercial banks provide:[13]

(*i*) lucrative opportunities of investment to the savers

(*ii*) funds for investment to the entrepreneurs, and

(*iii*) capital-formation to the country.

Entrepreneurial Development

The mere act of saving and its mobilisation cannot result in the formation of capital unless it is invested in the production of capital goods. This requires an adequate number of entrepreneurs. The entrepreneurial ability may be defined as the propensity of man to take calculated risks with confidence so as to make his enterprise a success. And the Commercial banks have got an important role to play in this field of entrepreneurial development. Commercial banks encourage entrepreneurial ability in two ways:[14]

(*i*) by providing timely and adequate amount of credit to those with technical skills and entrepreneurial talents who are not coming forwards on a higher economic plane for want of sufficient capital, and

(*ii*) by attenuating uncertainty and absorbing risk in arranging capital needed for their plans to be implemented.

The availability of bank credit enables entrepreneurs to harness innovations by bringing about new combinations of productive resources, drawing resources away from their existing comparatively low yielding employment and employing unemployed resources. This helps the economic system to get on to a higher plane of economic activity.

Credit and Purchase of Goods and Services

Economic development demands an adequate and flexible amount of credit. The basic function of credit is to enable business firms and individuals to purchase goods and services despite their inability or their desire to pay. Commercial banks are the major suppliers of credit in the capacity of both "residual suppliers" and "primary suppliers" of credit when they meet all the credit needs of individuals as well as business firms when the latter have little savings of their own.[15]

A commercial banking system provides more credit than its primary resources through the process of credit-creations, of course, within the limits set in by the volume of primary deposits, the necessary liquidity requirements and the size of the money market. Commercial banks, through their process of creation of credit, bridge the gap between actual savings and desired savings warranted for a rapid rate of economic development. The absence of desired savings otherwise would have limited the productive activities in the economy to the extent that the savings are actually available for investment.[16] Apart from this, the gap is also bridged by mobilising actual savings of the community which would otherwise be reduced due to major imperfections in the financial markets and the consequent immobility of funds including small and scattered savings – lying either idle or spent on luxury goods, jewellery, and other unproductive purposes.

Stabilises the Prices

The erratic behaviour of prices is not helpful in the steady and rapid rate of economic growth. It demands stability of prices of goods and services. Commercial banking system, through its decisions either to provide or not to provide credit, has also got an important role play in stabilising prices. The direction of the flow of credit has an important bearing on price stability. Credit, which stimulates production, has one type of impact and credit[17]. Even the credit, which goes to production purposes, can have different repercussions depending on the time lag between the increase in demand and the increase in supply, which the credit generates. If too much credit goes to longer gestation uses, it can have an adverse effect on the price level.

Helps the Government

Commercial Banks facilitate the activation of the Government motive force for economic development. They provide help in arranging finance to the Government through various methods like direct credit to the Government and various Government agencies: and through subscribing public debt and investing money in various Government securities. This process of credit supply enables the Government to implement various schemes of development. The banks also help the planning commission to achieve targets through their co-ordinate working with the

Commission. By providing credit to the needy in the countryside, they help the balancing of the economic development, and thereby, decentralise it, Their working also indirectly helps the Government to solve many problems like shortage of savings, rising prices, unemployment, unbalanced development, lack of entrepreneurship etc. They also help Government in reducing the social cost of supplying currency to the public[18].

Thus, the banking industry has been playing various roles in the transformation of the development process of the economy through branch expansion, deposit mobilisation, priority sector lending etc., This has resulted in the conversion of class banking into mass banking.

Metamorphosis of the Banking Sector

Up to late 1960s, banks were mainly engaged in financing organised trade, commerce and industry, but since then, they have been actively participating in financing of Agricultural, Small-scale, Micro-credits to Self Help Groups, business and demotic borrowers also. As Indian economy faced a great economic crisis, drastic changes were taken in all the sectors of the economy.[19] After the nationalisation of major banks in 1969, new banks in the private sector could not be set up in India for more than two decades through there was no legal bar to that effect. The Narasimham Committee on financial sector (1991) recommended the establishment of such banks in India. The Reserve Bank of India, therefore, issued guidelines for the setting up of new private sector banks to be financially viable and technologically up-to-date from the start. They are expected to start functioning in a professional manner, so as to improve the image of commercial banking system and to strengthen the confidence of the depositing public.[20]

Economy developed during 2005-06 on account of the initiatives taken by the government and the RBI. The government has set agriculture as its major priority area and has directed the banks and financial institutions to increase credit to the farmers. Accordingly, banks have increased credit to the agricultural sector. The RBI in its annual policy statement has advised the banks to be fair and transparent with regard to the charges for various services offered. It has not only directed the banks to display the charges and penalties on their websites and branches but has also constituted a working group to examine how reasonable these charges are. This will go a long way in furthering the scope of the Fair Practice code (FPC) in India.[21]

Besides the best practices and benchmarks in the industry, Capital is seen as a very important parameter in measuring the strength of a financial entity. In the current fiscal year, many of the banks have boosted their capital base by adding debt, equity, hybrids; RBI has prescribed innovative instruments, etc., to their portfolio. Some of the banks which have raised equity through public offerings include the Union Bank of India, the South Indian Bank, the ICICI Bank, the Andhra Bank and the Bank of Baroda.[22]

While on the domestic front, consolidation will increase the scales, acquiring banks abroad could surely help the Indian banks to widen their reach and service and serve their customers better. While Indian banks are going global, foreign banks are entering India. The foreign banks which are already functioning are looking forward to adding new product line and improving their business.[23]

The entry of private sector, has led to provide better service to the customer in all aspects. This has led to competition among the banks making them devise ways and means to provide qualitative service and thereby attract the customer. Consequently, a change in the relationship between the customer and the banking has also been contemplated, which is necessary in the changing scenario. Besides, powerful market forces like global competition for deposits, loans and underwriting fees, increasing customers, demand, shrinking profit margins and the need to keep pace with new the technologies are transforming the banking into a financial service market.[24]

However, apart from the increase in the shares of the private corporate sector, the government sector has been making efforts. The result is the share has shown a steep rise from 10.1 per cent in March 2006 to 14.5 per cent in March 2007. Indian banking has been under going a lot of positive change to the extent of making itself progressively sound and stable. After displaying accelerating tendency for several quarters, growth in bank credit picked up in the third quarter of 2006 and grew at the rate of 15.3 per cent in 2005-06. In 2006-07, annual growth of bank credit in India has more than doubled to about 31 per cent. In contrast, total deposits of the banking system have grown only by 13 per cent over the same period. As a result, the credit –to deposit ratio reached a record 65 per cent in March 2006 and the incremental credit-deposit ratio exceeded 100 per cent. A similar trend is seen to be continuing in 2006-07.

The trends in credit deployment show that there has been a structured shift in credit delivering towards sectors other than agriculture and industry mostly towards services and retail. The share of priority sector that had hovered around 32-33 per cent up to 2005-06 has increased to 35.3 per cent in 2006-07. How ever, the share of agriculture has remained almost stagnant around 12 per cent during the period under review with some improvement in 2006-07. The share of credit to small-scale industries has fallen from 14.0 per cent in 1994-95 to 7.8 per cent in 2006-07. Over the last eight years, the share of industry in the total loan portfolio of commercial banking has declined. This share has fallen from 53.5 per cent in 1996-97 to 37.7 per cent in 2006-07. The share of the credit to sectors other than agriculture and industry in outstanding gross bank credit, which was 31.4 per cent in 1996-97, now accounts for almost 45.5 per cent of total gross bank credit.[25]

While the performance of the Indian economy as well as the Indian Banking in the fiscal year 2006-07 has been good, there are some important challenges which the Indian banking is facing. The foremost challenge is to maintain the asset quality in a high credit growth environment. Though steps have been taken by RBI to strengthen the financial sector and maintain financial stability, maintenance of asset quality is becoming important. The second important challenge is to get ready for implementing the Basel II[26] norms. RBI has been categorical in saying that it is going ahead with implementing the internationally accepted Basel II Accord by March 2007 and all commercial banks have to gear up for that. Though most of the Indian banks have a superior Capital Adequacy Ratio (CAR) of around 12 per cent, they could face problems if they do not increase the capital base further. The Capital charge for market risk has not been covered until recently and the operational risk is not at all accounted for according to the present accord.

The third major challenge is to prepare for the enforcement coming from the RBI road map – allowing foreign banks and putting them on a level playing field by 2009.[27] Allowing a free hand for the foreign bank would, to an extent, change the dynamics of competition in the banking industry. Even though, the public sector banks will be untouched due to regulatory restrictions, some of the private banks will be acquired by the foreign banks. Some of the banks have already started entering into strategic alliances with foreign partners. Though India has many banks, none of them has reached the global scale and are nowhere compared to the global banking giants. The ongoing developments in the economy should scale up.

It is in this background, the present study has been initiated by the researcher emphasising the banker-customer relations in two public sector banks – State Bank of India and Andhra Bank, and two corporate sector banks –ING Vysya Bank and ICICI Bank. It's a well-proven and documented fact that customer retention is a much more efficient and cost-effective mechanism for revenue and profitability growth vis-à-vis new customer acquisition. The above analysis shows that much of the activity in the banking and financial services space remains focused around customer acquisition rather than retention. In fact, if customer retention is combined with leveraging knowledge about existing customers to increase wallet-share, the possibilities can be limitless. This idea constitutes the central concern of this thesis.

The foremost contention of the thesis is that there is a large database of knowledge about existing customers that is available, but is seldom effectively used by banks and other financial institutions. For example, apart from demographic profile, personal and family income details and a host of other background information influence banks.

The second contention of the thesis is that the real-time customer segmentation is a key benefit provided by Customer Relationship Management (CRM), enabling banks to differentiate their 'AAA' customers from the less-profitable ones. As a result, once identified, the 'AAA' customers can be provided with the best quality of service and attention, whether it is in terms of personalised service or minimum call-hold time. This ensures that 'AAA' customers feel wanted and important which thereby enables banks to prioritise their investments in time, effort and money. The CRM enables endless possibilities to improve customer satisfaction, retention and profitability. Using a combination of robust CRM technology and processes, banks can take their business to another level, emerging with not just higher growth rates but also better return on investment for their shareholders.[28]

Though technology and its applications have remained the subjects of debates from time to time, contribution of technology in the field of business, health, education, entertainment, information and communications and, of course, banking is growing day by day. For most of the people, it is more a question of how to exercise options of people in using technology to promote CRM.[29] Public sector Banks, which have large portfolios in terms of business and employment, are at various stages of migrating to new systems. As a matter of fact, this new strategic system may generally be identified with "core Banking" aided by ATM networks. This has its bearing on the banker-customer relationship. Therefore, the thesis examines the impact of technology on the customer-banker relationship.

The shift from Branch counter to e-channels has indeed enhanced customer service and convenience. The dream of anytime, anywhere banking is a reality now. With facilities like mobile alerts, customers get real-time information about transactions in their accounts.[30] However, customer experiences in resolving their problems through interactive voice response systems/call centres have not been satisfactory in most cases. The warmth and human touch is missing in these mechanical media, leaving many a customer to contemplate the benefits of talking to the good old bankers. Also, in the absence of channel integration, customers are unable to get identical information about their accounts across the channels. The silver lining for customers is that they can shift to competitor banks easily if they are not satisfied with the services from the present bank.

The banker- customer relationship depends on the ability to provide personalised services to every customer, every time everywhere. In this manner, the banking amply improves the quality services by customer relationship. Every bank is making efforts to increase customer satisfaction, building asset levels expanding relationship that includes insurance and brokerage services, reducing operational costs and building profitability. Launching of new products such as internet banking, mobile banking, debit cards/credit cards widening tie-ups with other banks/agencies for providing better services, setting up of internet care centre for internet banking are welcome trends at present.[31]

Banks are diversifying their activities in several ways for several advantages like earnings of the non-interest incomes; Benefits get through entry de-regulation and the resulting intensified competition may leave banks with no choice but to engage in risk-taking activities in the fight for market share in the field of banker- customer relationship. This could result in a possible reduction in total earnings and as such, banks would have to find alternative sources of income. Diversification helps to reduce information asymmetry by processing inside information on clients and monitoring their performance, indirectly creating opportunities to earn non-interest income and sustain profitability. Diversification may help banks in stabilising their income by engaging in varied activities, there by reducing the cost of funds. It promotes efficiency by allowing banks to utilise inside information arising out of long-term relationship with their clients, Banks can engage in activities like under writing of securities at a much lesser cost than others.[32]

Along with the above activities, some other steps at gross route level may improve the banker and customer relationship viz., the conditions to open the account in the bank, penalty for less than minimum balance in the account, Locker and issue cheques chares, Debt-card/Credit–card system connected with other institutions/ companies, expansion of withdrawal facilities with other banks issue of loans without surety or guarantee, fast services by computerisation. These dimensions are very essential to improve relationship between banker and Customers. As such the study focuses on these issues.

Obviously, in the present competitive environment in the banking, the success of the banking depends on the ability to understand changing customer needs and to turn that understanding into a competitive advantage. It is hoped that the future would be very favourable to the banks provided if they explore the technology to optimum level with the twin objective of improving quality of services and convenience at affordable costs that promote banker-customer relations. The present study has concentrated on the role and services of the banks to the various sectors of the economy. The nature and scope of relationship between banker and customer, services extended by the banks and the problems faced by customer with bankers and also the problems faced with customer by the banker in operating banking activities constitute a major part of the study area.

The banking sector has been providing a variety of services to different categories of customers. In providing the services, banks have to fulfil certain legal obligations which are necessary for establishing the relationship between banker and customer[33]. The study postulates that the common legal formalities to be observed by a banker with customer may include the following:

(*a*) Legal formalities for opening and closing of accounts.

(*b*) Rules and regulations related to deposit of cash, withdrawal of cash, issue of passbook and cheque book etc.

(*c*) Provision of physical facilities like seating arrangement, parking space for vehicles, availability of required vouchers and drinking water facilities etc.

(*d*) Installation of ATMs and their services.

(*e*) Provision of Debit Card/Credit Card, On line, Internet and other technology related services.

(*f*) Sanction of loans for different purposes

(*g*) Changes in the policy relating to levy of changes on various services and schemes.

(*h*) Issues relating to complaints and the manner in which they are solved.

As there is need for a strong customer-banker relationship, banks have been providing services to the following groups in society.

(1) Depositors who deposit money in different accounts like Saving Bank Account, Current Account, Fixed Deposits and others.

(2) Borrowers who approach banks for loan purpose are:

(*a*) Farmer Community

(*b*) Small Scale Industries

(*c*) Large and medium scale industries

(*d*) Retail traders, and Small business

(*e*) Exports and Education loans

(3) Other services like issue of Demand Drafts, TT, MT and collection of utility bills like telephone and taxes.

In view of the above analysis, it is felt that there is need for undertaking a study on these aspects to suggest measures for improve banker–customer relationship. The study makes an attempt to seek answers to the following issues:

The perception of the customers as to the services provided to them by the banks under the study vis a vis, the perception of bankers as to their customers whose transactions with their banks are deemed significant.

The problems faced by the banker-customer in relation to each other in the context of providing various latest services.

REFERENCES

1. Narasimham. M. "Financial Sector Reforms: The unfinished agenda", *Southern Economist*, October 15, 1993, p.15.
2. Varshneya, J.S. "What Banks have done for rural development?", *Yojana*, July 16-31, 1988, p. 6.
3. Basu, K. and Jindak (eds.) "*Microfinance-Emerging Challenges*", Tata McGraw Hill Publishing Company, New Delhi, 2002, pp. 59-65.
4. Basu, S.K. "*Commercial Banks and Agricultural Credit-A study in Regional Disparity in India*, Allied Publishers (P) Ltd, Bombay, 1979, pp. 108-109.
5. Vasudevan, A. "Central Banking for Emerging Market Economics", *Academic Foundation*, New Delhi and "Money & Banking", 2003, pp. 77-98.
6. Dreze, J. and Amartya Sen. "*Indian Economic Development and Social Opportunity*", Oxford University Press, New Delhi, 1997, pp. 67-72.
7. Rajendra Bail, R. "*Deposit Mobilisation by Commercial Banks – A study*", University Post-Graduate Centre, Khammam, Kakatiya University, 1986, pp 223-227.
8. RBI Report on Trend and Progress of Banking in India, 1970, p. 61.
9. Rangarajan, C. "*Innovations in Banking–The Indian experiences: impact on Deposits and Credit*" Oxford and IBH Publishing Co., New Delhi, 1982, pp. 89-90.

10. Simha, S.L.M. (Ed). "*Reforms of the Banking System*", Institute for Financial Management Research, 1973, pp.165-169.
11. Brahmanad, P.R. "*Freeing banks to lend more*", The Hindu Business Line, October 30, 1994, pp.22-25.
12. Levine, Ross, "Financial Development and Economic Growth: Views and Agenda", *Journal of Economic Literature*, 1997, 35(2).
13. Janakiraman, R. "*Indian Banking By 2000 A.D*", edited by Vinayakam, N, Kanishka Publishers, Delhi, 1995, p. 23.
14. Srinvasan. R. and Sriram, M.S. "Micro-Finance and Introduction", *IIMB Management Review*, June 2005, Unpublished Ph.D. Thesis, pp. 201-205.
15. Sabnavis, "Review of Reforms–Agenda for the Future", *IBA Bulletin*, 1995-96, pp.108-109.
16. Khandelwal, B.N. "*Exchange Banking in India*", Jhalani Publications Delhi, 1965, pp. 63-64.
17. Cameron, R. "*Banking and Economic Development*", Some lessons of History, Oxford University Press, New York, 1972, pp 165-169.
18. Radha, T. "*Impact of Banking sector reforms in Commercial Banks in India*", Andhra University, Visakhapatnam, Ph.D. Thesis, 2002, pp. 208-211.
19. Hanihar, T.S. "Metamorphosis of Indian Banking", *Chartered Financial Analyst,* Dec. 1999, p. 14.
20. Tanuja R. Nemivant, "Turnaround in Banking Performance: Back in the Black", *Chartered Financial Analyst*, August 1998, p. 33.
21. Vasudevan, T.M.C., Shyamji Mehrotra, Chandgadkar, D.M. "*Co-operative Banking Operations*", Macmillan India Limited, 2007, p. 56.
22. Vasant Desai, "*Banks and Institutional Management*", Himalaya Publications, 2006, pp.187-90.
23. Pain, P.K., Pethe, P.M. "*International Banking Operations*", Macmillan India Limited, 2007, pp.220-222.
24. Indian Institution of Banking & Finance, "*Legal Aspects of Banking Operations*", Macmillan, 2005, pp. 23-28.
25. RBI Bulletin, "*Coping with Liquidity Management: A Practitioner's View*", January 2006; "*Economic Growth, Financial Deepening and Financial Inclusion*", June 2006; "*Development of Financial Markets in India*", November 2007.
26. Caruana, Jaime. "*Announcement of BESEL-II" Remarks at the press conference announcing the publication of Basel-II,* 2004, p. 88.

27. Balamohandas, V. Andhra Bank Endowment Lecturer on "*Indian Banking Yesterday, Today and Tomorrow*", A seminar paper presented in Andhra University on 19th July, 2005.
28. Ramesh. V. Kang. K.S., Singh, U.P., Jagannathan, P., Smt. Sudha Venkat Ram. "*Information Technology, Data Communications & Electronic Banking*, 2nd edn., Macmillan India Limited, 2007, pp 52-56.
29. Mishra, D. "Banking Sector reforms – A great turnaround", Member of the Faculty, Reserve Bank Staff College, Madras, *The Journal of the Indian Institute of Bankers*, July-Sept, 1995, p. 58.
30. Yeeram Raju, "Looming Challenges to Indian Banking", *Indian Management*, Nov. 1999, p. 24.
31. Zeihaml Valerie A., Parasuraman, A., Bery Leonard, L. "*Delivering Quality Service*", The Free Press, a division of Macmillan, Ind., New York, 1990, pp. 31-35.
32. Sudhir M. Joshi, Ashish Parthasarthy, Mundra, S.S., Vasant Godse. *Theory and Practice of Treasury & Risk Management in Banks*, Taxmann Publications Private Limited, 2006, pp.111-115.
33. Zacharias, K.D., Ravindranath, C.P., Kulkarni, P.R., Gopalakrishnan, B. *Legal Aspects of Banking Operations*, Macmillan India Limited, 2005, p. 128.

CHAPTER

Review of Literature and Research Design

In this chapter, an attempt is made to define the Research Problem, Review of exciting literature, Objectives and Methodology of the study. Besides, the Need and Significance along with Limitations have also been dealt with in this chapter.

Research Problem

Economic liberalization, globalization, information technology revolution, changing customer requirements and increasing competition have posed a lot of challenges to the existing banking sector in India. With E-Banking, the brick and mortar structure of the tradition banking gets converted into a click and portal model thereby giving real shape to the concept of virtual banking. The new generation and foreign banks have expanded banking services through ATMs, Internet Banking, Mobile banking, Home banking etc.,

Now the major objective of both private and public sector Indian Banks is to attract a large customer base by offering more delivery channels, giving more importance to customer relationships. It is in this context that this study has been carried out to find out the level of awareness of customers on various banking services.

The most productive resources of the Bank are its Customer relationships. The Banks invest their major share of profits in the development of their relations with the customers. These development processes include service activities — both financial and non-financial activities. These service activities help the customers to boost up their deposit mobilisation and promote their role in the Banking sector. But the Banker is unable to know whether these service activities have achieved their objectives or not. Hence, a study of 'Banker and customers relationship' in the changing scenario of banking industry has been called for and taken up.

Banking sector is basically a service sector in the present day competitive service sector. The Customer plays a very significant role in achieving the objectives of business. The banking sector always displays a statement on customer relationship in every branch of the Bank. In this context, it is appropriate to quote Mahatma Gandhi[1] who stated that, *"Customer is the most important person ever in this office- in person or by mail. A customer is not dependent on us. We are dependent on him. A customer is not an interruption of our work ... he is the purpose of it. We are not doing a favour by serving him ... he is doing us a favour by giving us the opportunity to do so. A Customer is not someone to argue or match wits with. Nobody ever won an argument with a customer. A customer is a person who brings us his wants. It is our job to handle them profitability to him and to ourselves."*

This statement indicates the importance of Customer relationship in the banking sector. The service sector today is emphasising the importance of People, Process and Physical evidence to impress upon the customer and build relationship through these three P's. Hence, the present study aims at the study of Banker-Customer relationship in both public and private sector banks.

Review of Literature

There are several research publications on the Banking sector and its related activities. Research activities have been taken up by the Government of India, the Reserve Bank of India, the Banker Associations, the Academic Institutions and a host of Individuals about various operations of banks. The literature, available has been reviewed and presented.

Policy Issues

A descriptive and analytical study made by Rangarajan[2] (1982) focussed on the significant changes, issues, and problems that have taken place in the Indian Banking System since the nationalisation of 14 major commercial banks in 1969, particularly in the field of deposit mobilisation and credit deployment and suggested new approach to lending through district credit plans, village adoption scheme credit camps and groups system. The study covered the period between 1972-79.

Performance

Kaveri (1982)[3] evaluated the performance of nationalised banks in rural, semi-urban, urban and metropolitan centres by selecting a sample of 1206 branches. He came to the conclusion that branches, which are getting losses, had a higher credit-deposit ratio in rural and urban areas. This study shows the need to explore customer management relationship.

Gangadhar Khan (1978)[4] evaluated the functioning of commercial banks in both public and private sectors on the basis of criteria like expansion of banking services, encouraging bank habit, adaptation of new techniques and innovations in lending by commercial banks in rural areas. A study on profitability of 14 nationalised banks by Dhanjagan and Selvarajan (1983)[5] proved that 7 banks have more earning capacity. Similarly, another study "Banks since nationalisation", a Study of Economic Research Division of Birla Institute of Scientific Research (1981),[6] that covered the study period 1968-67, gave a comparative performance between the nationalised major commercial banks (14) and major private sector banks (13). The study concluded that the performance of the private sector banks has been noteworthy. This shows the need to study the public and private sectors putting together.

A study on deposit mobilisation, which is an aspect of customer management relationship, by private sector banks in India was conducted by Katilya Perumal (1982).[7] It concluded that among the private sector banks, the Vysya bank Ltd., established a lead role in the mobilisation of deposits over other private sector banks.

Satyam Murthy (1991)[8] who made a study of profitability trends in scheduled commercial banks during the period 1970-82 observed that mounting over dues has become a major impediment for improving the profitability of banks in India.

Robert (1992)[9] also made a study of profitability in public sector banks in India and made a similar observation as made by Satyam Murthy in his study.

Similar studies on profitability of private sector commercial banks was made by Vinod Kumar (1984)[10] who concluded that the Vysya Bank Ltd., has been making rapid strides in improving its profitability over the other private sector commercial banks.

Mathur (1978)[11] studied the role of public sector banks as an instrument for the rapid growth of the Indian economy in general and working of SBI and its associates in particular, and observed that their development role is noteworthy.

From the above, studies it can be said that most of the private sector banks and some public sector banks performed profitably. Vysya Bank in private sector and SBI and its associates in public sector performed creditably. The lending practices in rural areas need innovative approach. Credit-deposit ratio and over dues are to be controlled for profitable operations. All these are guided by the factors of customer management relationship.

Customer Orientation and Service

Kannaji Rao (1994)[12] made a study of marketing of services in commercial banks with special emphasis on the marketing operations of Andhra Bank and observed that the banks made significant changes in the product, price, place, and promotion strategies to reach the target market more effectively. A similar study was also conducted by Gopal Saxena (1992)[13] to review the marketing strategies of State Bank of India and concluded that the bank is ahead of other public sector banks in adopting new technology to improve their products in order to enhance their satisfaction of their customers.

The Government of India appointed a working group on customer service in banks under the Chairmanship of Talwar (1977).[14] The group submitted its final report in 1977 in which 176 recommendations were made to improve the customer service.

The study made by Rajiv Upadhyaya (1985)[15] concluded that customer service rendered by banks in India was of poor quality and most of them were not even conscious of their responsibility towards the community and special groups.

A comparative study of public and private sector banks of large and small size was organised by Narayana (1988)[16] on customer service in commercial banks. Based on the reported attitudes of consumers it concluded that the attitude of banks staff towards customers should undergo a qualitative change in all the banks to improve service which are less satisfactory.

Social Responsibility Areas

The studies made by different researchers on the social responsibility areas are briefly presented in Corwin and Theibolt have a case analysis of the employment and promotion of minorities in specific banks.

Mellow (1980)[17] in his study points out that over the span of 11 years the commercial banks have succeeded in channelising sizable amount of credit to priority sectors. However, qualitatively such as extension of credit lacked in director and failed to fulfil the social objective of planning.

Rama Jyothsna Ratna Kumari (1990)[18] in her study on "Priority sector lending by commercial banks: a study of Vysya Bank Guntur division concluded that the Vysya Bank made stupendous progress in regard to advancing to priority sector. Its performance outranked the performance of public sector banks.

Ramesh (1989)[19] made a case study of Andhra Bank during the period (1969-87) and concluded that the performance of the bank in respect of priority sector lending has been found to be very impressive in spite of certain lapses in the maintenance of growth rates among individual components of priority sectors.

Anil Kumar (1985)[20] made a study on performance evaluation of 14 nationalisation banks with special reference to priority sector lending during 19700-80. He observed that their advances to each priority sector and advances of banking industry are positively related. The relationship is more strong and significant only in the case of advances to agriculture, small-scale industries and exports but not so in case of other social priority sector areas like road and water transport operators, retail trade, small business, professionals, self-employed and education. Ashok Kumar Bohra (1987)[21] in his analytical study on the role of lead banks in rural financing in the State of Rajasthan, observed that the lead banks are very much necessary for the promotion of rural financing in the country.

Small Scale Industries

Rama Krishna (1962)[22] in his thesis emphasised the importance and need for financing small-scale sector. He dealt with all the external sources of finance for small-scale sector such as state aid to this sector, State Financial Corporations, Commercial Banks and Co-operative Banks.

Satish Bahadur Mathus (1992)[23] in his study on the role of commercial bank in lending to small scale sector concluded that small scale sector in India is facing serious problems which are to be addressed by commercial banks in India.

Brahmanandam (1983)[24] studied on the financing small scale industries by commercial banks in Guntur District. He found that the overall performance of commercial banks in funding small scale industries in the district however was not satisfactory when compared to the performance of banks in this respect in the state, Southern States and the country.

Finance to Agriculture

In a study of agriculture financing in Bihar State, Mukherjee (1976)[25] has brought out the practical difficulties as problems of bankers in agriculture financing. Ravi Kumar Bhola (1983)[26] studied the role of scheduled commercial banks in India in promoting agricultural development during 1969-81. He maintained that the scheduled commercial banks played a significant role in promoting agricultural development an suggested measures to improve recovery of advances from agriculture.

Self-employment

A survey was organised by Daniel (1987)[27] on the role of commercial banks in financing the scheme for self-employment to educated unemployed youth in Karnataka State. He concluded that the assistance provided under the scheme was inadequate to the beneficiaries.

Artisans and Minorities

Nagaraj (1988)[28] in a study about rural artisans points out that though rural artisans were included in weaker sections, the credit flow to them has been found to be very meagre. The studies examined relationship between overall advances and priority sector lending and performance of banks in lending to priority sector areas.

Social Reporting

Approach: Dave (1991)[29] discussed the issues regarding measurement of corporate social reporting. He suggested that social report of the firm should include contribution to the environment, consumption, product improvement, human resources and community investment. His plea was to develop a suitable format for social reporting after identifying the information needs in accordance with social goal.

Guruswamy (1991)[30] found that social audit in TISCO was very descriptive but not accounting oriented. He observed that none of the leading private sector enterprises have quantified their social activities. He pleaded for a suitable legislation for all the companies to make adequate disclosure of their activities to the society.

Samiuddin and Hifzur-Rehman (1991)[31] observed that conventional measurement of profitability and growth as reflected in profit and loss account and balance sheet is not adequate enough to reveal the extent of contribution a business house has made to the community. While making a survey of social reporting practices in India companies, they concluded that it was unlikely that a systematised basis of reporting should be developed quickly in near future unless tremendous efforts were made by academicians, companies and the Government.

Sharma (1991)[32] examined the scope of public interest reporting by business firms in India. He divided the reporting contents into business interests (ROI, leverage, contribution to state exchequer, expenditure on R&D etc.,) and public interests (wages to value added index of real wages, index of accidents, taxes to value added, employment to weaker sections, product quality improvement , pollution index etc.).

Panda (1993) [33] dealt with the need of social reporting by the public sector enterprises and suggested a system and taxonomy of social reporting in the Indian context. It comprises (a) contribution to state economy (net profit contribution, value added foreign exchange gain, energy saved contribution to exchequer etc., (b) contribution to HRD-employment generation, development and welfare, (c) contribution to environment-equipment, pollution type, costs of pollution, (d) contribution to consumers- product satisfy, after sales service index, product R&D complaints etc., (e) contribution to community by way of road construction, education, games and sports etc. All these suggest the need for customer management relationship in the banking sector.

Recent Studies

Arun & Turner's Study (2002)[34] on Financial Sector Reforms in Developing Countries: The Indian Experience is based on the premise that the success/failure of financial sector reforms depends heavily on country specific factors and makes an attempt to examine these factors in the Indian context. The financial sector reforms analysed in this paper include the deregulation of interest rates, increasing competition and foreign ownership, and the introduction of financial supervision. We argue that an economic rationale for a gradualist approach to financial reform is that it is stability enhancing. Furthermore, it could suggested that India's complex political economy has resulted in a gradual approach to reform, and this approach has been successful along the dimension of banking stability.

Patrick T. Harker (2002),[35] in a study on Customer Efficiency: Concept and its impact on E-Business Management states that the continued development of e-business models has triggered a dramatic transition of customers' roles in a variety of service production and delivery processes. In the co-production of service, the scale and scope of customers' participation have been significantly transformed and enhanced by new e-business models and technology. This transition calls for a new understanding of customers' roles in service delivery systems. The concept of customer efficiency is crucial for the successful management of systems where customers are actively engaged in service production and delivery processes. This article presents the concept of customer efficiency management (CEM), studies its relationship with other key customer characteristics, and explores its potential impact on e-business management "Banking and Financial Services in India: Marketing Redefined" by Renu Sobti (2003)[36] shows that Banking and financial services form the core of the economic system of a country. A financial system refers to the whole gamut of institutional arrangements which help mobilise financial surpluses of an economy and transfer them to areas of financial deficit.

Banking sector is an integral part of the financial system of a modern industrial economy. The role of commercial banks is particularly important in developing countries like India. The present book critically examines the various issues related to banking and financial services in the Indian economy. With liberalisation of the economy and restrictions eased by the WTO, customer service has assumed added significance. This will not only improve the operational efficiency of the banks but also augment their bottom line. The book will be useful for bankers, research scholars, academicians, government officials and students of economics, commerce and business management.

Matthias Gouthier and Stefan Schmid (2003)[37] in their Customers and Customer Relationships in Service Firms: The Perspective of the Resource-Based View point out that In many publications on service management and marketing, the customer is said to be an important resource of the service firm. This is not surprising, since a basic characteristic of services is the participation of the customer in the production process. However, up to now, there has been no theoretical discussion as to whether and why customers - as well as relationships with customers - are really important resources of the service firm. The present paper draws on the resource-based view within strategic management. It explores the potential of the resource-based view for analysing customer roles and customer relationships within service firms, and it discusses managerial implications for customer relationship management.

Satish Jayachandran, Kelly Hewett , Peter Kaufman (2004)[38] in their study argue that An organisation's customer response capability, its competence in satisfying customer needs through effective and quick responses, is critical for sustained success. In this article, the authors examine how customer knowledge process influences customer response capability. They highlight two dimensions of customer response capability, customer response expertise and customer response speed. It is observed that apart from its direct positive association with customer response expertise and speed, the customer knowledge process also diminishes the positive association between risk propensity and these dimensions of customer response capability. The influence of customer response expertise and speed on performance is also examined. The hypotheses are tested using survey data collected from a sample of retailing firms and the findings triangulated using qualitative data collected through depth interviews with managers. The results highlight the importance of customer knowledge in enhancing customer response capability.

Shun Yin Lam, Venkatesh Shankar, M. Krishna Erramilli, and Bysan Murthy (2004)[39] believe that Although researchers and managers pay increasing attention to customer value, satisfaction, loyalty, and switching costs, not much is known about their interrelationships. Prior research has examined the relationships within subsets of these constructs, mainly in the business-to-consumer (B2C) environment. The authors extend prior research by developing a conceptual framework linking all of these constructs in a business-to-business (B2B) service setting. On the basis of the cognition-affect-behaviour model, the authors hypothesise that customer satisfaction mediates the relationship between customer value and customer loyalty, and that customer satisfaction and loyalty have significant reciprocal effects on each other. Furthermore, the potential interaction effect of satisfaction and switching costs, and the quadratic effect of satisfaction, on loyalty are explored. The authors test the hypotheses on data obtained from a courier service provider in a B2B context. The results support most of the hypotheses and, in particular, confirm the mediating role of customer satisfaction.

Sundaram (2005)[40] in a seminar on customer relationship management held at the PKR Arts college for Women in Gobichettipalayam, focused on the need to develop customer banker relationship and improving service quality in the banking industry. He said winning the customer favour and loyalty by satisfying their wants, is the need of the hour. Non-disclose of facts, misleading advertisement and biased attitude has made customer relationship management all the more important. The motto of today's business should be 'hi-tech services through hi-tech applications'.

2.3 Research Gap

From the survey of literature, it is evident that

(*a*) There are very few studies with their direct focus on customer-banker relationship. The research on Banker- Customer relationship in the changing scenario is inevitable as is suggested from the recent studies reviewed so far.

(*b*) There are studies to know the attitudes of different banks in terms of specific functions like agriculture, small scale industries, micro-credit etc. But they focused little on the relationship aspect between the banks and the customers. Hence there is need to study the attitudes of the customers of banks and the bankers as well.

This study fills the gap by attempting to studying at micro level, the relationships of specific bankers as well as attitudes of bank customers in the present changing scenario The problem faced by bankers in providing various services to customers and the expectations of the customers is also highlighted.

Need for the Study

A review of relevant literature shows that the Banking sector is studied extensively by the researchers. However, most of the studies are confined either to policy issues, performance of nationalised banks in rural, semi urban, urban and metropolitan branches. Evaluation of the functioning of commercial bank in both public and private sectors, new approach to lending through direct credit plans, study of profitability trends in Scheduled commercial banks, Profitability of private sector Commercial banks, Studied the role of public sector banks as an instruments for the rapid growth of the Indian economy, studied lending practise in rural areas need innovative approach analysis of function areas of the banks, credit management or the banks social responsibility, lending and recover policy of the banks, lending to priority sector etc.,

Though there are some studies on customer orientation, these studies may be conducted emphasising mainly the marketing approach of the banks, moreover these studies are macro in nature. There are no specific studies in banking sector highlighting the importance of Banker-Customer relationship, which is highly essential in this present day competitive environment. Hence, the need for the present study.

Importance of The Study

The success of new services like Internet banking, mobile banking, ATM facility, home banking, priority banking, insurance products, investment and financial advisory services, demat account, 24 hour tele-banking etc., is highly depends upon its usage by the customers. The present study is an attempt to examine how far the banks in Andhra Pradesh have succeeded in popularizing their new banking services. The study also tries to find out the reasons for low level of awareness of customers on various services and products. The findings may help the banks to widen their customer base and to detect the deficiencies in their present services and can be of useful for policy formation in this sphere.

Objectives of the Study

The main objective of the study is to study the relationship among the banks and their customers. The study mainly aims at analysing the service rendered by the select banks, the relations maintained by the banks with their customers and identifying the degree of satisfaction among customers.

The detailed objectives of the research study are:

1. To understand various services provided by the selected banks under the study to society in general and to their customers in particular.
2. To examine the nature and scope of relationship between the banks and customers in the light of changing competitive scenario in the banking sector.
3. To elicit the opinions of bankers on customer requirements, customer services, customer care, and customer satisfaction.
4. To examine the feelings of customers on the services received from their respective banks.
5. To highlight the challenges and problems faced by both the bankers and the customers in the light of the changing scenario in the banking sector and thereby.
6. To suggest suitable strategies and measures that would help build up a strong relationship between the bankers and the customers.

Hypotheses

The study examined the following hypotheses:

- The relationship between banker and customer is being affected during the post reform period, because of various developments, changes and challenges that have taken place in the banking sector in the recent past.

- There has been a significant change in the banker and customer relationship in the select districts in the recent past i.e., after reforms.
- There has been no significant difference in the views of customers and Bank officers of both Public and Private sector banks in the select districts.

Scope of The Study

The study is based on the responses of Bank officers and customers towards Relationship in the changing scenario of banking sector. The survey has considered the metropolitan, semi-urban and rural areas while selecting the sample banks for the study. The study covers both the customers and the Bankers and provides them an opportunity to express their views and impressions along with making suggestions. The study is limited to four select Banks i.e., State Bank of India (Government Bank), Andhra Bank (Leading Nationalised Bank in Andhra Pradesh), ING-Vysya Bank (Old Private Sector Bank), and ICICI Bank (Leading New private sector Bank), and Covers all types of Customers i.e., Agriculturist (Farmers), Business people, Micro creditor (Self Help Group People), SSI (Small-scale Industrialist) and others (including salaried employees, Housewife's, students, old people.

Methodology of The Study

Sample

The present study is an exploratory research work. It is based on both Primary and Secondary data.

Selection of Study Area and Banks

The study is conducted in coastal Andhra Pradesh. There are eight districts in Coastal Andhra Pradesh. Out of cight districts, three districts viz., Visakhapatnam, East Godavari and Guntur have been selected for the present study. For the purpose of the study, Visakhapatnam District has been selected because it is an Industrially developed district in

Coastal Andhra. The East Godavari District has been selected as it is a developed district in Agriculture sector and hailed as the "Rice Bowl" of Andhra Pradesh. The Guntur District has been selected as it is the flourishing centre of Trade and Business.

The researcher has addressed the authorities of the public sector and private sector banks under the study for permission to collect information from customers and officers of the banks under the study. The researcher has personally visited the headquarters of some of the banks and sought permission from the authorities to undertake the research activity. The researcher has received permission from the following banks.

1. State Bank of India
2. Andhra Bank
3. ICICI Bank Ltd.
4. ING Vysya Bank Ltd.

The sample was drawn in such a way that it consists of banks of: (a) Public sector, and (b) Private sector. As it is difficult to cover all customers and officers of all the banks, a sample of customers and officers is preferred.

Selection of sample

All together one hundred eighty Bankers and three hundred Customers are taken as a sample for the present study at random basis. While selecting the sample, care has been taken to see that the sample represents all services offered by all the banks. Thus, the views and the opinion of the select sample represent such actual services of the banks as Agriculture, Small-scale Industries, Micro-Finance, Business (Retail loans) and others.

The details relating of the sample have been provided in the following tables. Table-I depicts the sample of Visakhapatnam District, Table-II and Table-III provide the details of sample relating to the Guntur and East Godavari Districts.

Table 2.1: Visakhapatnam District

Occupation wise customers particulars

Customers	Visakha-patnam	Anaka-palle	Yelaman-chili	Payaka-raopeta	Total
Agricultural	—	10	05	05	20
S.S.I.	15	05	—	—	20
S.H.G.	—	05	10	05	20
Business	05	05	05	05	20
Others	05	05	05	05	20
Total	25	30	25	20	100

Bank-wise customers particulars

Customers	Visakha-patnam	Anaka-palle	Yelaman-chili	Payaka-raopeta	Total
S.B.I.	07	10	08	05	30
A.B.	08	10	07	05	30
I.C.I.C.I.	05	05	05	05	20
ING	05	05	05	05	20
Total	25	30	25	20	100

Bank-wise officers particulars

Customers	Visakha-patnam	Anaka-palle	Yelaman-chili	Payaka-raopeta	Total
S.B.I.	08	04	02	01	15
A.B.	08	04	02	01	15
I.C.I.C.I.	15	—	—	—	15
ING	10	02	02	01	15
Total	41	10	06	03	60

Table 2.2: Guntur District

Occupation-wise Customers Particulars

Customers	Guntur	Chilaka-luripet	Narasa-raopet	Sattena-palli	Total
Agricultural	10	02	02	06	20
S.S.I.	10	02	02	06	20
S.H.G.	05	05	05	05	20
Business	15	05	—	—	20
Others	15	05	—	—	20
Total	55	19	09	17	100

Bank-wise customers particulars

Customers	Guntur	Chilaka-luripet	Narasa-raopet	Sattena-palli	Total
S.B.I.	13	04	05	08	30
A.B.	12	05	04	09	30
I.C.I.C.I.	15	05	—	—	20
ING	15	05	—	—	20
Total	55	19	09	15	100

Bank-wise officers particulars

Customers	Guntur	Chilaka-luripet	Narasa-raopet	Sattena-palli	Total
S.B.I.	05	05	02	03	15
A.B.	05	05	03	02	15
I.C.I.C.I.	15	—	—	—	15
ING	15	—	—	—	15
Total	40	10	05	05	60

Table 2.3 : East Godavari District

Occupation wise Customers' Particulars

Customers	Kaki-nada	Rajah-mundry	Pedda-puram	Samalkot	Amala-puram	Vatal-palam	Anapa-rthy	Bicca-volu	Total
Agricultural	—	—	—	—	05	05	05	05	20
S.S.I.	03	03	04	10	—	—	—	—	20
S.H.G.	—	—	—	—	05	05	05	05	20
Business	10	10	—	—	—	—	—	—	20
Others	10	10	—	—	—	—	—	—	20
Total	23	23	04	10	10	10	10	10	100

Bank-wise Customers Particulars

Customers	Kaki-nada	Rajah-mundry	Pedda-puram	Samalkot	Amala-puram	Vatal-palam	Anapa-rthy	Bicca-volu	Total
S.B.I.	02	01	02	05	05	05	05	05	30
A.B.	01	02	02	05	05	05	05	05	30
I.C.I.C.I	10	10	—	—	—	—	—	—	20
ING	10	10	—	—	—	—	—	—	20
Total	23	23	04	10	10	10	10	10	100

Bank-wise Officers Particulars

Customers	Kaki-nada	Rajah-mundry	Pedda-puram	Samalkot	Amala-puram	Vatal-palam	Anapa-rthy	Bicca-volu	Total
S.B.I.	04	02	02	02	02	01	01	01	15
A.B.	04	02	02	02	02	01	01	01	15
I.C.I.C.I	10	05	--	--	--	--	--	--	15
ING	10	05	--	--	--	--	--	--	15
Total	28	14	04	04	04	02	02	02	60

Sources of Data Collection

Primary Data

The primary data are collected through personal interviews, observations and discussions with bank officers concerned and bank customers. A separate structural schedule was papered for bank officers and customers to collect the necessary information for the present study. Before preparing schedule, the researcher has conducted a pilot study separately for the bankers and customers with a view to collect primary information necessary for designing the schedule.

The collected Primary data are tabulated and analysed with statistical tools.

Secondary Data

Apart from this information, the researcher has verified Annual reports, Booklets, Periodically publication of all the four Banks to get information about the profile of the Banks under study. The researcher has also made personal visits to PUNE (Indian institute of Bank management) and Andhra University Central Library, Osmania University Central Library and Library of Bank Administrative Staff College of India to collect necessary information relating to the banks.

Method of Data Collection

Schedule

The schedule contains both open end and close and questions that enables one to know the response of both bank officers and customers to the relationship in the changing scenario of banking industry.

The schedule was administered to different categories of customers such as Agricultural, Self Help Groups, Business Customers, Small scale industries and other customers (Household, salaried employees, educational loan holders).

The schedule to customers covered the following aspects:

1. Bank account opening
2. Deposits particulars
3. Withdrawal
4. Physical facilities

5. Cheque book facility
6. Debit/Credit card
7. Problems faced in the above aspects

The questionnaire to bank officers covered the following:

1. Provision of various services
2. Developments in the technology
3. Change in the expectations of customers
4. Problems relating to above aspects.

Data Analysis

The acquired data has been subjected to simple statistical treatment and presented in the form of cross tables. The interpretations of tables (SPSS package has used for tabulation) are given under each table with Chi-square values. The succeeding chapters of the study contain the tabulations of data with f-test (ANOVA) and t-test analysis and their interpretation was constructed below the tables Percentages are also calculated at appropriate places.

Limitations of the Study

- The study was conducted with regard to only Three districts in Andhra Pradesh: 1) Visakhapatnam District, 2) Guntur District, 3) East Godavari District.
- The information collected through the schedule is presumed to be correct. The validity of information given by respondents is verified with cross checking.
- The details of Micro-credit customers and Small Scale Industrialist are not available from both private sector banks (ICICI Bank Ltd., and ING Vysya Bank Ltd.).
- Another limitation is that the study cannot cover mutual fund, Insurance, and financial product.

However, due care has been taken to see that the study findings and conclusions are not adversely affected by the above limitations. Hence, the suggestions given in the study are worthy of consideration by policy makers for better promotion relations any customer and banker in the changing scenario.

Plan of the Study

The study is presented in *Eight Chapters*. The *first chapter* is entitled "introduction" presents the importance of banks in economic development of a country. *Chapter two* reviews the available literature on banking sector in India. It also presents the need for the present study along with objectives, methodology and limitations of study. The *third chapter* reviews the profiles of all the banks selected for presented study. The *fourth chapter* analyses the changing trends in banking sector in India, its emphasis is on the banking sector reforms and the impact of globalisation on Indian banking sector. The conceptual frame work, bank–customer relationship is presented in the *fifth chapter*. It deals with all the banking services and the need for relationship with customer and society. The *sixth and seventh chapters* are based on field study. The sixth chapter, which is opinion survey on Customer Services, presents the opinions of Bank officers and the views of bank customers on banker–customer relations in the changing scenario. On the other hand, the *seventh chapter* concentrates on opinion survey of customers on customer and banker relationship. The *last chapter* deals with findings, conclusions and suggestions to strengthen the existing relationship with the customers.

REFERENCES

1. Philip Kotler, "*Marketing Management*", 10th ed., Prentice Hall of India, New Delhi, 2000, p. 49.
2. Rangarajan, C. "*Innovation in Banking: The Indian Experience impact on Deposits and Credit*, Oxford & IBH Publishers Co., New Delhi, pp.32-38.
3. Kaveri, V.S. "Performance Evaluation of Bank Branches", *The Journal of Indian Institute of Bankers*, October-December, 1982, 178-183.
4. Gangadhar Khan, "*Nationalised Banking and Economic Development*", Vora & Co. Pub. Pvt. Ltd., Bombay, 1978, pp.138-158..

5. Dhanjagan, R.S. and Selvarajan, V. "Profitability of 14 Nationalised Banks: Examination of Recent Trends", *South Economist, October 15,*1983, pp. 9-13.
6. Birla Institute of Scientific Research, "*Banks since Nationalisation*", Allied Publishers Pvt. Ltd., New Delhi, dt.1-9-1981, pp.58-62.
7. Katilya Perumal, "*Deposits Mobilisation by Private Sector Banks*", An Unpublished Ph.D. Thesis submitted to Annamalai University, Annamalainagar, India, 1982.
8. Satyam Murthy, B. "*Profitability Trends in Scheduled Commercial Banks in India Changing the period 1970-82 – An Analytical Approaches,* An unpublished thesis submitted to the University of Bombay, Bombay, 1991.
9. Robert, M. "*Profitability of Private Sector Banks in India since 1969*", An unpublished Ph.D. Thesis submitted to Madras University, Madras, 1992.
10. Vinod Kumar. "*Profitability of Private Sector Banks in India-1969,* An unpublished Ph.D. Thesis submitted to Meerut University, Meerut, 1984.
11. Mathur, O.P. "*Public Sector Banks in India in Indian survey – A case study of S.B.I.*" Sterling Pub. Pvt. Ltd., New Delhi, 1978, pp. 128-132.
12. Kannaji Rao, "*Marketing of Services in Commercial Banks: A Study of Marketing operations of Andhra Bank,*" Unpublished Ph.D. Thesis, Andhra University, Visakhapatnam, 1994.
13. Gopal Saxena, "*Marketing in Commercial Banks: A Study of S.B.I.*", Unpublished Ph.D. Thesis, Manipur University, Manipur, 1992.
14. Talwar, R.K. "Government of India, Report of the Customer Services in Banks", 1997, pp. 9-46.
15. Rajiv Upadhyaya, "Management of Commercial Banks in India: Public Relations and Customer Services, Deep & Deep Publications, New Delhi, 1985, p. 78.
16. Narayana, M.S. "*A Study of the Attitude of Customers*", An Unpublished M.Phil. Dissertation, submitted to Nagarjuna University, 1988, pp.208-209.
17. Mellow, L.D. "Bank Credit for Weaker Sections: Performance and Prospects", *A Journal of Indian Institute of Banks*, April-June, 1980, pp. 87-95.
18. Rama Jyothsna Ratna Kumari, V. "*Priority Sector Lending by Commercial Banks – A Study of the Vysya Bank Ltd, Guntur District.*", Ph.D. Thesis submitted to Nagarjuna University, 1990, pp.193-194.

19. Ramesh, "*Changing Role of Commercial Banks: A Study of Andhra Bank*", Ph.D. Thesis submitted to Nagarjuna University, 1989.
20. Anil Kumar, "*Performance Evaluation of the 14 Nationalised Banks in India with special reference to priority sector-1970-80*", Ph.D. Thesis submitted to Nagarjuna University, 1985.
21. Ashok Kumar Bohra, "*An Analytical Study of the Role of Lead Banks in Rural Financing Rajasthan: A Case Study*", Ph.D. thesis submitted to Jodhpur University, Jodhpur, 1987.
22. Rama Krishna, "*Finances for Small Scale Industries in India*", Published Thesis of Bombay University, Aisa Pub. House, 1962, pp. 182-190.
23. Satish Bahadur Mathur, "*Sickness in Small Scale Sector causes and cure with special reference to role of Commercial Banks*", Ph.D. Thesis submitted to Osmania University, Hyderabad, 1992.
24. Brahmanandam, G.N. "*Financing Small Scale Industries by Commercial Banks in Guntur District*", Ph.D. Thesis submitted to Nagarjuna University, Guntur, 1983.
25. Mukherjee, K.P. "Nationalised Banks and Agricultural in Bihar", *Journal of Indian Institute of Bankers*, July-September, 1976, pp. 143-147.
26. Ravi Kumar Bhola. "*Financing Agricultural by Commercial Banks*", Report of the Seminar held in 1968, RBI Publications, Bombay, 1983.
27. Daniel, "*Role of Commercial Banks in Financing, the Schemes for Poverty, Self Employment Schemes to educate unemployed youth – Regional Study of Hubli, Dharwad Corporation Area in Karnakata State*", Ph.D. Thesis submitted to Karnataka University, 1987.
28. Nagaraj, "*Problems of Rural Artisans*", *Khadi Gramodyog*, May 1988, pp. 52-53.
29. Dave, G.L. "Issues regarding measurement and reporting of corporation social performance", *The Indian Journal of Commerce*, Vol. XLIV, Part-II, No.167, 1991, pp. 92-96.
30. Guruswamy, "Corporation Social Responsibility particular in India", *The Indian Journal of Commerce*, Vol. XLVI, Part-II, No. 167, 1991, pp. 78-84..
31. Samiuddin and Hifzur-Rehman, Survey of Social Reporting Practices in Indian Companies, *The Indian Journal of Commerce*, Part-II, 1991, pp. 34-38.

32. Sharma, "A Case study for public interest reporting in India", *The Indian Journal of Commerce*, Vol. XLIV, Part-II, No. 167, 1991, pp. 70-72.

33. Panda, N.M. "Uniformity in Social Reporting: A pragmatic approach for public sector enterprise in India", *The Indian Journal of Commerce*, Vol. XLVI, Part-II, No. 175, 1993, pp. 1-11.

34. Arun, T.G. and Turner, J.D., "Financial Sector Reforms in Developing Countries - The Indian Experience", *The World Economy,* 25(3), 2002, pp. 29-45.

35. Mei Xue Patrick T. Harker, "Customer Efficiency Concept and Its Impact on e-Business Management", *Journal of Service Research*, University of Pennsylvania, Sage Publications, Vol. 4, No. 4, 2002, pp. 53-67.

36. Renu Sobti, "*Banking and Financial Services in India: Marketing Redefined by 2003*", New Century Publications, 4800/24, Bharat Ram Road, Ansari Road, Daryaganj, New Delhi, 2003.

37. Matthias Gouthier, Catholic University of Eichstätt-Ingolstadt, Germany Stefan Schmid ESCP-EAP European School of Management, Germany Marketing Theory, Sage Publications Customers and Customer Relationships in Service Firms: The Perspective of the Resource-Based View, Vol. 3, No.1, 2003, pp. 19-43.

38. Satish Jayachandran, University of South Carolina; Kelly Hewlett, University of South Carolina; Peter Kaufman, Illinois State University; *Journal of the Academy of Marketing Science,* Customer Response Capability in a Sense-and-Respond Era: The Role of Customer Knowledge Process, Vol. 32, No.3, 2004, pp. 19-33.

39. Shun Yin Lam Nanyang, Technological University; Venkatesh Shankar, University of Maryland; Krishna Erramilli, M. and Bysan Murthy, Nanyang Technological University; Customer Value, Satisfaction, Loyalty, and Switching Costs: An Illustration From a Business-to-Business Service Context, *Journal of the Academy of Marketing Science*, Vol. 32, No.3, 2004, pp. 29-31.

40. Sundaram, R. The Hindu - A Seminar on Customer Relationship Management held at the PKR Arts College for Women in Gobichettipalayam, focused on the need to develop customer banker relationship and improving Service Quality in the Banking Industry, dt. 09-01-2005.

CHAPTER

Profiles of Banks under Study

This chapter makes as attempt to present a profile of the banks under the study — State Bank of India, Andhra Bank, ING Vysya Bank and ICICI Bank. It explains the organisational structure, activities, operating system and customer care programmes of each bank under the study. This provides the necessary back ground for the present study.

Banking institutions come under the organised sector. Among these the commercial banks are the oldest institutions having a wide network of branches, commanding utmost public confidence and having a lion's share in the total banking operation. Initially, they were established as corporate bodies with share-holding by private individuals, but subsequently there has been a drift towards State ownership and control. Today 27 banks constitute the strong public sector in Indian commercial banking.[1]

Up to late 1960, banking institutions were mainly engaged in financing organised trade, commerce and industry. Since then, they have been actively participating in financing agriculture, small business and small borrower also. The commercial banks operating in India fall under a number of sub-categories on the basis of ownership and control of management[2] as is evident from the Chart 3.1.

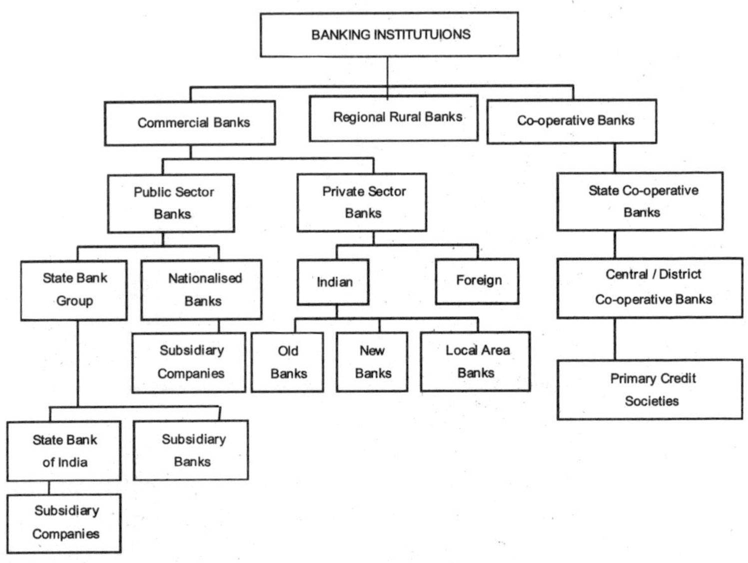

Public and Private Sector Banks

Public sector in Indian banking has reached its present position in three stages-first, the conversion of the then existing Imperial Bank of India into the State Bank of India in 1955 followed by the establishment of its seven subsidiary banks; Second, the nationalisation of 14 major commercial banks on July 19, 1969 and last, the nationalisation of 6 more commercial banks on April 15, 1980. One of them, New Bank of India was later on merged with Punjab National Bank. Thus, 27 banks constitute Public Sector in Indian Commercial Banking.[3]

After the nationalisation of major banks in 1969, new banks in the private sector could not be set up in India for more than two decades though there was no legal bar to that effect. The Narasimham Committee on Financial Sector (1991) recommended the establishment of such banks in India. The Reserve Bank of India, therefore, issued guidelines for the setting up of new private sector banks in India in January, 1993[4]. These guidelines aim at ensuring that the new banks are financially viable and technologically up-to-date from the start. They are expected to start functioning in a professional manner, so as to improve the image of commercial banking system and to win the confidence of the depositing public.

The new banks are required to be registered as public limited companies under the Companies Act, 1956, with an initial paid up capital of Rs.100 crore. They are to be governed by the provisions of Reserve Bank of India Act and the Banking Regulation Act, 1949 and shall comply with the directions issued by the Reserve Bank of India[5]. Ten new private sector banks have been established mainly by the financial institutions such as UTI, ICICI, IDBI, and HDFC. Times Bank was subsequently merged with another new bank HDFC Bank.

Profiles of the Banks under the Study

State Bank of India

State Bank of India is an India-based bank. In addition to banking, the Company, through its subsidiaries, provides a range of financial services, which include life insurance, merchant banking, mutual funds, credit card, factoring, security trading, pension fund management and primary dealership in the money market. It operates in four business segments: the treasury segment includes the entire investment portfolio and trading in foreign exchange contracts and derivative contracts; the corporate / wholesale banking segment comprises the lending activities of corporate accounts group, mid corporate accounts group and stressed assets management group; the retail banking segment comprises of branches in National Banking Group, which primarily includes personal banking activities, and other banking business. As of March 31, 2011, the Bank had a network of 18,266 branches including 4,724 branches of its five Associate Banks

The State Bank of India (SBI) has an extensive administrative structure to oversee the large network of branches in India and abroad. Its Corporate Centre is in Mumbai and 14 Local Head Offices and 57 Zonal Offices are located at important cities spread throughout the country. The Corporate Centre has several other establishments in and outside Mumbai, designated to cater to various functions. Its Colleges/Institutes/Training Centres are the seats of learning and research and development to spread the wings of knowledge not only to the employees of SBI but also other banks establishments in India and abroad. The Corporate Accounts Group is a Strategic Business Unit of the Bank set up exclusively to fulfil the specialised banking needs of top corporates in the country. The State Bank of India has 52 foreign offices in 34 countries across the globe. The State Bank of India invites the public to take a journey to understand the potential of not just a large but truly global organisation.[66]

The State Bank of India has an unbroken tradition of more than 196 years of banking. Its history is traced back to the Bank of Calcutta (1806) which received its charter as Bank of Bengal in 1809. There were two other Banks, Bank of Bombay (1840) and Bank of Madras (1843). These three banks were known as Presidency Banks. The Presidency Banks were authorised to conduct Government business and also to issue currency notes.

The three Presidency Banks were amalgamated to form the Imperial Bank of India (70 branches) in 1921. The Imperial Bank was conducting government business exclusively. The RBI was established only in 1935 pursuant to the recommendations of the Hilton Young Commission. After the formation of RBI, the Imperial Bank acted as its agent in doing government business and in maintaining currency chest and small coin depot. The RBI was first established as a Private Bank in 1935 and nationalised later in 1949. The All India Rural Credit Survey Committee (Gorwala Committee), 1955 recommended the formation of the State Bank of India. Accordingly, the SBI was formed as a state partnered and state sponsored bank. It took over the Imperial Bank of India. The SBI was formed under the State Bank of India Act 1955. It was established with the objective of taking banking to the interior and remote parts of India.

An important turning point in the history of State Bank of India is the launch of the first Five Year Plan of independent India, in 1951. The Plan aimed at serving the Indian economy in general and the rural sector of the country, in particular. Until the Plan, the commercial banks of the country, including the Imperial Bank of India, confined their services to the urban sector. Moreover, they were not equipped to respond to the growing needs of the economic revival taking shape in the rural areas of the country. Therefore, in order to serve the economy as a whole and rural sector in particular, the All India Rural Credit Survey Committee recommended the formation of a state-partnered and state-sponsored bank.

The All India Rural Credit Survey Committee proposed the take over of the Imperial Bank of India, and integrating with it, the former state-owned or state-associate banks. Subsequently, an Act was passed in the Parliament of India in May 1955. As a result, the State Bank of India (SBI) was established on 1 July 1955. This resulted in making the State Bank of India more powerful, because as much as a quarter of the resources of the Indian banking system were controlled directly by the State. Later on, the State Bank of India (Subsidiary Banks) Act was passed in 1959. The Act enabled the State Bank of India to make the eight former State-associated banks as its subsidiaries.

The State Bank of India emerged as a pacesetter, with its operations carried out by the 480 offices comprising branches, sub offices and three Local Head Offices, inherited from the Imperial Bank. Instead of serving as mere repositories of the community's savings and lending to creditworthy parties, the State Bank of India catered to the needs of the customers, by banking purposefully. The bank served the heterogeneous financial needs of the planned economic development.

The other important particulars of the Bank are (2011 March):

(*a*)	No. of Branches/Offices	=	99345
(*b*)	No. of Employees	=	383,347
(*c*)	Total assets	=	US$ 370 billion
(*d*)	Net Profit	=	Rs. 2,810 Cr.
(*e*)	Capital Adequacy Ratio	=	13.35% (Tier I: 9.22%; Tier II: 4.13%)
(*f*)	Net NPA/Net Advances	=	5.63% (Decreased from 6.03% IN 2006-07)
(*g*)	Deposits	=	Rs. 2,70,560 Cr.
(*h*)	Advances	=	Rs. 1,20,806 Cr.

SBI's Organisational Structure

The Bank has been making changes in its structure, systems etc in tune with environmental demands.

The Present Organisational Structure

The Bank has a 4-tier structure. The Central Office is the bank's apex policy-making body. The Central Office is now called Corporate Centre. The Management of the Bank vests with the Central Board consisting of a Chairman, 2 Managing Directors and other Directors. The term of office of a director is 3 years. At the Local Head Office, a Local Board is constituted. The Board comprises CGM (ex officio), Directors of the Central Board ordinarily resident in the area, one member elected by the local shareholders holding together not less then 2.5 per cent of the issued capital and others nominated by the Government in consultation with the RBI.

Areas that needed immediate attention:

(*a*) The Bank faced increased competition from domestic and foreign banks in respect of corporate customers.

Hence, the risk evaluation techniques had to be improved.

(*b*) The Money market, Forex market and Capital market had become volatile. The Bank had to equip itself in terms of skills and expertise, state of the art technology and appropriate structure.

The changes at the Central Office level were first introduced in 1994.

The following key changes were introduced at Central Office Structure:

1. **Lean Corporate Centre**: The numbers of top management positions at C.O. level were reduced. New designations were given to signify the importance of the roles.
2. **Introduction of independent business units as profit centres:** The Bank's markets have been identified and re-grouped as under

   (*a*) Corporate Banking

   (*b*) National Banking

   (*c*) International Banking, and

   (*d*) Associates and Subsidiaries

The bank has been opening specialised branches which are delivery platforms for meeting the banking needs of specific customer groups like Personal Banking customers, SSI units etc. Specialised Personal Banking Branches are opened in metro and urban areas and are equipped with the state-of-the-art technology. They are targeted at high networth individuals with the objective of providing them with a full average of services and products. These branches are technology driven, possess distinct brand image and prime ambience; these branches will be the launch pad for new products like internet banking, tale-banking and home banking.[7]

The Bank has the following Non-Banking subsidiaries in India:

1. SBI Capital Markets Ltd
2. SBI Funds Management Pvt. Ltd
3. SBI Factors & Commercial Services Pvt. Ltd
4. SBI DFHI Ltd.

The SBI is committed to customers' service. It says[8]:

(*i*) We promise that we will act courteously, fairly and reasonably in all our dealings with you.

(*ii*) We will make sure that our documents and procedures are clear and not misleading and that you are given clear information about our products and services.

(*iii*) When you have chosen an account or service we will give you clear information about how it works, the terms and conditions and the interest rates which apply to it.

(*iv*) We will help you use your account or service by sending you regular statements (where appropriate) and we will keep you informed about changes to the interest rates, charges or terms and conditions.

(*v*) We will deal quickly and sympathetically with things that go wrong by correcting mistakes quickly, handling complaints quickly and reversing any bank charges applied in error.

(*vi*) We will treat all your personal information as private and confidential, and operate secure and reliable banking and payment systems.

(*vii*) We will make public our Citizens' Charter, have copies available and make sure that our staff are trained to put it into practice.

The SBI expects their customers to[9]:

(*i*) Help us meet the "Know Your Customer (KYC)" guidelines at the time of opening the account

(*ii*) Take precautions that are indicated for protection of their accounts (*iii*) Avail services like Automated Teller Machine (ATM), Online banking, Electronic Clearing System (ECS), Electronic Fund Transfer (EFT) etc. if offered by the branch.

(*iv*) Avail nomination facility for their accounts and safe deposit lockers.

(*v*) Not to introduce any person not known personally for the purpose of opening account.

(*vi*) Pay service charges for non maintenance of minimum balances, return of cheques, remittances, collections etc. The details of charges are available in the Citizen's charter and also with our branches.

(*vii*) Provide valuable feedback on our services so as to enable us to correct our mistakes and improve our services.

The SBI has customer care service. The Customers of the Bank can meet senior executives of the Bank on 15th of every month (between 3.00 p.m. and 5.00 p.m.) without any prior appointment and discuss issues relating to their accounts/banking transactions. In case, the 15th of month is a holiday, customer can meet the officials on the next working day.[10]

In the event of excessive delay in resolving their problems, the customers can contact the help line of the Local Head Office, under whose control the branch functions.

Subsidiaries

The State Bank Group includes a network of eight banking subsidiaries and several non-banking subsidiaries. Through the establishments, it offers various services including merchant banking services, fund management, factoring services, primary dealership in government securities, credit cards and insurance.

The eight banking subsidiaries are:

State Bank of Bikaner and Jaipur (SBBJ)

State Bank of Hyderabad (SBH)

State Bank of India (SBI)

State Bank of Indore (SBIR)

State Bank of Mysore (SBM)

State Bank of Patiala (SBP)

- State Bank of Saurashtra (SBS)
- State Bank of Travancore (SBT)

Products And Services Personal Banking

SBI Term Deposits SBI Loan For Pensioners

SBI Recurring Deposits Loan Against Mortgage of Property

SBI Housing Loan Loan Against Shares & Debentures

SBI Car Loan Rent Plus Scheme

SBI Educational Loan Medi-Plus Scheme

Other Services

Agriculture/Rural Banking

NRI Services

ATM Services

Demat Services

Corporate Banking

Internet Banking

Mobile Banking

International Banking

Safe Deposit Locker

RBIEFT

E-Pay

E-Rail

SBI Vishwa Yatra Foreign Travel Card

Broking Services

Gift Cheques

Profile of the Andhra Bank

The "Andhra Bank" was founded by the eminent freedom fighter Dr.Bhogaraju Pattabhi Sitaramayya. The Bank was registered on 20th November, 1923 and it commenced business on 28th November, 1923 with a paid up capital of Rs 1.00 lakh and an authorised capital of Rs 10.00 lakhs. The Bank has crossed many milestones and the Bank's Total Business as on 30.09.2006 stood at Rs.56,113 crores with a Clientele base over 1.48 crores. The Bank is rendering services through 1811 Business Delivery Channels consisting of 1233 branches, 116 Extension Counters, 425 ATMs and 37 Satellite Offices spread over 21 States and 2 Union Territories as at the end of Sep., 2006. All Branches are 100 per cent computerised, 1026 units viz., 917 Branches, 94 Extension Counters, 15 Service Centres networked under Cluster Banking Solution and providing "Any Branch Banking (ABB)". Real Time Gross Settlement (RTGS) Facility has been introduced in 600 Branches. To provide value-added services to Customers, the Bank has set up its own 425 ATMs as on 30.09.2006.[11] Besides, ATM sharing arrangements with several Banks including SBI, ICICI Bank, IDBI Bank, UTI Bank, SBI, HDFC Bank, Indian Bank, Corporation Bank and 17 other banks under National Financial Switch provide Bank customers access to 15500 ATMs throughout the country. The Andhra Bank is a pioneer in introducing Credit Cards in the country in 1981 and the business turnover under Credit Cards increased to Rs.513 cr. as on 30.09.2006 registering a growth rate of 27.39%.

The Andhra Bank has launched Mobile ATM and ATM Compatible Kisan Vikas Card recently. The Bank has recently has opened its Representative Office in Dubai and is planning to open more such offices in Doha, Muscat, Riyadh and Kuwait shortly in order to reach the NRIs staying in the Middle East Countries. The Bank has introduced Internet Banking Facility (AB INFI-net) to all customers of cluster linked branches. Rail Ticket Booking Facility is made available to all debit card holders through IRCTC Website through a separate gateway. The Bank's Corporate Website is available in English and Hindi Languages communicating the Bank's image and information. A Website in Telugu language is under construction. The Bank has been given 'BEST BANK AWARD' a banking technology award by IDRBT, Hyderabad for extensive use of IT in Semi Urban and Rural Areas on 02.09.2006. Thus, the Bank accords utmost importance to customer satisfaction by offering innovative and need based financial products and services using state-of -the art technology.

Financial Details

Total Business volume of the bank in the third quarter of the 2008-09 financial year stood at Rs. 95, 822 Crores, while the Total Deposit volume during the same tenure was Rs. 53,795 Crores.

As of 31st of December, 2008, Andhra Bank had a client base of more than 18.5 Million customers with 2194 Business Delivery Channels. Till the same date, the bank had 1,410 branches spread across 22 states and 2 Union Territories, out of which 1,067 branches have been enabled with Centralized Core Banking Solution (CBS). While the total number of ATMs summed up to 685, the bank had a Per Employee Productivity of Rs 6.92 Crore.

The Andhra Bank has Corporate Identity. 'Togetherness 'is the theme of this logo where the world of banking services meets the realm of ever changing customer needs and establishes a link that is like a chain, inseparable. The logo also denotes a bank that's prepared to do anything, to go to any lengths, for the sake of the customer. The blue pointer on the top represents the philosophy of a bank that's always looking for growth and newer, and challenging, more promising directions .The keyhole indicates safety and security. The colours red and blue represent fusion of dynamism and solidity. At a time when the performance of the bank, the prospects of the bank, and even the perceptions of the bank are vibrantly different, and poised as we are at the threshold of a new millennium, this modernised logo is a tribute to the Andhra Bankers who are the true creators of the image of the bank. Shri K Ramakrishnan took charge as Chairman and Managing Director of Andhra Bank in June, 2005.[12] Two Specialised Corporate Finance branches are catering exclusively to the needs of the corporate clientele. Corporate terminals are offered to high value corporate customers. 60 Corporates are availing these services. Cash Management System (CMS) is introduced to improve and enhance effective cash supervision of our corporate clients.

The Bank's lending to Priority Sector, as a portion of Net Bank Credit (NBC) was 42.42 per cent at the end of March 2007, against the stipulated norm of 40 per cent. Such advances have registered a growth rate of 20.27 per cent from Rs.4322 crore as on the last reporting March 2006 to Rs.5198 crore as on March 2007. The Bank focused attention on the flow of credit to agriculture and allied activities during the year 2006-2007. The Agri Business Centres on the lines of the Personal Banking Centers and small scale industries lending centres are successfully functioning in 37 branches of the Bank. The Bank is having 3 specialised Agri Finance Branches and 6 designated Agri Hi-Tech branches to cater to the needs of high value and Hi-tech agriculture. The Agriculture lending through these branches has crossed Rs.133.38 crore[13].

Further branches have extended financial assistance to 4040 beneficiaries under Golden Jubilee Rural Housing Finance Scheme, during the year 2006-2007. Sanction of Educational Loans under Dr. Pattabhi Vidyajyothi Scheme to students for pursuing higher studies in India and abroad has been taken up as a thrust area. The advances to weaker sections stood at Rs.1242.63 crore as on 2006 In the area of financing the poor through the intermediation of Self Help Groups (SHGs), the Bank had so far credit linked 1,26,811 SHGs (cumulative) with disbursement of Rs.332 crore.

In addition to normal Banking operations, the Bank as a responsible and responsive corporate citizen, has invested a part of its profit for community welfare. The bank underlines the importance of the retail banking along with other banks in India.

Credit/ATM/debit Cards

Credit Card: The Bank has achieved Credit card business turnover of Rs.591.50 crore with a card base of 1,03,289 as against Rs.551 crore in the previous year. The card is made attractive by offering lowest service charges on card usage. The VISA card is also made compatible with our ATMs, Cash drawing facility is made available on domestic and international VISA cards. The Bank established Master Card connectivity to the our ATMs for domestic and international Master Cards.

The Bank has introduced "Master Card Electronic" as a value addition for its term Deposit holders. The deposit holders of the Bank can obtain this card without producing any documents. It also offers attractive Insurance coverage.

Debit/ATM Cards

The Bank's Debit card in association with VISA was launched on 12.05.2003. It facilitates the cardholders to draw cash from any ATM across the world with VISA logo, besides providing access to the Merchant establishments / Point of sale Terminals for purchase of goods and services. The Bank has enrolled 692 numbers of merchants during the year. The turnover on Andhra bank Cards has increased from Rs.117 crore during the year 2005-2006 to Rs. 160 crore for 2006-2007 with annualised growth of 37 per cent.

Customer Service and Marketing

Various recommendations of the Government, RBI and IBA have been implemented by the Bank. However, despite this, there is the need to revamp and bring about an overall improvement varied in nature.

1. **Customer Complaint Redressal:** The complaints received are dealt with promptly and expeditiously. During the period between 01.04.2006 and

31.03.2007, the Customer service department received 403 complaints and no complaint is pending as on 31.03.2007.

2. **Citizen charter:** The Bank has published Model Citizen charter captioned Essentials, in bi-lingual form, which contain information on – common practices followed by the branches, Fair Banking practices , Gist of Banking Ombudsman scheme-2002, Redressal of complaints. The same is kept in the Bank's website, too.
3. **Specialised Client Relationship Officers**: The Bank has 305 specialised CROs to act as a bridge between the customer and the Bank. These CROs market the products and reach out to new customer groups like Government Departments, corporate Clients, High value clients etc to increase the market share of the Bank.
4. **Booklets and Brochures:** As a part of enhancing information to Customers, the bank has brought out booklets and brochures on its unique features of ATM, Know Your Currency, Deposit Schemes, Personal Banking Schemes, facilities available to NRIs.
5. **Customer Service Centre:** On behalf of all branches of Public sector Banks and branches of Jammu & Kashmir bank in twin cities of Hyderabad and Secunderabad, the Bank is acting as coordinator of "Customer Service Centre".
6. **Adhoc Committee on Procedures and Performance Audit of Public Services**: An Adhoc Committee was constituted at Head Office, under the leadership of General manger Marketing to review systems in place by providing better services to the customers and simplifications of procedures and practices for different activities.
7. **ISO 9001:2000 Certification**: The Bank has identified 50 branches from various Zones for ISO

9001: 2000 certification in the FY 2003-2004 of which six branches were certified and the rest are in the process of certification. As on 31.03.2006, 53 branches are certified.

Branch Expansion

The Bank has its branches spread over 21 states and 2 Union territories of which 73.58% (830 branches) of branches are located in Andhra Pradesh. During the year, the Bank opened 28new branches (including up gradation of Extension Counters). With this as at the end of 31 March 2007, the Bank had 1573 Delivery Channels constituting 1128 branches, 129 Extension Counters and 44 Satellite Offices and 272 ATMs.

The population Group-wise classification of branches is as follows:

Sl. No.	Category	Number	Percentage to total No. of Branches
1.	Rural	381	34
2.	Semi-Urban	317	28
3.	Urban	277	24
4.	Metro	153	14
	Total	**1128**	**100**

A major thrust was given to consolidation of the existing branch network. 296 branches are acting as focal point branches for collection of direct taxes, 39 branches are handling pension payments, and all these branches are fully computerised.[14]

Products and Services

The products and services provided by the bank are mainly categorized into businesses of Retail, Corporate, NRI, MSME, and Agricultural industries. Under the Retail Business, the bank offers Deposits, Loans, Cards, DMAT Services, Payment

Services, Insurance, and Mutual Funds to individual customers. Under the Corporate Business, the bank offers Loans & Advances, Project Appraisal services, and Syndication of Loans to the business entities. Under the NRI business segment, the bank offers Deposit schemes, Loans, Remittance services, and Investment services to the Non Resident Indians. Under the MSME business segment, the bank offers different schemes that aimed at providing loan and transaction services to Micro Small and Medium Enterprises(MSME). Some of the MSME schemes available are OTS Scheme, Composite loan scheme, Open cash credit(OCC), Artisans Credit Card(ACC), AB Laghu Udhyami Credit Card(LUCC), AB Power Tools(Shakti), Technology upgradation fund scheme(TUFs), Credit guarantee fund trust for small industries(CGTSI), AB Doctor Plus...etc. Under the Agriculture business segment, bank provides different credit schemes to farmers, Women Empowerment schemes, and Andhra Bank Rural Development Trust(ABRDT) helps Rural Self Employment Training Institutes(RSETIs).

Following are the various *Deposit Schemes* available -

- AB Savings Accounts
- AB Current Accounts
- AB Term Deposits
- AB Arogyadaan Scheme
- AB Bancassurance Life
- AB Bancassurance (Non Life)
- Retail Loans
- Agricultural Loans
- Corporate Banking
- NRI Banking
- NRI Products and Services
- NOSTOR details for remittance
- Western Union Money Transfer

Following are the various *Technology Products* available:

- Internet Banking

- Credit cards (Either on the basis of Fixed Deposit or latest Income Tax returns)
- Multi City Cheque Facility
- On-Line Tax Accounting System (OLTAS)
- Real Time Gross Settlement (RTGS)

Instant Funds Transfer

- ATM Services
- Any Branch Banking
- Electronic Clearing Service (ECS)
- National Electronic Funds Transfer

Profile of ING Vysya Bank

The ING Vysya Bank Ltd., is an entity formed with the coming together of erstwhile, Vysya Bank Ltd. a premier bank in the Indian Private Sector and a global financial powerhouse, ING of Dutch origin, during Oct 2002. The origin of the erstwhile Vysya Bank was pretty humble. It was in the year 1930 that a team of visionaries came together to found a bank that would extend a helping hand to those who weren't privileged enough to enjoy banking services. On the other hand, ING group originated in 1990 from the merger between National–Nederlanden NV, the largest Dutch Insurance Company and NMB Post Bank Group NV. Combining roots and ambitions, the newly formed company was called "Internationale Nederlanden Group". Market circles soon abbreviated the name to I-N-G. The company followed suit by changing the statutory name to "ING Group N.V.".

1930	Set up in Bangalore
1948	Scheduled Bank
1985	Largest Private Sector Bank
1987	The Vysya Bank Leasing Ltd. Commenced
1988	Pioneered the concept of Co branding of Credit Cards
1990	Promoted Vysya Bank Housing Finance Ltd.

1992	Deposits cross Rs.1000 crores
1993	Number of Branches crossed 300
1996	Signs Strategic Alliance with BBL., Belgium. Two National Awards by Gem & Jewellery Export Promotion Council for excellent performance in Export Promotion
1998	Cash Management Services, & commissioning of VSAT. Golden Peacock Award - for the best HR Practices by Institute of Directors. Rated as Best Domestic Bank in India by Global Finance (International Financial Journal - June 1998)
2000	State -of - the -art Date Centre at ITPL, Bangalore.RBI clears setting up of ING Vysya Life Insurance Company
2001	ING-Vysya commenced life insurance business.
2002	The Bank launched a range of products & services like the Vys Vyapar Plus, the range of loan schemes for traders, ATM services, Smartserv, personal assistant service, Save & Secure, an account that provides accident hospitalization and insurance cover, Sambandh, the International Debit Card and the mi-b@nk net banking service.
2002	ING takes over the Management of the Bank from October 7th , 2002
2002	RBI clears the new name of the Bank as ING Vysya Bank Ltd, vide their letter of 17.12.02
2003	Introduced customer friendly products like Orange Savings, Orange Current and Protected Home Loans
2004	Introduced Protected Home Loans - a housing loan product
2005	Introduced Solo - My Own Account for youth and Customer Service Line – Phone Banking Service
2006	Bank has networked all the branches to facilitate 'AAA' transactions i.e. Anywhere, Anytime & Anyhow Banking

It's been a long journey since then and the Bank has grown in size and stature to encompass every area of present-day banking activity and has carved a distinct identity of being India's Premier Private Sector Bank.

In 1980, the Bank completed fifty years of service to the nation and the Bank made rapid strides to reach the coveted position of being the number one private sector bank in the post 1985 period. In 1990, the Bank completed its Diamond Jubilee year. At the Diamond Jubilee Celebrations, the then Finance Minister Prof. Madhu Dandavate, had termed the performance of the bank 'Stupendous'. The bank celebrated its 75th anniversary (Platinum Jubilee year) in 2005[15].

The long journey of seventy-five years has had several milestones. The Bank was established in 1930 at Bangalore. It became a Scheduled Bank in 1948. It is the largest private sector bank in 1985. It commenced business in 1987 as The Vysya Bank Leasing Ltd. In 1988 it pioneered the concept of Co branding of Credit Cards and by 1990 it promoted Vysya Bank Housing Finance Ltd. By 1992, the Deposits of the Bank crossed Rs.1000 cores. Its number of branches crossed 300. In 1996 the Bank signed Strategic Alliance with BBL., Belgium and received two National Awards by Gem & Jewellery Export Promotion Council for excellent performance in Export Promotion. In 1998 it introduced Cash Management Services, & commissioning of VSAT. and received Golden Peacock Award - for the best HR Practices by Institute of Directors. rated as the Best Domestic Bank in India by Global Finance.[16]

The Bank progressed and by 2000 the bank started State -of - the -art Date Centre at ITPL, Bangalore. RBI cleared setting up of ING Vysya Life Insurance Company, as a result of which in 2001 ING-Vysya commenced life insurance business. In 2002 the Bank launched a range of products & services like the Vys Vyapar Plus, the range of loan schemes for traders, ATM services, Smart service, personal assistant service, Save & Secure, an account that provides accident hospitalisation and insurance cover, Sambandh, the

International Debit Card and the mi-bank net banking service. In the same year RBI cleared the new name of the Bank as ING Vysya Bank Ltd, vide their letter of 17.12.2002,[17] it introduced customer friendly products like Orange Savings, Orange Current and Protected Home Loans in 2003. in the year, 2004 the bank introduced Protected Home Loans - a housing loan product and in the subsequent year, it in introduced Solo - My Own Account for youth and Customer Service Line – Phone Banking Service. in 2006 Saral Savings - No Frills Account for the common man has been introduced.

In terms of pure numbers, the performance over the decades can better be appreciated from the following table:

Performance of ING Vysya Bank Ltd., during 1940-2010

(Rs. in millions)

Year	Networth	Deposits	Advances	Profits	Outlets
1940	0.001	0.400	0.400	0.001	4
1950	1.40	5.30	3.80	0.09	16
1960	1.60	20.10	13.50	0.13	19
1970	3.00	91.50	62.80	0.74	39
1980	11.50	1414.30	813.70	1.13	228
1990	162.10	8509.40	4584.80	50.35	319
2000	5900.00	74240.00	39380.00	443.10	481
2001	6527.00	81411.10	43163.10	371.90	484
2002	6863.24	80680.00	44180.00	687.50	483
2003	7067.90	91870.00	56120.00	863.50	456
2004	7473.20	104780.00	69367.30	590.01	523
2005	7094.00	125693.10	90805.90	381.80	536
2006	1019.67	133350.00	102320.00	90.60	575
2007	11101.90	154185.70	119761.70	889.0	626
2008	14260.00	204980.00	146500.00	1569.00	677
2009	15940.00	248900.00	167510.00	1888.00	857
2010	2223.00	258650.00	185070.00	2422.00	866*

Source: Complied from ING Vysya Annual Reports & Publications.

In totality, the bank comprises of 380 branches, 42 ECs, 28 Satellite Offices and 127 ATMs. Besides, the Bank also has Internet Banking – mi-bank and Customer Service Line for Phone Banking Service.

The ING has gained recognition for its integrated approach of banking, insurance and asset management. Furthermore, the company differentiates itself from other financial service providers by successfully establishing life insurance companies in countries with emerging economies, such as Korea, Taiwan, Hungary, Poland, Mexico and Chile. Another specialisation is ING Direct, an Internet and direct marketing concept with which ING is rapidly winning retail market share in mature markets. Finally, ING distinguishes itself internationally as a provider of 'employee benefits', i.e. arrangements of non-age benefits, such as pension plans for companies and their employees.[18]

The ING's mission is to be a leading, global, client-focused, innovative and low-cost provider of financial services through the distribution channels of the client's preference in markets where ING can create value.

The immediate benefit to ING Vysya Bank ltd is the pride of having become a member of global financial services giant, with an asset base of 1159 billion euros, net profit of 7.21 billion euros as of December 31st 2005. Further, the presence of the group in over 50 countries, employing over 117000 people, serving over 60 million customers across the globe, only multiplies the credibility, not only across the country but also across the globe. The pride of this global identity, the back up of a financial power house and the status of being the first Indian International bank, would also greatly enhance productivity, profitability resulting in improved performance for the bank to translate into higher returns, to all the stake holders.

The bank as a part of its Corporate Social Responsibility has partnered with Parikrama Humanity Foundation. Parikrama Humanity Foundation is a non-profit company aiming to unleash the potential of slum children in urban

India. Their mission is to help the poor break their cycle of poverty and live meaningfully through tools necessary to succeed in a knowledge based world.

Profile of ICICI Bank

ICICI Bank is India's second-largest bank with total assets of Rs. 4,062.34 billion (US$ 91 billion) at March 31, 2011 and profit after tax Rs. 51.51 billion (US$ 1,155 million) for the year ended March 31, 2011. The Bank has a network of 2,563 branches and 7,440 ATMs in India, and has a presence in 19 countries, including India. ICICI Bank offers a wide range of banking products and financial services to corporate and retail customers through a variety of delivery channels and through its specialised subsidiaries in the areas of investment banking, life and non-life insurance, venture capital and asset management.

The Bank currently has subsidiaries in the United Kingdom, Russia and Canada, branches in United States, Singapore, Bahrain, Hong Kong, Sri Lanka, Qatar and Dubai International Finance Centre and representative offices in United Arab Emirates, China, South Africa, Bangladesh, Thailand, Malaysia and Indonesia. Our UK subsidiary has established branches in Belgium and Germany.

ICICI Bank's equity shares are listed in India on Bombay Stock Exchange and the National Stock Exchange of India Limited and its American Depositary Receipts (ADRs) are listed on the New York Stock Exchange (NYSE).

ICICI Bank offers a wide range of banking products and financial services to corporate and retail customers through a variety of delivery channels and through its specialised subsidiaries and affiliates in the areas of investment banking, life and non-life insurance, venture capital and asset management. The Bank set up its international banking group in fiscal 2002 to cater to the cross border needs of clients and leverage on its domestic banking strengths to offer products internationally. The

Bank currently has subsidiaries in the United Kingdom, Russia and Canada, branches in Singapore, Bahrain, Hong Kong, Sri Lanka and Dubai International Finance Centre and representative offices in the United States, United Arab Emirates, China, South Africa and Bangladesh. The UK subsidiary has established a branch in Belgium. ICICI Bank is the most valuable bank in India in terms of market capitalisation.

ICICI Bank's equity shares are listed in India on the Bombay Stock Exchange and the National Stock Exchange of India Limited and its American Depository Receipts (ADRs) are listed on the New York Stock Exchange (NYSE). The Bank has formulated a Code of Business Conduct and Ethics for its directors and employees.

On June 5, 2006, the ICICI Bank, with free float market capitalisation[19] of about Rs. 480.00 billion (US $ 10.8 billion) was ranked third amongst all the companies listed on the Indian stock exchanges.

The Bank was originally promoted in 1994 by ICICI Limited, an Indian financial institution, and was its wholly-owned subsidiary. The ICICI's shareholding in ICICI Bank was reduced to 46% through a public offering of shares in India in fiscal 1998, an equity offering in the form of ADRs listed on the NYSE in fiscal 2000, ICICI Bank's acquisition of Bank of Madura Limited in an all-stock amalgamation in fiscal 2001, and secondary market sales by ICICI to institutional investors in fiscal 2001 and fiscal 2002. The ICICI was formed in 1955 at the initiative of the World Bank, the Government of India and representatives of Indian industry. The principal objective was to create a development financial institution for providing medium-term and long-term project financing into Indian businesses. In the 1990s, the ICICI transformed its business from a development financial institution offering only project finance to a diversified financial services group offering a wide variety of products and services, both directly and through a number of subsidiaries and affiliates like ICICI Bank. In 1999, ICICI become the first Indian company and the first bank or financial institution from non-Japan Asia to be listed on the NYSE.[20]

After consideration of various corporate structuring alternatives in the context of the emerging competitive scenario in the Indian banking industry, and the move towards universal banking, the managements of ICICI and ICICI Bank formed the view that the merger of ICICI with ICICI Bank would be the optimal strategic alternative for both entities, and would create the optimal legal structure for the ICICI group's universal banking strategy. The merger would enhance value for ICICI shareholders through the merged entity's access to low-cost deposits, greater opportunities for earning fee-based income and the ability to participate in the payments system and provide transaction-banking services. The merger would enhance value for ICICI Bank shareholders through a large capital base and scale of operations, seamless access to ICICI's strong corporate relationships built up over five decades, entry into new business segments, higher market share in various business segments, particularly fee-based services, and access to the vast talent pool of ICICI and its subsidiaries. In October 2001, the Boards of Directors of ICICI and ICICI Bank approved the merger of ICICI and two of its wholly-owned retail finance subsidiaries, ICICI Personal Financial Services Limited and ICICI Capital Services Limited, with ICICI Bank. The merger was approved by shareholders of ICICI and ICICI Bank in January 2002, by the High Court of Gujarat at Ahmedabad in March 2002, and by the High Court of Judicature at Mumbai and the Reserve Bank of India in April 2002. Consequent to the merger, the ICICI group's financing and banking operations, both wholesale and retail, have been integrated in a single entity[21]. Free float holding excludes all promoter holdings, strategic investments and cross holdings among public sector entities.

The ICICI Bank has better customer relations. The ICICI Bank disseminates information on its operations and initiatives on a regular basis. The Banks' website serves as a key investor awareness facility, allowing stakeholders to access information on ICICI Bank at their convenience. The Bank's investor relations personnel are dedicated to playing a proactive role in disseminating information to both the analysts and the investors they respond to specific queries as below:[22]

"We believe that, as in everything else, you deserve the best in banking too. Therefore, we constantly strive to cater to all your financial needs with world class products. If you need any information or assistance about a service or a product, please let us know. We are here to assist you". The ICICI Bank is now making its presence felt in international markets. Mrs. Gupte is at the helm of ICICI Bank's global foray, which includes operations in the USA, Canada, UK, United Arab Emirates, Singapore, China, Sri Lanka, Russia, South Africa and Bangladesh. She is responsible for ICICI Bank's international relationships and businesses in the retail, corporate and technology areas and for forging international alliances required for the domestic businesses.

The Bank is today a technology and retail banking leader in India. In 2004, ICICI Bank received the "Best Bank in India" award from Business India and "India's Most Customer-Friendly Bank" from Outlook Money amongst several other awards. The Bank also continues to gain recognition internationally with numerous awards including the Best Bank in India by Euro money, Global Finance, Asian Banker Journal and the Banker.[23]

Customer Data Yields Dividends at ICICI

This key player in India's banking sector is the first of its kind to turn to CRM. by Tim Walters Customer focus. cross-selling. and one-to-one marketing. ICICI's management believes in customer focus, in seeing each customer's complete financial picture. It also is determined to stay ahead of the competition by integrating and analysing customer data using the latest in data warehousing technology.

The ICICI has plenty of data to work with from its more than 10 million customers. With 364 branches, 46 extension counters, a network of 1,050 ATMs, multiple call centres and well-developed Internet banking, the Mumbai-headquartered banking giant can provide financial services all over India. Its customers often use multiple channels, and they are increasingly turning to electronic banking options. Business from the Internet, ATMs and other electronic channels now comprises 50% of all transactions, up from 5 per cent just two years ago.

In the process of growing its business to this level, The Bank has distinguished itself from other banks through customer relationships. Chanda Kochhar, Executive Director says, "In an increasingly competitive environment where customers are becoming more demanding and financial services are getting commodities, the ICICI realised the key differentiator would be customer focus.[2424] Anju Das. "Financial Inclusion an Economic Growth Driver".

Investor Relations

ICICI Bank disseminates information on its operations and initiatives on a regular basis. The ICICI Bank website serves as a key investor awareness facility, allowing stakeholders to access information on ICICI Bank at their convenience. ICICI Bank's dedicated investor relations personnel play a proactive role in disseminating information to both analysts and investors and respond to specific queries.

REFERENCES

1. Sharma, Harish, C. *"Nationalisation of Banks in India"*, Sahitya Bhavan, Agra, 1970, p. 9.
2. Kabra, K.N. and Suresh, R.R. "*Public Sector Banking*", Peoples' Publishing House, New Delhi, 1970, pp.133-134.
3. Vashisht, A. *Public Sector Banks in India*, H.K. Publishers, Delhi, pp.154-58.
4. Maheswari, S.N. & Paul, P.R. *Banking Theory and Practice*, Kalyani Publishers, New Delhi, 1994, pp.23-25.

5. Subramanian, K. Velayudham, T.K. *Banking Reforms in India: Managing Change*, Tata McGraw Hill Publishing Co., Ltd., New Delhi, 1997, p. 9.
6. www.state bank of India.htm
7. Di Vanna, Joseph. A. *"The Future of Retail Banking"*, Palgrave Macmillan, New York, 2004, pp.78-79.
8. Nayyar, S.K. *HRD in State Bank of India*, Vinsro Publications, New Delhi, 2000, pp.89-90
9. State Bank of India (2005-06) Annual Report pp. 12.
10. Ruma.R. "Training Policy and Program in the State Bank of Hyderabad–An Evaluation study, Osmania University, Hyderabad, 1996, pp. 122-125.
11. Annual Report of Andhra Bank: 2005-06, p. 8.
12. Rama Krishna, K. Chairman & Managing Director, Andhra Bank; Andhra Bank Endowment Lecture on 19th July 2005 at Andhra University, Visakhapatnam.
13. Ramakrishnan, K., CMD, Andhra Bank Deccan Chronicle, (English News Paper), October 2, 2006, p. 16.
14. Andhra Bank Endowment Lecturer on Betting on Human Potential vital Need for Success of An Organisation by Dr. K. Rama Krishna, Chairman & Managing Director, Andhra Bank on 27th July 2007 at Andhra University, Visakhapatnam..
15. www.ingvysyabankltd.in.org.
16. *International Financial Journal*, June 1998.
17. Annual Report of ING Vysya Bank 2000-06.
18. Jain, C.M., Shurveer S. Bhanawat, "Productivity of Human Resources in Banking Industry", *Indian Journal of Accounting,* Vol. XXXVI (1), December 2005, p. 15.
19. www.banker & customer relations.com
20. www:icicibankltd.htm
21. *Ibid.*
22. Banker's Report 2006 & 2007 of ICICI Bank.
23. Satyabhusan Dash, Ed. Bruning, Kalyan Ku Guin, "The Moderating Effect of Power Distance on Perceived Interdependence and Relationship Quality in Commercial Banking: A Cross Cultural Comparison, *Journal of International Journal Bank Marketing*, 2006, Vol. 24, Issue 5.
24. Anju Das. "Financial Inclusion an Economic Growth Driver", *Professional Banker,* February 2007, The ICFAI University Press, p. 34 .

CHAPTER

Changing Trends in Banking Sector in India

This chapter is devoted to discuss the changing trends in the banking sector in India. It deals with the growth and performance of the Indian banks before and after the period of financial reforms. And the challenges and the future of banking sector in India have been extensively dealt with, with reference to the developments.

The Present scene of banking industry received a face lift with the constitution of three important committees much as the Narasimham committee, the Khan committee and the Verma committee. The Narasimham committee was instrumental in forcing Indian banks to become globally competitive. It suggested measures like capital adequacy norms, income recognition, asset classification, entry of private sector banks etc., with more focussed private sector banks making a pitch for corporate accounts through better servicing public sector banks felt the first heat of competition. The Khan committee recommended the setting up of universal banks. Preference was given to financial institutions which could provide a whole range of corporate financial solutions under one roof, which could include term lending, working capital finance, project advisory services etc. The Verma committee, suggested the need for voluntary retirement in the banking sector.

The banking system in India has a significant role to play in the rapid growth of economy through planned efforts.[1] The first five year plan emphasised that the banking system had to be fitted into the scheme of development to make the process of saving and their utilisation economically productive and socially purposive. The importance of banking system as a dynamic force of development started increasing over the successive five year plans in conformity with national policies, priorities and objectives. In this chapter an attempt is made to review the trends of banking in India under three important phases – pre-nationalisation, post-nationalisation and post- reform periods in order to cover the important milestones in Indian banking sector. In this context, the emerging challenges that the banks have to face have also been discussed.

Genesis of Banking in India

The history of formal commercial banking in India can be traced back to the 18th century.[2] The first commercial bank in India was the Hindustan Bank, which was set up by an English agency house in Calcutta in 1770. Nevertheless, the origin of modern commercial banking in India can be associated with the setting up of the first Presidency Bank, viz., the Bank of Bengal, in Calcutta in 1806. Two other presidency banks were set-up in Bombay and madras in 1840 and 1843 respectively. Majority of the equity of these banks was privately held and the East Indian Company also had some shares. These banks acted as bankers to the government and were also given the right of note issue. This right was subsequently taken over by the government in 1862. Later on, all the Presidency Banks were merged to form the Imperial Bank.

One major development during pre-independence period was that setting up of the Reserve Bank of India (RBI) in 1935 as the Central Bank of the country. At the time of Independence, there were 640 banks out of which only 96 were Scheduled Banks and rest was non-scheduled banks.

Banking was concentrated in urban and metropolitan areas and distribution credit was skewed in favour of large industry and trading sectors. Against this backdrop, strengthening of the banking system was one of the major challenges during the post-independence era.

Banking during 1949-1969

In the two decades, following the enactment of Banking Companies Act 1949, the Indian banking system underwent amazing changes – graphically, structurally and functionally. The banking system adopted itself along with Reserve Bank of India to the changing economic scenario. The period also witnessed RBI's efforts towards the institutionalisation of savings in order to orient the credit system to the changing needs of a developing economy. During the same period efforts were made for the consolidation and strengthening of the banking structure and organisation so as to improve the quality of service, enlarging of geographical and functional spread of banking activities. The Indian commercial banking system thus, was regulated and controlled mainly under the provisions of banking company's act 1949. The primary object of the measure of the protection of interest of depositors, along with strengthening and expanding the banking system was to cater to the growing needs of our economy.

Following independence, the development of rural India was given a priority. To cater to the needs of the rural areas, an official committee was created which recommended that the imperial bank which was the functioning bank in India, should be taken over by a state partnered and state-sponsored bank. By an act of Parliament, the State Bank of India (SBI) was constituted on July 1st 1955.[3] With its creation more than a quarter of the resources of Indian banking system thus passed to the direct control of the state. Subsequently in 1959, the State Bank of India (subsidiary bank) Act was passed enabling the SBI to take over the seven former state associate as its subsidiaries. This marked a significant set-up in the launch of a state-controlled banking system in India.

The trends in Indian banking during 1950-1969 displayed that the Indian banking sector demonstrated its ability to have vigorous branch expansion and there by bringing down the population per office from 64,000 to 70,000. Even in the case of deposit mobilisation and credit deployment, impressive performance was recorded during the same period[4].

Table 4.1: Trends in Indian Banking during 1950–1969

Sl. No.	Particulars	31st Dec. 1950	31st Dec. 1967	31st Dec. 1969
1.	No. of scheduled commercial banks	92	75	73
2.	No. of offices	2732	6816	8262
3.	Deposits (Rs. in millions)	754	3683	4646
4.	Bank credit (Rs. in millions)	370	2492	3599
5.	Credit deposit ratio	41.1	67.7	77.46
6.	Investments (Rs. in millions)	361	1142	1361
7.	Cash balances	119	387	275
8.	Population for office	70000	73000	64000
9.	Average deposit per office (lakhs)	22	57	56
10.	Average credit per office (Lakhs)	12	39	44
11.	Per-capital deposits (Rs.)	27	77	88
12.	Per-capital credit	14	54	68
13.	Deposit as per cent of GNP	9.1	12.5	15.5
14.	No of employees ('000)	—	184	211
15.	No. of depositors (lakhs)	32.9	140.1	161.1
16.	No. of borrowers (lakhs)	3.0	10.5	12.8

Source: Compiled from RBI publications.

Growth during 1969-1991

'Social control' of bank credit flows, with priority sector lending as a major focus, was an important objective of bank nationalisation. Restrictions on advances by banking companies were initiated to ensure that bank advances were available not only to large- scale industries and big business houses, but were also directed, in due proportion, to vital sectors such as agriculture, small-scale industries and exports.

Since 1969, there has been a considerable spread of banking habit in the economy with banks being able to garner a large amount of savings. However, by the 1980s there was a general feeling that the operational efficiency of banks in India was on the downturn with declining profitability, growing Non-Performing Assets (NPAs) which were already high and a low capital base. Inadequate internal controls and lack of suitable disclosure norms led to many problems which were kept undercover. The quality of customer service did not keep pace with the increasing expectations.[5] All these factors paved the way to the next phase of nationalisation in 1980 which raised the public sector banks share of deposit form 86 per cent (1969) to 92 per cent (1980). A second phase of bank nationalisation saw six more private banks getting nationalised in 1980. Domestic private banks and foreign banks were allowed to coexist with the Public Sector Banks (PSBs), but their activities were closely monitored and highly restricted through regulated entry and strict branch licensing. With the nationalisation of banks, a large number of regulatory measures were adopted by the RBI to attain a desired sectoral allocation of credit, e.g., subsidised lending rates to priority sectors, provision of refinance facilities, setting up of credit guarantee schemes, rural and semi-urban branches, ceiling on deposit rates and differential lending rates depending on borrower's level of income and type of loan. These measures resulted in phenomenal growth of the banking system, especially that of the PSBs. In fact, during the early 1990s PSBs owned nearly 90 per cent of total business in the banking industry.

Post-nationalisation Period

During the post nationalisation period, branch expansion was undertaken on a massive scale with an aggressive branch licensing policy supported by lead bank scheme. As many as 51,958 branches were opened during 1969-1991. The branches were spread even in the remote and non-banked areas. Deposits were mobilised by launching several innovative schemes and the deposits of banks went up to Rs.2,01,199 crores by the end of March, 1991 from only Rs.4,646 crores in June, 1969. Advances also grew to Rs.1, 21,865 crores from Rs.3, 599 crores during the same period. This supports the view that banks had a spectacular growth in terms of branch expansion, deposit mobilisation and deployment of credit during 1969-1991.[6]

The banks during this period functioned in a heavily regulated and controlled environment coupled with administered interest rate structure, quantitative restrictions on credit flows, high reserved requirements and preemption of considerable share of lendable resources in favour of priority and government sectors. However, a reversal of the process started with the introduction of large-scale banking de-regulation and reforms in the banking sector as a part of the overall economic reforms in India in 1991.

Indian Banking prior to Financial Sector Reforms

The Indian banking was purely carried in a traditional way before the adoption of financial sector reforms and banks were adopting accrual system of accounting. The balance sheets were inflated with illusory income as the income recognition was purely based on accrual system, which weakened the very fundamentals of banking sector. The evils of the system promoted for remedial measure on priority. The banks were under stringent control and banking were to maintain Cash Reserved Rations & Security Leveraged

Rations which were raised from 3 per cent and 25 per cent to 15 per cent and 38.5 per cent by the end of 1991.[7] A higher SLR forced the banks to maintain a larger portion of their funds with the RBI. Direct credit programme held by the government led to the deterioration in quality of loans, growth of overdue and consequent erosion of profitability. Banks were asked to shift from security oriented credit to purpose oriented credit without proper appraisal of credit applications followed with no collateral requirements and no post credit supervision and monitoring. Political and administrative interference caused serious damage to policies of banks as loan melas were contrary to the principle of sound banking

Programmes like Integral Rural Development Programme,[8] priority sector lending and Differential rate of interest schemes resulted in non-commercialisation of banking business and affected adversely the profitability of banks. Many banks, especially public sector banks suffered from mounting expenditure due to phenomenal increase in branch banking, growth in staff, staff promotions and extension of bank credit to priority sectors as well as under various schemes at concessional rates of interest. Thus, despite impressive quantitative achievements in resource mobilisation and credit advancement, several distortions that occurred over the years weakened several private and public sector banks and, therefore, they were unable to meet the challenges of competitive environment. Against this background, the financial sector reforms which include obviously reforms for banking sector were initiated with the following major objectives:

- To Eliminate financial repression that prevailed earlier.
- To Create an efficient, productive and profitable financial sector industry.
- To Enable price discovery, especially by the market determined interest rates so as to help in efficient allocation of resources.

- To Offer operational and functional autonomy to institutions.
- To Make financial sector ready to face the increasing international competition.
- To Open the external sector in a calibrated fashion, and
- To Promote the maintenance of financial stability even in the presence of domestic and external shocks

Banking Industry at Glance

The publication profiles 82 scheduled commercial banks, comprising of 28 Public Sector Banks, 25 Private Sector Banks and 29 Foreign Banks, as defined by the RBI. The group of Public Sector Banks (PSBs) includes nationalised banks, SBI & its Associates and IDBI Ltd .*

With the purpose of gaining a deeper understanding of the Indian banking industry, an overall profiling of the industry has been attempted in this section. This study considers only the 82 banks profiled in this publication. The data for the study was collated through responses received directly from banks, from sources in the public domain like annual reports, the RBI documents and the bank websites. Various parameters like efficiency, growth, productivity, etc., have been examined for gaining insights.

Total Assets

Total assets for the 82 scheduled commercial banks combined stood at Rs 27,785,739 mn in FY11, of which Public Sector Banks had the largest share of 72.5%, followed by Private Sector Banks of 20.2% and Foreign Banks at 7.3%.

The asset base of SBI & Associates in FY06 stood at 24.9% of the total assets for the 82 banks profiled. In other words, excluding SBI & Associates, the asset base of Public Sector Banks was 47.6% of total assets of scheduled commercial banks.

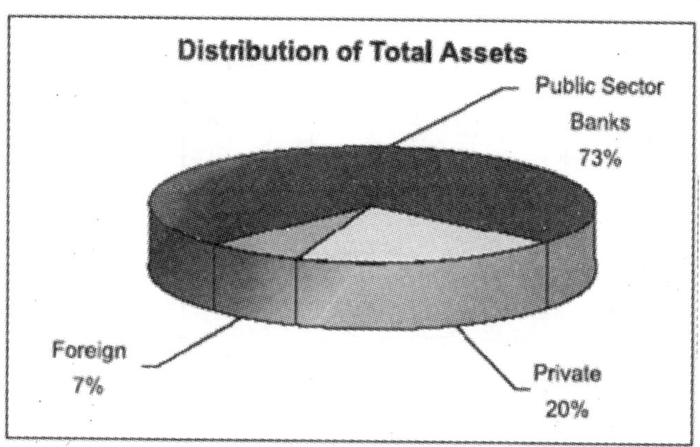

*During the year FY11, two domestic banks were amalgamated - Ganesh Bank of Kurundwad with Federal Bank Ltd and Bank of Punjab Ltd with Centurion Bank Ltd to become Centurion Bank of Punjab Ltd, while one foreign bank, UFJ Bank Ltd merged with Bank of Tokyo-Mitsubishi Ltd. ING Bank NV closed its business in India. In Sept, 06, The United Western Bank Ltd was placed under moratorium, leading to its amalgamation with Industrial Development Bank of India Ltd. in Oct, 2006, Sangli Bank, another Private Sector Bank was merged with ICICI Bank. Ganesh Bank of Kurundwad, Sangli Bank and The United Western Bank have therefore been excluded of the publication.

The assets for all the profiled banks have grown at a rate of 22.6% over the previous year. It was observed that the asset base of Private Sector Banks was growing more rapidly compared to the other bank groups. Total assets of private banks grew by 16% in FY10 and 33% in FY11, over the previous year. The asset base of Foreign Banks grew by 13% in FY10 and by 30% in FY11 mainly driven by the growth in advances of four banks in this group. The Public Sector Banks maintained a decent year-on-year growth of 15% and 19% in the respective years. However, it should be noted that the growth of Public Sector Banks is on a very high base.

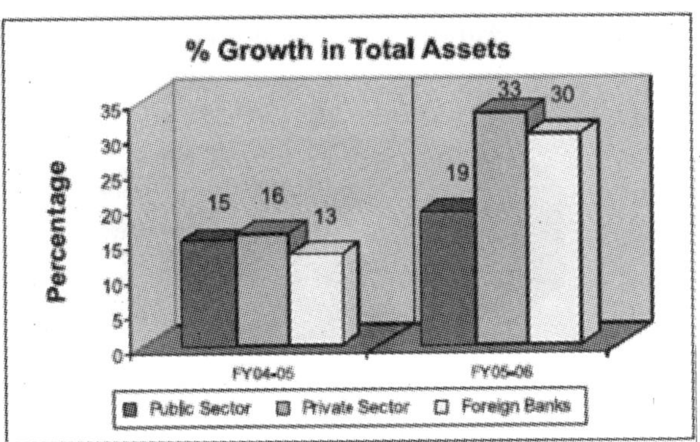

Total Income

The total income for the 82 banks stood at Rs 2,215,280 mn in FY06, of which the Public Sector Banks held the highest share of 72.7%, Private Sector Banks at 19.5% followed by 7.8% for the Foreign Banks. The SBI & Associates accounted for 36.6% of the total income for Public Sector Banks; having a combined income of Rs 589, 096.6 mn which is slightly higher than one fourth of the total income of the 82 banks profiled.

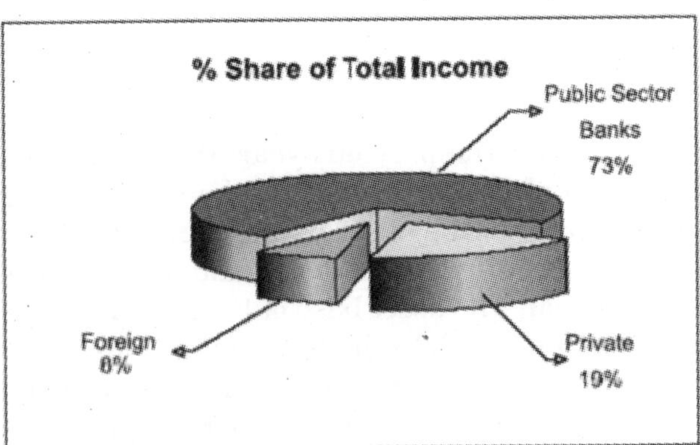

The top ten banks classified on the basis of their respective total income accounted for nearly 56% of the total income of the 82 banks. Of these top ten banks, 8 banks were Public

Sector Banks while the remaining two were Private Sector Banks.

Non-Interest Income/Total Income

The non-interest income for all the 82 banks profiled in this publication on an average stood at 22.1% of the total income. Among the bank groups, non-interest income was the highest for Foreign Banks at 31%, followed by Private Sector Banks at 19.8%; indicative of the value-added services these banks offer. For Public Sector Banks, non-interest income was just 15.3% while interest income was a high 84.7%. Non-interest income includes fee income components such as commission, brokerage and exchange transactions, sale of investments, corporate finance transactions, M&A deals; and any other income other than the interest income generated by the bank.

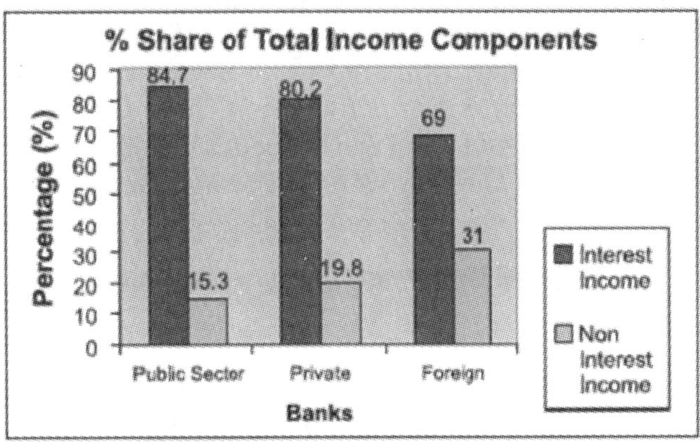

Net Profit

The net profit for the profiled banks together stood at Rs 248,281.5 mn for FY06. The top ten banks, based on the net profit classification, accounted for nearly 58.5% of the total net profit of all the 82 banks. These top ten banks included 6 Public Sector Banks, two Private Sector Banks and two Foreign Banks. Interestingly, of these top 10 banks, four banks that managed to make it to the top ten on the basis of net profit do not feature among the top ten on the basis of total income.

Bank group-wise, Public Sector Banks continued to dominate with a 66.6% share in the net profit. The share of Private Sector Banks in the total net profit stood at 21%, followed by Foreign Banks having a 12.4% share in the total net profit. Within the Public Sector Banks, SBI & Associates accounted for 36% of the total Public Sector Banks' net profit, or nearly one-fourth of the total net profit of the 82 banks profiled. There are 5 banks, 4 foreign and one private, out of the profiled 82 banks, which made losses in FY06.

Infrastructure

Banks across all three groups have been rapidly increasing their infrastructure to tap the under served markets, though Public Sector Banks are dominant all across in all regions. As of Mar 06, the total number of branches of the profiled banks operating in the country was 54,346, of which 88% of the branches belonged to the Public Sector Banks (PSBs), indicative of the extent of penetration these banks have in the country. Another 11% of the branches belonged to Private Sector Banks and the rest were of Foreign Banks.

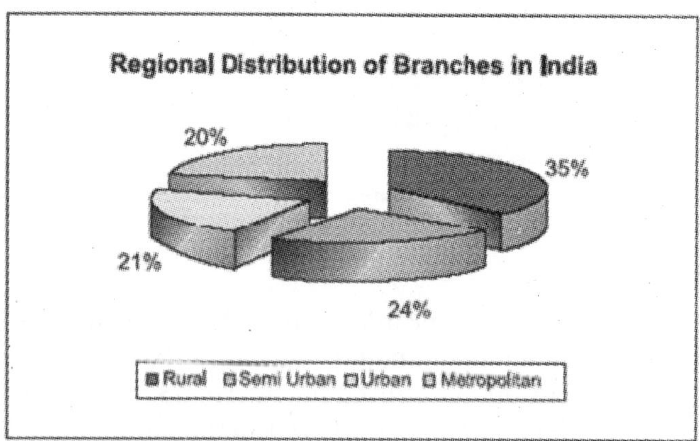

Region-wise, the concentration of branches was highest in the rural areas, accounting for almost 35% of the total.

The rural segment is entirely dominated by Public Sector Banks with 95% of the total rural branches belonging to PSBs. 23% of the branches of PSBs are located in semi urban area, while 19% branches are in the metropolitan regions. The immense reach of PSBs can be seen by the fact that almost 62% of total PSB branches are in rural & semi-urban areas.

Group-wise, the presence of Private Sector Banks was largely in urban areas with almost 30% of their branches in this region.

As of Mar11, the total numbers of ATMs installed by profiled banks were 21,047. Public sector banks once again accounted for the largest share of installed ATMs with 12,608 machines, followed by the Private Sector Banks with 7,584 ATM's. Foreign Banks have installed 855 ATMs around the country.

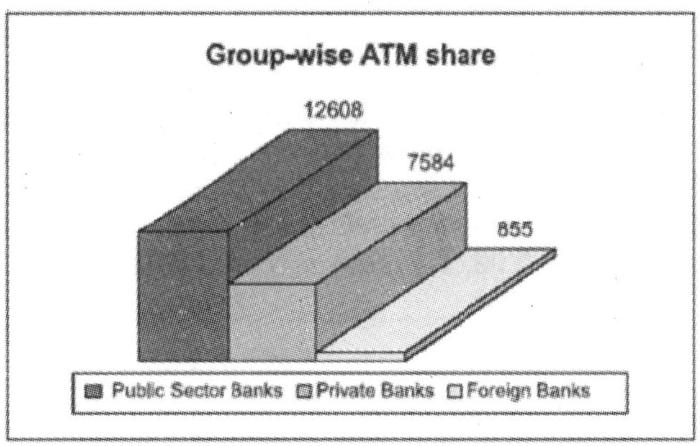

Growth in Deposits, Advances & Retail Credit

Deposits

The overall deposit growth for the profiled banks was at 18.2% for FY11. Group-wise, deposits of Private Sector Banks witnessed a robust growth of 39.2%, closely followed by Foreign Banks at 31.7%. For Public Sector Banks the deposits grew at about 13% for the same time period. The share of

Private Sector Banks in total deposits has been rising gradually, while that of Public Sector Banks has been declining over the years.

Growth in Deposits, Advances & Retail Credit

Group	Deposits	Advances	Retail Credit
Public Sector Banks	12.9	30.7	35.0
Private Banks	39.2	44.0	48.3
Foreign Banks	31.7	30.0	—

*The above figures are represented as an average % growth over FY11

Advances

Advances for all the profiled banks have grown at about 32% YoY and that made by Private Sector Banks grew at the highest rate of 44% for FY11 followed by a growth of 30.7% for Public Sector Banks and 30% for Foreign Banks. Among the major components of total advances, there was no relative change in the percentage share of Bills Purchased and Discounted, over the last three years. Cash Credits, Overdrafts and Loans have shown a yearly decline of 4% in FY10 as a part of total advances. Correspondingly, Term Loans have been growing and constitute a large component of advances. In FY09, Term Loans constituted 49.4% of Total

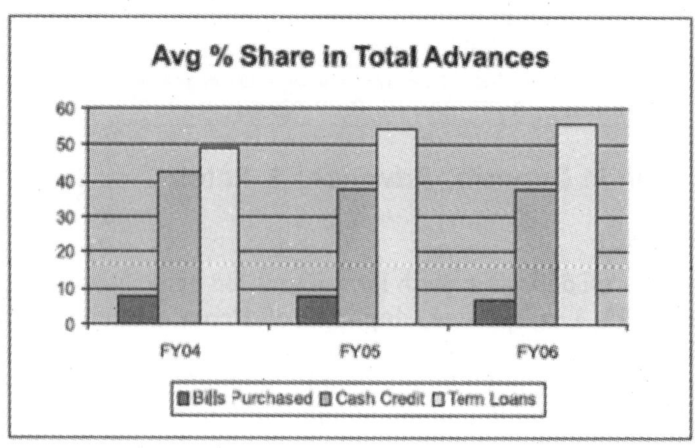

Advances, which increased to 54.2% in FY05, and further to 55.7% in FY11.

Group-wise Average Growth in Term Loans

Group	FY05	FY06
Public Sector Banks	59.8	32.2
Private Banks	38.7	48.9
Foreign Banks	37.2	30.2

*All figures in %age.

In FY06, Term Loans across the profiled banks grew on an average of 35.9%. Term Loans provided by the public sector banks showed robust growth of 59.8% in FY05 which almost reduced to half and stood at 32.2% in FY06. The growth shown by Private Sector Banks has varied too, with 38.7% growth in FY05 and 48.9% in FY06. Foreign Banks, however, have shown a lower growth in term loans in FY06 as compared to FY05, which grew by 30.2% in FY06 as against a growth of 37.2% in FY05. This growth in all three bank-groups can largely be attributed to the growth in retail credit and the overall economy, among other factors.

Retail Credit

Retail credit for the Public Sector scheduled commercial banks increased by 35%, which was significantly higher than the profiled banks' overall credit growth of 32%. The retail advances by the Private Banks grew by 48.3%, which too was well above the overall growth.

Credit Deposit Ratio

The Credit-Deposit ratio (C-D ratio) is the proportion of loan-assets created by the bank from the deposits received. Among the 82 banks profiled, the aggregate C-D ratio stood at 70.1% in FY06 as compared to 62.7% in FY05. Among the profiled bank-groups, foreign banks had the highest C-D ratio of 85.8% in FY06, which was slightly lower than that of FY05. An opposite trend was seen with private banks, where in their C-D ratio stood at 73.4% in FY06, higher than 70.9% for FY05. Public sector banks too showed a growth in their C-D ratio at 68.2% as compared to 59.5% in FY05. As seen earlier, the high rate of bank credit growth during the last two years has resulted in this unique behaviour of credit-deposit (C-D) ratio.

Priority Sector Advances/Total Advances

As instructed by the RBI, a target of 40% of net bank credit was stipulated for priority sector lending by domestic scheduled commercial banks, both in the public and private sectors. Within this, sub-targets of 18% and 10% of net bank credit had been stipulated for lending to agriculture and weaker sections, respectively.

In FY06, the average credit to the priority sector by the profiled Public Sector Banks accounted for 41.6% of their total credit, a little above the stipulated target level of 40%. In FY05, the profiled private banks lending to the priority sector constituted 39.6% of their total advances. The Public Sector Banks contributed 15.6% of their total credit to the agriculture sector and private banks contributed 11.9% for the same, both falling short of the stipulated sub-targets of 18%.

Operating Efficiency

Net NPAs to Net Advances (Net NPAs/Net Advances)

On an average, the net NPA/Net Advances ratio for the 82 banks was 1.4% in FY06. Of this, the net NPAs to net advances ratio for the Public Sector Banks was estimated to be 1.4%, closely followed by Private Sector Banks at 1.8%. For Foreign Banks, the ratio was much lower at 0.9%.

The graph below depicts that the asset quality of all the banks has been improving for the past couple of years. It is evident that there has been a sharp decline in non-performing loans of Public Sector Banks and Private Sector Banks.

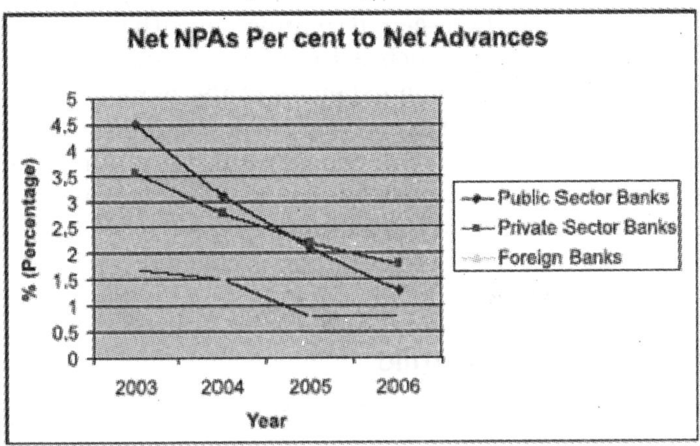

Operating Expenses

The operating expenses are those expenses that cover the day-to-day functioning of the bank like employee costs and charges for normal running of business. Among the profiled 82 banks, the ratio of operating expense to total expense for the Public Sector Banks was 26.5%, Private Sector Banks was 28.4%, while for Foreign Banks the ratio was nearly one-third of their total expenses and stands a little higher compared to their peers.

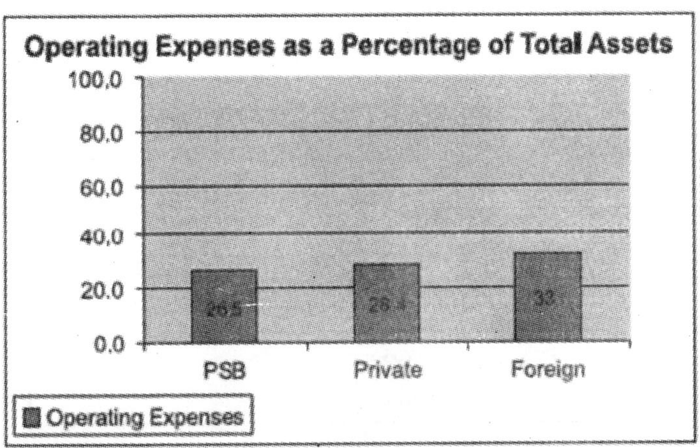

Intermediation cost is the ratio of operating expense to total assets, and when seen in conjunction with non-interest income explains how much is the non-interest income able to cover up the operating expenses of the banks. This gap (the excess of operating expenditure over non-interest income as a percentage to total assets) has been narrowing considerably over the past few years. Among the profiled banks, for Public Sector Banks this gap was 0.9%, for private banks 0.4% and for Foreign Banks it stood at 0.2% for the year ending Mar 06.

Capital Adequacy Ratio

The Capital Adequacy Ratio is a measure of the amount of a bank's capital expressed as a percentage of its risk weighted credit exposures. The RBI guidelines require a capital adequacy ratio of 9%. All the banks profiled in this publication have a capital adequacy ratio of above 9%; with most of the banks placed well above the 9% mark.

Return on Assets

In the list of 82 banks profiled, the return on assets for Foreign Banks was highest at 1.5%, followed by Private Sector Banks at 0.9%; and Public Sector Banks at 0.6%. The graph depicts that the return on assets bounced back smartly

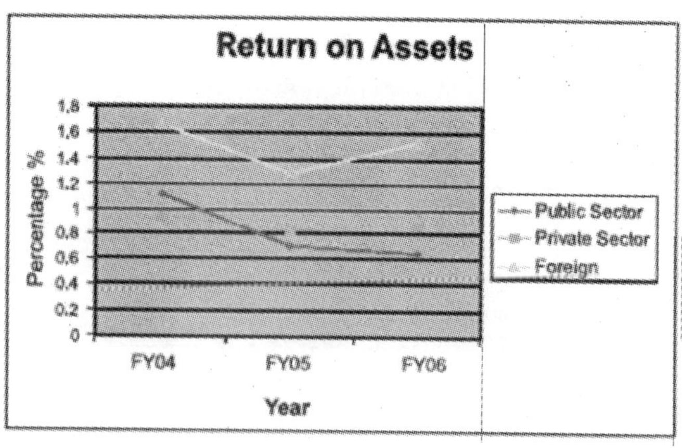

for Foreign Banks after the slight decline it witnessed in FY05. The return on assets for the Private Sector Banks has more or less remained the same with just a slight decline in it. While the return on assets for Public Sector Banks shows a very sharp decline.

Return on Equity

Of the 82 banks profiled in the publication, the Return on Equity for Public Sector Banks was estimated to be the highest amongst its peers at 16%, closely followed by Private Sector Banks at 11.1% and 9.2% for Foreign Banks.

As shown in the graph depicting the trend in Return on Equity over the last four years, it is observed that the Return on Equity for Private Sector Banks fell drastically from 21.1% in the year 2003 to 11.1% in the year 2006. The Return on Equity for Public Sector Banks too showed a sharp decline from 21.8% in 2003 to 16% in 2006. As for Foreign Banks, the return on equity showed a marginal decline from 11% in 2003 to 9.2% in 2006.

One of the reasons for the declining RoE could be the large amount of resources raised from primary capital market to strengthen the capital base. As per RBI data ,the equity capital for public sector banks jumped close to five times from

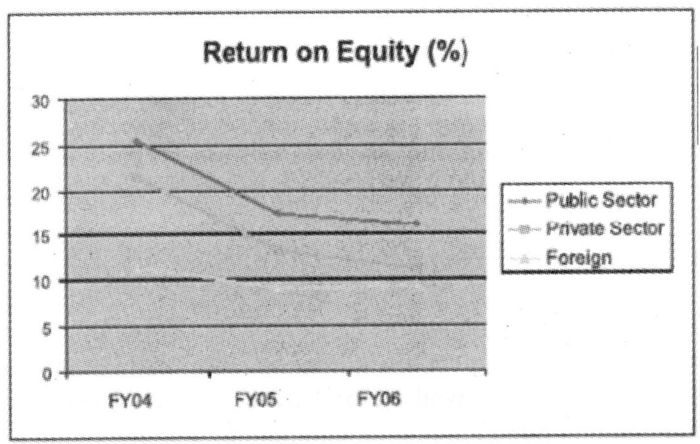

Rs 11040 mn in 2003-04 to a whopping Rs. 54130 mn in the year 2005-06. The private sector banks which had a low capital base in 2003- 04, also witnessed a huge jump in equity capital and ended the year with an equity capital of Rs. 56540 mn in 2005-06.

Net Interest Margin

It is defined as the excess of interest income over interest expense, as an percentage to total bank assets. Broadly speaking, this ratio reflects the allocative efficiency of financial intermediation, a lower ratio being indicative of upper efficiency. The net interest margin in FY06 stood at 3.5% for Foreign Banks its due to the fact that tradionally, the Foreign Banks can mobilise low-cost deposits. ; followed by 3.4% for Private Sector Banks and 3.13% for Public Sector Banks.

Productivity

Business per employee is the total revenue generated on a per employee basis where as Net Profit per employee gives an indication of the ability of labour to generate profit. However, both can be used as tools for measuring the efficiency of an organisation with respect to its human assets.

In FY11, the Foreign Banks on an average generated business worth Rs 101.27 mn per employee, which was the highest among the various bank groups. The business generated per employee by public sector and private banks stood at Rs 41.64 mn and Rs 49.54 mn respectively.

Correspondingly, the profitability per employee for Foreign Banks was highest at Rs 2.20 mn per employee, followed by private banks with Rs 1.87 mn per employee. Public sector banks showed an aggregate Rs 0.21 mn profitability on per employee basis. This indicates that profit generation with respect to its human resource is highest in Foreign Banks followed by private banks, and lowest in Public Sector Banks.

Narasimham Committee on Banking Sector Reforms

The Government of India appointed a high-power committee on financial system under the Chairmanship of M. Narasimham in 1991 to assess the problems of Indian banking industry. This committee submitted its report in the same year. The report contained far-reaching recommendations for reforms in the banking sector providing important inputs to the overall economic reforms of the 1990s. The salient features of this bank–related reforms included the following:

Introduction of stricter income recognition and asset classification norms

Introduction of higher capital adequacy requirements

Introduction of higher disclosure standards in financial reporting

Introduction of phased deregulation of interest rates

Lowering of statutory liquidity ratio (SLR) and cash-reserve ratio (CRR) requirements.

The RBI pursued a strategy to introduce the attainment of capital adequacy ratio (CAR) at 8 per cent by banks in a phased manner. Based on the recommendation of the Narasimham committee II on banking sector reforms, the minimum CAR was enhanced to 9 per cent March 31, 2000. Other measures based on the recommendations of Narasimham committee–II,[9] included:

- A risk weight of 20 per cent for investment in government guaranteed securities issued by public sector undertakings (PSUs);
- 20 per cent risk weight on state government guaranteed advances which remain in default as on March 31,2000 and 100 per cent weight in the case of continued default after March 31, 2001;
- Risk weight of 2.5 per cent to account for market risk for government and approved securities;
- 100 per cent risk weight on the foreign exchange open position limit.

Thus, the objectives of reforms were to strengthen the Indian banks, make them internationally competitive and encourage them to play an effective role in accelerating the process of growth. The reforms process also initiated measures for improving the productivity, efficiency and profitability of the banking system. It was also recognised that the Indian banking system should be placed on par with international standards in respect of capital adequacy and other prudential norms. The operational rigidities in credit delivery system were to be removed to ensure allocation efficiency and achievement of social objectives. With an objective to inculcate competitive efficiency in the banking system, entry of private sector banks with a minimum start-up capital of Rs.100 crore with promoter's contribution of 25% thereof has been allowed by the RBI.

The policy initiatives taken in this regard were largely based on the recommendation of Narasimham committee I & II on financial sector reforms and banking sector reforms, respectively. The major initiatives undertaken in pursuance of the recommendations of the committee may be categorised under deregulation, prudential measures, competition and enabling measures. Financial sector reforms were undertaken as part of overall economic reforms. Moreover, the approach towards financial sectors in India as mentioned by the RBI Governor, Dr. Y.V. Reddy,[10] is based on *pancha sutra* or five principles namely

(1) continuous and appropriate sequence of reform measures
(2) introduction of norms that are mutually reinforcing
(3) introduction of complementary reforms across sectors
(4) development of financial institutions
(5) development of financial markets.

Trends During 1991 to 2011

The trends in Indian Banking during 1991-2011[11] are portrayed in Table 4.2. The data portrayed in Table 2 reveals the trends in Indian banking that took place during post-nationalisation period viz., period before reforms and period after reforms. It is evident from the data, that the bank achieved remarkable progress during the post reform period despite facing several new challenges.

Table 4.2: Statistics Relating to Scheduled Commercial Banks at Glance during–1991-2011

	March 1991	March 2011
	1	2
Number of Commercial Banks	276	290
(a) Scheduled Commercial banks	272	286
Of which : Regional Rural Banks	196	196
(b) Non – Scheduled Commercial Banks	4	4
Number of Bank offices in India	60220	69071
(a) Rural	35206	32227
(b) Semi–urban	11344	15288
(c) Urban	8046	11806
(d) Metropolitan	5624	9750
Population per Office (in thousands)	14	16
Aggregate deposits of Scheduled Commercial Banks In India (Rs. in millions)	201199	1542284
(A) Demand deposits	38300	245948
(B) Time deposits	162898	1296342
Credit of scheduled Commercial Banks in India(Rs. in crores)	121865	865594
Investment of scheduled Commercial Banks in India(Rs. in crores)	75817	675868
Deposits of scheduled Commercial Banks per Office(Rs. in lakhs)	202	2265
Credit of scheduled Commercial Banks per office(Rs. in lakhs)	202	1330

	1	2
Per capita deposit of scheduled Commercial Banks (Rs.)	2368	14313
Per capita credit of scheduled Commercial Banks (Rs.)	1434	8404
Deposits of Scheduled Commercial Banks as Percentage to Gross National Product (at current prices)	48.1	61.7
Scheduled Commercial Banks advances to prioritySectors (Rs. in crores)	44572	277047
Share of priority sector advances in total Credit of scheduled Commercial Banks (%)	37.7	33.7
Credit deposit ratio(%)	60.6	56.1
Investment – deposit ratio (%)	37.7	43.8
Cash – Deposit Ratio (%)	17.6	5.6

Source: RBI Statistical Tables Relating to Banks of respective years.

A glance at this table reveals the following:

- Massive branch expansion was undertaken by the banks to increase banking access even to remote areas during post-nationalisation and pre-reform period. However, in the post-reform period, this process was slowed down in the name of consolidation.
- The commercial banks were compelled to open more rural branches as a consequence of nationalisation, while in the post-reform period more bank offices were set up in urban, semi-urban and metropolitan areas basing on the viability factor.
- The productivity of bank in terms of deposits and advances per office had been on the gradual rise in the post-nationalisation period and it was further improved during post-perform period.
- Though there has been absolute increase in the level of commercial bank advances towards priority sector

throughout the period under consideration, it is constrained to observe that there was a reduction in the share of bank finance to priority sector in total advances.

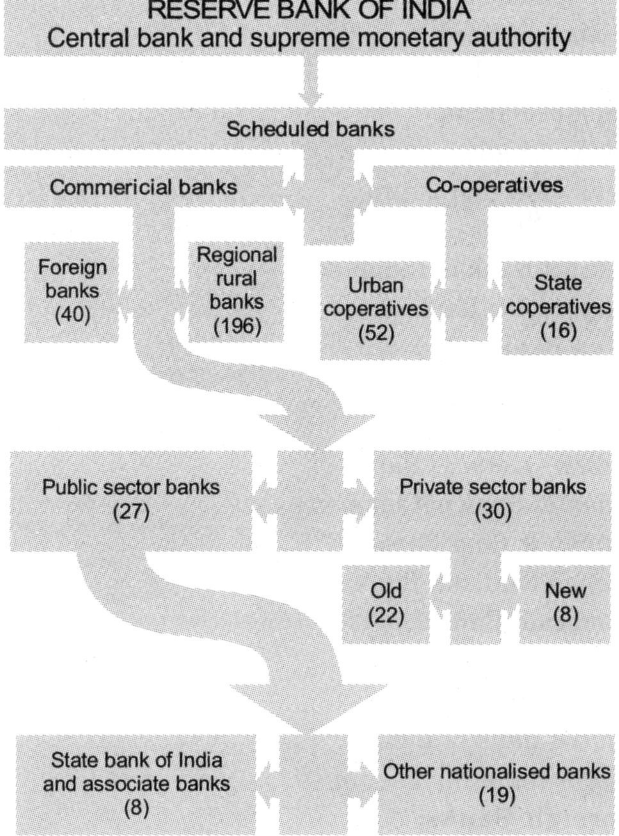

List of Commercial Banks in India

SBI & Associates:

State Bank of India

State Bank of Bikaner & Jaipur

State Bank of Hyderabad

State Bank of Indore
State Bank of Mysore
State Bank of Patiala
State Bank of Travancore

Nationalised Banks:

Allahabad Bank
Andhra Bank
Bank of Baroda
Bank of India
Bank of Maharashtra
Canara Bank
Central Bank of India
Corporation Bank
Dena Bank
IDBI Bank Ltd.
Indian Bank
Indian Overseas Bank
Oriental Bank of Commerce
Punjab & Sind Bank
Punjab National Bank
Syndicate Bank
UCO Bank
Union Bank of India
United Bank of India
Vijaya Bank

Foreign Banks:

ABN Amro Bank
Abu Dhabi Commercial Bank
American Express Banking Corporation
Antwerp Diamond Bank
AB Bank
Bank International Indonesia

Bank of America
Bank of Bahrain & Kuwait
Bank of Ceylon
Bank of Nova Scotia
Bank of Tokyo Mitsubishi UFJ
Barclays Bank
BNP Paribas
Calyon Bank
Chinatrust Commercial Bank
Citibank
DBS Bank
Deutsche Bank
Hongkong & Shanghai Banking Corporation
JP Morgan Chase Bank
JSC VTB Bank
Krung Thai Bank
Mashreq Bank
Mizuho Corporate Bank
Oman International Bank
Shinhan Bank
Societe Generale
Sonali Bank
Standard Chartered Bank
State Bank of Mauritius
UBS AG

Other Scheduled Commercial Banks:

Axis Bank
Bank of Rajasthan
Catholic Syrian Bank
City Union Bank
Development Credit Bank
Dhanalakshmi Bank
Federal Bank
HDFC Bank

ICICI Bank

IndusInd Bank

ING Vysya Bank

Jammu & Kashmir Bank

Karnataka Bank

Karur Vysya Bank

Kotak Mahindra Bank

Lakshmi Vilas Bank

Nainital Bank

Ratnakar Bank

SBI Commercial & International Bank

South Indian Bank

Tamilnad Mercantile Bank

Yes Bank

Cooperative Banks in India Other than the above mentioned banks, there are some co-operative banks in India and the names are given below:

Adarsh Co-Operative Bank Ltd.

Sadhna Sahakari Bank Ltd.

Vishweshwar Sahakari Bank Ltd.

Deogiri Nagari Sahakari Bank Ltd.

Sanmitra Sahakari Bank Ltd.

Ajantha Urban Co Op Bank Ltd.

Shri Chhatrapati Rajashi Shahu Urban Co Op Bank Ltd.

Banking Ombudsman Scheme

The Reserve Bank of India introduced the scheme of Banking Ombudsman in June 1995, under the provision of the Banking Regulation Act. 1949.[12] The scheme covers all scheduled commercial banks and all scheduled primary cooperative banks having business in India. The scheme provides for expeditious and inexpensive solution of customer complaints. The Banking Ombudsmen appointed under the scheme have the authority to look into the following complaints:

(*a*) Concerning deficiency in service such as:

(*i*) Non-payment/inordinate delay in the payment/ collection of cheques, drafts, bills, etc.

(*ii*) Non-issue or drafts to customers and others.

(*iii*) Non-adherence by bank branches to prescribed working hours.

(*iv*) Failure to honor guarantee/letter of credit by banks.

(*v*) Claims in respect of unauthorised/fraudulent withdrawals from deposit accounts.

(*vi*) Complaints regarding operations in accounts maintained with banks.

(*vii*) Complaints from exporters in India.

(*viii*) Complaints from non-resident Indians having accounts in India.

Strategic Banking

Liberalisation and globalisation polices require an open system approach. Changes like convertibility of the rupee, market determined exchange rate system etc. pose new challenges. Better risk management and new work culture become necessary. The emergent situation called for an aggression laced with caution which require ability to identify, anticipate, manage and mitigate risks that are well known today as also those that are likely to appear tomorrow.[13] An altogether new work culture with the domination of IT products at work environment, concern for relationship, instant transactions at global level became necessary. The three tasks of banking in this era are.

Managing Competition

It refers to acquiring competitive size and launching competitive measures. Competition is possible only among equals. As foreign banks are relatively large in size, the challenge before the Indian banks is to acquire a competitive size. Mergers and acquisitions provide a quick step forward in this direction. In the wake of changing client expectations and behaviours as well as emerging challenges, commercial banks will require to change the way they have been looking at product offerings, pricing, and delivery of services. For instance, the following measures seem to be the order of the day.

- — Introduction of technology driven product lines.[14]
- — Changing from cost plus basis to seeking remuneration for value addition.

Technology management

The enormous challenges in this new era can be met effectively only when the banking institutions also make knowledge an engine for growth. One may find that knowledge management is concerned with.

- Creating new information by research, and
- Managing existing information in people, process and physical resources.

Technological upgradation is a sine qua non for banking sector reforms, particularly to achieve better customer service, internal control, house-keeping and augmenting productivity and profitability.[15] Concerted efforts have been made to achieve bank mechanisation and computerisation both at macro and micro level on the lines recommended by Rangarajan committee.[16] The Committee on Technology issues relating to payment system, Cheques clearing[17] and securities settlement in the banking industry (Saraf Committee) also make far reaching recommendation. In addition to these, a committee on Technology upgraduation in banking sector was constituted with representation from the Government, RBI, Banks & Academic institutions connected with information technology. The Indian Financial Network (INFINET), a wide area satellite based Network[18] using VSAT technology was jointly set up by RBI and institute for development and research in banking technology at Hyderabad in June 1999. The RBI in co-ordination with Indian Bank's Association, banks and other sectors of the financial system is proactively dealing with the year 2000 problem. For this purpose a high level working group with members from banking, regulatory, supervisory and information technology departments of the RBI, representatives of IBA, Commercial banks and the National Institute of Bank Management has been constituted.

Universal Banking

The latest trend the world over is the move towards universal banking. There are instances like Deutsche Bank, and Citibank which provide a complete range of services under one roof. ICICI has emerged as the first financial institution in India which has made an attempt to convert itself into a truly universal bank. And it has skillfully exploited the mergers route to reach this end. The merger of ITC classic finance provided with a huge deposit base in the east while the merger of Anagram Finance provided ICICI with a huge retail network in the west. Another such move was the reverse merger of Centurion Bank into 20th Century Finance[19].

Internet Banking

The Internet facility has given another facelift to the banking services all over the world[20]. There are a variety of ways that the Internet is going to affect the paradigm of banking industry in the future. India has just about made to the first transition from physical cash to "anytime money and anywhere money". This trend is more pronounced among foreign banks operating in India and private sector banks. The public sector banks are still behind the technology race. Some private sector banks like ICICI bank are entering into the realm of Internet banking while other foreign banks are ready to join the race.

Anytime and Anywhere Banking

The networking of compurterised branches enables customers to operate their account through any branch of the bank once they become the account holder of any branch[21]. The introduction of Automated Teller Machines facilitates the customers to transact with the bank all through the 24 hours. At Present ATMs are city-oriented in our country. Gradually the facilities of ATMs are likely to be introduced in other parts of the country also.[22]

Relationship Banking

With the operation of central computers, it is now possible to access the entire chain of accounts for a customer. These accounts may be current savings, fixed deposits type or mutual funds or credit cards or loan accounts etc. This helps in identifying the larger customer segments and designing product mix strategies to benefit both the bank and the customer. Hence, technology has now become 'market differentiated' and is clearly used as a competitive edge.[23]

Smart Cards Technology

The Smart Card technology is relatively a new comer to the retail payment scene. A smart card has an integrated circuit with a microprocessor chip embedded in it, which gives it enormous versatility. It performs calculations, maintain records, and acts as an electronic purse storing electronic money. It is essentially a chip or a memory card. A Project called SMARS (Small Rupees System) was undertaken by Indian Institute of Technology, Powai, the Institute for Development and Research in Banking Technology, Hyderabad, hardware and Software vendors and two commercial banks (State Bank of India and Canara Bank) have worked in concert as partners. The RBI has involved itself in the project to encourage market participants to develop a common technical infrastructure with a view to promoting the inter-operability of competing car schemes as well as to encourage wider acceptability of this sophisticated retail payment mode[24]. The success of the smart card projections depends on the efficiency of the inter-institutional clearing and settlement arrangements associated with the product.

Pushpa System

The Saraf Committee[25] on Upgradation of Technology in the payment system had given some leads to the banks on the new services which can be introduced. One of its suggestions pertains to the payment mode for the utilities and services. PUSHPA system (Paying Utilities, services Hasslefree payment system) is designed to simplify the bill payment for everybody i.e., customers, utility companies and banks. This system can be used for payment of electricity bills, insurance premiums, municipal taxes, vehicle taxes, school/college fees etc. It gets ready data file of paid cases from the clearinghouse. With the changes in technology the time has come form saying no to cash and yes to pushpa system which is user friendly to all the groups. This system has to make a real beginning in the country.

Challenges for Banking Industry

The process of globalisation of Indian economy will be further intensified in future. In such an environment, Indian commercial banks will have to equip themselves to meet the challenges of competition from within the country as well as from outside. And as they proceed to do this, they have to ensure that their foundation remains sound and that the desire to grow fast play in the same league as their competitors does not, in the least, detract their attention from principles of sound and prudent banking[26]. Some of the major challenges that the banking industry is likely to face can be summarised as under.

Competition from Global Majors

Indian commercial banks need to possess matching financial muscle as far competition is possible only among equals. In the days of on going revolution in information and communication technology, the challenges before the Indian banks is therefore to acquire a competitive size. Mergers and Acquisitions provide a quick step forward in this direction offering opportunities to share synergies and to reduce the cost of product development and delivery. Mergers, amongst bans will no more be a rare phenomena but a common business process.

Threats from New Banks

The entry of new private sector banks as in the case of other countries also resulted in a paradigm shift in the ways of banking in India. Equipped with latest technology, and technologically driven product lines, these have aroused customer's expectations very high. The market has changed drastically in that it has become largely customer centric. This situation calls for an aggression for an aggression laced with caution, and involves a highly efficient management of both liabilities and assets. The corner stone of such a management will be the ability to identify, anticipate, manage and reduce risks that are well known today as also those that will appear in relation to the products of tomorrow.

Self-regulation by Banks

In the liberalised milieu, regulation and self-regulation will go hand in hand. An effective self-regulatory organisation for the banking industry to monitor activities of the members, lay down the ground rules and settle disputes among members amicably is a logical development.

Thus, banks are required to reorient themselves with the changing environment in order to extend better service to all kinds of customers as per the changing requirement coping with all kinds of changes that are taking place in the environment and banking sector. It is not out of context here to quote the words of the former Governor of the Reserve Bank of India, Dr. Bimal Jalan, in his inaugural address at BECON, in January 2001,[27] "the long term vision for India's banking system to transform itself from being a domestic one to the global level may sound far fetched. However, it is not beyond our capacity provided we have the will and the determination."

REFERENCES

1. RBI Bulletin, "*Economic Growth, Financial Deepening and Financial Inclusion*", July-November, 2006, pp. 1305-1320.
2. Balamohandas, V. Andhra Bank endowment Lecture on "*Indian Banking Yesterday, Today and Tomorrow*", A seminar paper presented in Andhra University on 19th July, 2005.
3. Ranganadha Chary, A.V. and Paul, R.R. "*Banking & Financial System*", Kalyani Publications, (2003) pp 123-125
4. www.rbi.org.in
5. Saxena, K.S. "Management of Assets", *Journal Banking and Finance*, June 1989. p. 16.
6. Narasimham, M. *Report of the Committee on the Financial System*, 1991, p. 52.
7. Reserve Bank of India, *Report on Trend and Progress of Banking in India 1990-91,* p. 19.
8. NABARD, "*Progress of SHG – Bank Linkage in India 2003-04*, Mumbai, 2004, p. 22.
9. Narasimham, M., Chairman, *Report of the committee on Banking Sector Reforms*, 1998, pp.16-34.
10. Reddy, Y.V. "*Economy: Challenges for Policy Makers*", Speech at the Colegio de Economists Madrid, Spain, "*Monetary and Financial Sector Reforms in India: A Central Banker's Perspective*", November 23, 2000.
11. www rbihist@vsnl.net
12. Varshney, P.N. "*Banking Law and Practice*", Sultan Chand & Sons, New Delhi, 2005, p. 54.
13. RBI Bulletin, 2003. "*Transforming Indian Banks: In Search for a Better Tomorrow*", and "*Some Apparent Puzzles for Contemporary Monetary Policy*", January 2005, p. 17.
14. Rangarajan, C., Chairman & Deputy Governor, "*Committee on Computerisation in Banks*", Reserve Bank of India, 1988, p. 22.
15. Jain, C.M., Shurveer S. Bhanawat Dharmalingam Venugopal, *Technology in Banks: Some Thoughts for the Future* in *Professional Banker*, The ICFAI University Press, August 2004, p.14.
16. Rangarajan, *Banking Sector Reforms : Rationale and Relevance*, 1998, p.19.

17. Damle, Y.B., Convenor & Advisor. "Working Group to consider feasibility of introducing MICR/OCR Technology for Cheque Processing, Management Services Department, Reserve Bank of India, 1982, p. 23.

18. Iyer, T.N.A., Chairman & Executive Director, "Committees on Communication Network for Banks and SWIFT implementation", Reserve Bank of India, 1987, p.34.

19. Rao & Pallavi, "Bankable Banks", *Business Standard*, New Delhi, August, 2004, pp. 67-70.

20. Shesunoff, A. "The wait is over for Internet Banking", *ABA Banking Journal*, New York, Vol.1. No.91, 1999, p. 13.

21. Haranath, G. and Sathish, A.S. "The impact of the Internet on Competition in the Banking Industry" by Porters' five force model', *The Journal of Banking information Technology and Management,* Vol. 4, No. 1, January-June 2007, p 27.

22. Shere, K.S. "*Committee for proposing Legislation on Electronic Funds Transfer and other Electronic Payments*", Chairperson & Principal Legal Adviser, Reserve Bank of India, 1995, p. 23.

23. Panda, Tapan Kumar, "Service Quality Value Alignment through Internal Customer Orientation in Financial Service – An Exploratory study in Indian Banks", Publisher *Scholarly Article,* 2001, p. 22.

24. Ramani, D. "The E-Payment System" in E-Business, *ICFAI Journal,* May, 2007, p. 5.

25. Saraf, W.S. Chairman & Executive Director, "Committee on Technology Issues relating to Payments System, Cheque Clearing and Securities Settlement in the Banking Industry, 1994, Reserve Bank of India, p. 67.

26. Subhaqsish Roy, "*New Challenges for Banks*", The Hindu Business Line (daily newspaper), dt.March 13, 2007.

27. *Indian Banks Association Bulletin*, June 2005, p. 23.

CHAPTER

Nature and Scope of Relationship between Banker and Customer

The present chapter deals the nature and scope of relationship between bankers and customers. It provides the theoretical background for the empirical study which constitutes the core of the thesis. It explains the different kinds of relationships between customers and bankers. The emphasis of the chapter is on the banker customer relationship through account, deposits and attractive saving schemes.

The relationship that exists between a banker and his customer is significant. This significance is due to the interdependence of both the parties. In this context, the terms "Banker" "and "Customer" have been explained. The term "Banking" is defined 'as accepting for the purpose of lending or investment, of deposits of money from the public, repayable on demand or otherwise, and withdrawal by cheques, a draft order or other wise as per "Section 5(B) of 1949 Banking regulation Act. The term "Customer" of a bank is not defined by law. Ordinarily a person who has an account in a bank is considered its customer. In Sir. John Puget's view "To constitute a customer there must be some recognizable course or habit of dealing in the nature of regular banking business." This definition of a customer of a bank lays emphasis on the duration of the dealings between the banker and the customer and is, therefore, called the duration theory."

According to Hart "a customer is one who has an account with a banker or for whom banker habitually undertakes to act as such.

Broadly speaking, a customer is a person who has the habit of resorting to the same place or person to do business. So far as banking transactions are concerned, he is a person whose money has been accepted on the footing that the banker will honor up to the amount standing to his credit, irrespective of his connection being of short or long standing.

A customer of a banker need not necessarily be a person. A firm a joint stock company, a society or any separate legal entity may be a customer, and includes a Government department and a corporation incorporated by or under any law explanation to Section 45-Z of Banking Regulations Act 1949.[1]

A person who does not deal with the banker in regard to the essential functions of the Banker i.e., accepting of deposits and lending of money, but avails of any of the services rendered by the banker, is not called a customer of the Banker. For example:- any person without a bank account in his name may remit money through a bank draft, encash a cheques, deposit cash in the bank to be credited to the account of the LIC or any Joint Stock company issuing new shares. But he will not be called a customer of the banker as his dealings with the banker are not in regard to the essential functions of the banker. Such dealings are considered as casual dealings and are not in the nature of banking business.

Thus, to constitute a customer the following essential requisites must be fulfilled.[2]

- A Bank account - Savings, Current or Fixed deposits must be opened in his name by making necessary deposit of money, and
- The dealing between the banker and the customer must be of the nature of banking business.

General relationship between Banker and Customer

In addition to his primary functions, a banker renders a number of services to his customer. The relationship between them primarily is that of a creditor and debtor. A Banker also acts as an agent or trustee of his customer if the latter entrusts the former with agency or trust work. In such cases, the banker acts as a debtor, an agent and a trustee simultaneously but in relation to the specified business.

The Relationship between a banker and a customer is that of as a debtor and creditor On the opening of an account, the banker assumes the position of debtor. He is not a depository or trustee of the customer's money because the money handed over to the banker becomes a debt due from him to the customer.

The creditor has the right to demand his money from the banker, and the banker is under an obligation to repay the debt as and when he is required to do so, But it is not necessary that the repayment is made in terms of the same currency notes and coins, The payment of course, must be made in terms of legal tender currency of the country.

A depositor remains a creditor of his banker so long as his account carries a credit balance. Banker relationship with the customer is reversed as soon as customer's account is overdrawn. Banker becomes creditor who has taken a loan from the banker and continues in that capacity till the loan is repaid. Though the relationship between a banker and his customer is mainly that of a debtor and creditor[33]

- The creditor must demand payment
- Proper place and time of demand
- The Demand must be made in proper manner

Types of Deposit Accounts

The deposit accounts are a source of banker and customer relationship. There are different kinds of deposits. In this category are included the deposits with the bank for a fixed period which is specified at the time of making the deposit.

Such deposits are, therefore, called Fixed Deposits or Term Deposits. A Fixed deposit is repayable on the expiry of the specified period, chosen by the depositor to suit his purpose and to enable him to get back the money as and when he needs it. For example, if a person intends to utilise his money for any purpose after a few years, he may deposit it for 3,5 or 6 years, whereas if his purpose is to meet some urgent need in the near future, the fixed deposit may be made for 3,6 or 9 months. As the date of repayment of a fixed deposit is determined in advance, the banker need not keep more cash reserves against it and can utilise such amount more profitably.

The banker, therefore, offers higher rate of interest on such deposits because the depositor parts with liquidity for definite period. Fixed deposits have grown in importance and popularity in India during recent years. There are Fixed Deposit Schemes for Senior Citizens. Reserve Bank of India has also permitted the banks to formulate fixed deposit schemes specially meant for senior citizens on which they may offer higher and fixed rates of interest as compared with normal deposits. These schemes will also incorporate simple procedure for automatic transfer of deposits to nominees of such depositors in the event of death.

For opening a fixed deposit account a depositor is required to fill in an application form wherein he mentions the amount of the deposit and the period for which deposit is to be made. He also gives his specimen signature. A Fixed Deposit Receipt is thereafter issued to the depositor, acknowledging the receipt of the sum of money specified therein, to be repaid at the expiry of the period mentioned therein along with interest at the specified rate. Reserve Bank of India has made it absolutely necessary to indicate on the Fixed Deposit Receipt the date of receipt, the period for which the deposit has been accepted and due date, as also the applicable rate of interest.

A variant of the savings bank account is the recurring deposit or cumulative deposit account introduced by banks in recent years. This account is intended to inculcate the habit of saving on a regular basis as an inducement is offered in the form of comparatively higher rate of interest. A depositor opening a recurring deposit account is required to deposit an amount chosen by him, generally a multiple of Rs.5 or 10, in his account every month for a period selected by him. The period of recurring deposit varies from bank to bank. Banks open such accounts for periods ranging from 1 to 10 years.

The rate of interest on the recurring deposit account stands favourably as compared to the rate of interest on the saving bank account because the former partly resembles the fixed deposit account. According to the directive of the Reserve Bank, banks are required to ensure that the rates of interest offered by them on recurring deposits are generally in accord with the rates prescribed for various term deposits. The rate of interest is, therefore, almost equal to that of the fixed deposit account.

In case a depositor is compelled to close the account before its maturity, the bank pays no interest if the deposits are made for less than 3 months, interest at 1½ per cent is payable for deposits made up to 6 month, up to 4 per cent for deposits made up to 12 months and 1 per cent below the rate applicable to a recurring deposit of the period for which the deposit has actually run in case deposits are held for over year. The accounts are transferable from one branch to another without charge.

The recurring deposit account can be opened by any person, more than one person jointly or severally, by a guardian in the name of a minor and even by a minor. While opening the account, the depositor is given a Pass Book which is to be presented to the bank at the time of monthly deposits and repayment of amount. Installments for each month should be paid before the last working day of that month. Accumulated amount with interest will be payable after a month of the payment of the last installment.

The Reserve Bank of India publishes[4] the classification of deposits with the commercial banks under two broad heads, namely: (*i*) Demand Deposits, and (*ii*) Time Deposits. The various types of deposits included in these heads are as follows:

Demanded Deposits include: (*i*) Current deposits, (*ii*) demand liabilities portion of savings bank deposits, (*iii*) margins held against letter of credit / guarantees (if payable on demand), (*iv*) balances in overdue fixed deposits, cash certificates and recurring deposits, (*v*) outstanding telegraphic and mail transfers, demand drafts, (*vi*) unclaimed deposits, (*vii*) credit balances in cash credit accounts and (*viii*) deposits held as security for advances which are repayable on demand.

The Deposits include: (*i*) fixed deposits, (*ii*) cash certificates, recurring deposits, (*iii*) time liabilities portion of savings bank deposits, (*iv*) staff security deposits (*v*) margins held against letter of credit if not payable on demand, and (*vi*) fixed deposits held as security for advances.

It is to be noted that the savings deposits are apportioned in both of the above categories. The portion which be withdrawn notice is treated as demand deposits and the rest as time deposits.

As suggested by the Working Group on the Money Market (Chairman N. Vaghul), Reserve Bank of India has permitted the banks to issue Certificates of Deposit Reserve Bank has issued guidelines also in this Regard, which have been relaxed from time to time.

Certificates of Deposit can be issued by scheduled commercial banks only and not by the Regional Rural Banks. Through CDs banks accept short term deposits of substantial amounts from the investors who have liquid funds for temporary period. Such CDs can be issued to individuals, corporations, companies, trusts, funds, associations, etc. Non-resident Indians (NRIs) may subscribe to such certificates but on a non-reportable basis and such CDs cannot be endorsed to another NRI in the secondary market.

A large number of Indian citizens and aliens of Indian origin live abroad and are in a position to save a good deal of money. The Government of India realised the urgency of mobilising their savings in the from of bank deposits in India and have, therefore, offered them certain concessions and incentives to remit money to India for investment[5]. Banks in India at present operate various types of deposit accounts for nationals abroad both in Indian Rupees and foreign currencies. These accounts may be opened by Non-Resident Indians or by Overseas Corporate Bodies.

Savings Bank Accounts

Savings bank accounts are another source of banker and customer relationship. A savings bank account is meant for the people of the lower and middle classes who wish to save a part of their current incomes to meet their future needs and also intend to earn an income from their savings. The banks, therefore, impose certain restriction on the savings bank account and also offer a reasonable rate of interest. The need of keeping cash reserves against such deposits is comparatively larger vis-à-vis the fixed deposits but smaller as against the current deposits, because of the restrictions on the number of withdrawals.

With the extension of banking facilities during the last decade and the growth of banking habit amongst the people, the savings deposits of all scheduled commercial banks have gone up substantially playing a vital role in banker and customer relationship[6]. The customer may deposit any amount in the savings bank account subject to a minimum of Rs500. The banks do not accept cheques or other instruments payable to a third party for the purpose of deposit in the savings account. Banks prescribe the minimum balance that is to be maintained in the savings Bank accounts. For this purpose they take into consideration the cost involved in maintaining and servicing such account. They also levy specific charges, if the minimum balance is not maintained.

Current Accounts

Current accounts constitute another area of banker and customer relationship. A current account is a running and active account which may be operated upon number of times during a working day. There is no restriction of the number and the amount of withdrawals from a current account. As the banker is under an obligation to repay these deposits on demand, they are called demand liabilities of a banker. To meet such liability, the banker keeps sufficient cash reserves against such deposits vis-à-vis the savings and the fixed deposits. Current accounts suit the requirements of big businessmen, joint stock companies, institutions, public authorities and public corporations, etc., whose banking transaction happen to be numerous on every working day[7]. Special characteristics of the current account are as follows:

1. A current account is meant for the convenience of his customers, who are relieved of the task of handling cash themselves and to take the risk inherent therein. Thus the primary deposit accounts which are meant to solicit the savings of the people.
2. As the banker undertakes to make payments and to collect the bills, drafts, cheques etc., any number of times daily, the operating cost, i.e., the cost of bank personnel, involved in current account is considerable. It is, therefore, customary for the banks not to pay any interest on the credit balance in the current account. The Reserve Bank directive prohibits the payment of interest on current accounts. No countervailing interest is payable on any current account maintained by a borrower with any bank. Banks may pay interest on current account of Regional Rural Banks at half per cent below the borrowing rate fixed for the RRB by the sponsor bank. Since May 1983, banks have been permitted to pay interest on balances lying in current accounts in the name of a deceased depositor from the date of death of the depositor till payment to the legal heirs.

Interest on such amount shall be payable at savings bank deposit rate.[8]

3. The State Bank makes no charge for keeping an account provided the balance maintained is sufficient to compensate the bank for the work involved. In case of unremunerative accounts involving lot of work but without the maintenance of sufficient balances, the banker charges incidental expenses from the customer. The public sector banks now impose a uniform "Ledger folio charge" of Rs.20 per folio (i.e., one side of the ledger page) on accounts having average balance below Rs. 25,000).
4. A current account carries certain privileges which are not given to a savings bank account-holder, e.g.,
   (*i*) Third party cheques and cheques with endorsements may be deposited in the current account for collection and credit.
   (*ii*) Overdraft facilities are given in case of current accounts only.
   (*iii*) The loans and advances granted by the banks to their customers are not given in the form of cash but through the current accounts. Current accounts thus earn interest on all types of advances granted by the banker.

Attractive Savings Schemes

After the de-regulation of interest rates on deposits banks have introduced various attractive savings schemes[9]. These have their bearing on banker and customer relationship. Some of the deposit schemes are as follows:

(1) Re-investment Plan. This is just like fixed deposits with the difference that deposits are accepted for a fixed period ranging between 12 and 120 months and interest, though calculated periodically, is payable at the time of maturity. This plan provides for the re-investment of interest also. In case of premature

withdrawal or renewal under such plan, compound interest with quarterly rests at prescribed rate is to be allowed. If an advance is granted against a deposit under re-investment scheme, accrued interest is also to be taken into account for determining the margin.

(2) Cash Certificates. These certificates are issued with different face values payable after specified maturity periods. The issue prices for different maturity periods are specified in advance; for example, one can get a Cash Certificate with face value of Rs.100 after 12 months by paying its discounted value. Thus interest is payable on maturity.

(3) Multi Option Deposit Scheme, State Bank of India has introduced this scheme to provide liquidity to term deposits and other facilities. Under this scheme, term deposits are accepted in conjunction with Savings Bank / Current a/c or both. The facility of withdrawal is permissible in units of Rs.1000 through Savings Bank a/c without attracting any penal rate of interest. The remaining amount continues to earn interest at contracted rate.

(4) Savings Accounts linked with Fixed Deposits. Under this scheme the depositor specifies the maximum amount in his savings bank account, beyond which the balance is to be automatically transferred to a fixed deposit account the maturity of which is decided by him.

(5) Super Savings Account. Bank of Baroda has launched this scheme wherein a range of benefits are given to depositors.

Banker as Trustee

A banker is a debtor of his customer in respect of the deposits made by the latter, but in certain circumstance he acts as a trustee also. On the other hand, if a customer instructs his bank to purchase certain securities out of his deposit with the latter, but the bank falls before making such purchase, the bank will continue to be a debtor of his customer (and not a trustee) in respect of the amount which was not withdrawn from or debited to his account to carry out his specific instruction. The relationship between the banker and his customer as a trustee and beneficiary depends upon the specific instructions given by the latter to the former regarding the purpose of use of the money or documents entrusted to the banker.

Banker as Agent

A Banker acts as an agent of his customer and performs a number of agency functions for the convenience of his customers.[10] For example, he buys or sells securities on behalf of his customer collects a cheques on his behalf and makes payment of the various dues of his customer, e.g., Insurance premium etc.

Special Relationships

The Aim of this research study is to investigate the strength of banker and customer relationship in bank service. A model that relates service quality and satisfaction to relationship strength is presented. The empirical part of the research is based on a qualitative study concerning customers and banker relationship from micro - level in India. A Look at the definitions of relationship in the Banker and Customer relationship literature reveals that the concept rarely is defined directly at all. The literature often, discusses activities the firm should engage in to develop, maintains and enhance relationship with customer. Assumed consequences of good relationship with customers are often discussed as well. Within, Industrial, Micro credit, Agricultural, Business and General relationships have been studied more in depth

Although the ideal is that both parties should be positively committed to the relationships, as suggested within the interaction – net work approach of banking industrials marking, this kind of relationship is not usual in consumer market when talking about consumer services, the focus has to be on the customer side.

If a firm through direct marketing approaches repeatedly a customer, and if the customer buys nothing from the firm, there is no relationship. It might be concluded that the firm is engaged in relationship marketing with the aim of creating a relationship with the customer.[11]

Thus a customer who has purchased twice from the company, feels some positive commitment to it, and/or has bonds with it has a stronger relationship than some one who gas purchased twice without being committed and/or having bonds. Bonds can be studied at both company and individual levels. A customer may be committed to, and have a social bond to a specific person in the company, without feeling commitment and trust for the company, as a whole.[12]

The operationalisation of the measures have been developed specifically for our study. The relationship strength is a multidimensional measure consisting of relationship commitment and relationship loyalty. Relationship commitment is the extent to which the customer favours a particular bank and spreads positive information by word of mouth. A strong commitment is characterised by the customer showing an active interest in the company and speaking well of it. A weak relationship commitment exists when customers are disappointed and / or spread negative views by word of mouth. Customers may also be indifferent. Relationship loyalty can be measured by many measures e.g. as the number of bank relationship, intensity of usage, concentration of usage, length of relationship and expressed as the customer's own perceived and verbally expressed loyalty. Their actual behaviour which is the base for the traditional loyalty concept might differ from their own perception of loyalty. Strong relationship loyalty would be characterised by fewer bank relationships, higher intensity of usage relative to other banks greater concentration of usage, longer relationship and higher expressed loyalty. Those customers who are customers in more than one bank may perceive it as easier to change the main bank. Customer's relationship to banks were found to be very strong. Most customers have used the same bank for more than 15 years and up to the time of their retirement.

Banking services need to keep in view the requirements of the Swadesh groups and also focus their attention on globalisation efforts.[13] They require a balancing effort. The technology driven foreign banks have aroused customer's expectations high. In the wake of new client expectations, satisfying the customer requires a new approach labelled as Relationship marketing.

Activities of Commercial Banks

Primary Functions of Commercial Banks

Deposit Acceptance: Being a short term credit dealer, the commercial banks accept the savings of public in the form of following deposits:

- Fixed term deposits
- Current A/c deposits
- Recurring deposits
- Saving A/c deposits
- Tax saving deposits
- Deposits for NRIs

Lending Money

A second major function is to give loans and advances and thereby earn interest on it. This function is the main source of income for the bank. Overdraft facility: Permission to a current A/c holder of withdrawal more than to what he has deposited.

Loans & Advances

A kind of secured and unsecured loans against some kind of security. Discounting of bill of exchange: in case a person wants money immediately, he/she can present the B/E to the respective commercial bank and can get it discounted.

Cash credit : Facility to withdraw a certain amount of money on a given security.

Secondary Functions of Commercial Banks

Agency functions: Bank pays on behalf of its customers as an agent and gets paid fee for agency functions such as:

- Payment of taxes, bills
- Collection of funds through bills, cheques etc.
- Transfer of funds
- Sale-purchaseof shares and debentures
- Collection/Payment of dividend or interest
- Acts as trustee & executor of properties
- Forex Transactions
- General Utility Services: locker facility

Credit Creation

It is one of the most outstanding function of commercial banks. A bank creates credit on the basis of its primary deposits. It further lends the money which people has depositted with the bank also charge interest on this money, which is much higher than what it actually pays to depositer. Thus bank generates money for itself.

Scope of Relationship among Banker and Customers

The commercial banks in India are to perform a variety of roles such as promotion of the interest of the depositors, giving fair and adequate return on the deposits, assisting the people who are in need of financial assistance to raise their standard of living, upliftment of the downtrodden in the society, a more responsible and accountable role to Government, safeguarding the rights and interests of the employees, and apart from all these roles, in the commercial banks have to earn profits to sustain their existence and to do justice to all these roles. Hence, the objectives of modern banking industry are primarily two fold economic responsibilities.[14]

As a result of many structural changes, commercial banks have gained more power and prominence in the economy. Their performance affects the whole of the economic system since they constitute an important element in the total financial system of the country. The establishment of these banks for the attainment of Good relationship has aroused many expectations in the public. Press and Parliament. The real justification for their existence depends on how efficiently and effectively they discharge these relationships. Considering all the relevant aspects of the Indian economy, viewing various arguments for and against nationalisation of these banks and keeping in view all the structural changes the various responsibilities of these banks may be as under. These responsibilities may be grouped under the following heads

(1) Maintain good relationship with customers
(2) Maintain Good relationship with society
(3) Maintain good relationship with Government
(4) Maintain good relationship with other financial institutions
(5) Maintain good relationship with employees

Relationship with Customers

The whole philosophy of the commercial banking centres on the service to its customers. Customers of a commercial banks are those who have bank accounts in their names and such accounts are used essentially for the business of banking i.e., accepting the deposits and lending of money. Thus, both the suitors and borrowers are termed as customers of a commercial banks. Both individuals institutions and the corporate bodies may be included in the term customers of a banks. Depositors are lenders of money to the community through banks. Apart from comparatively higher rates of interest, they are also interested in the safety and liquidity of funds. Easy approach to the bank office, courteous behaviours of banks employees, stable, efficient and quick service particularly at counters, convenient banking hours etc., are the expectations of the customers of a bank. This leads to good image of banks, which boosts the confidence of the customers.

As the rates of interest are being regulated by RBI, the management of these banks cannot do much in this respect. However, it should try to see that these expectations are fulfilled. Through insurance of deposits, yet good behaviour and efficient, prompt and stable service should be ensured by the management. Borrowers are the purchasers of services of these banks. They are always interested in good service easily and efficiently available and that too without any cumbersome procedures.

Hence, the management should ensure that credit is granted in time, adequately and easily. As purveyors of credit, the management of these banks should grant credit to all those who deserve it and to those sectors the financing of which helps to maximise the use of scarce resources. Credit should also be followed by constancy of service particularly in the case of financing priority an the neglected sectors. Credit should be given for approved purposes where the proposals should be technically feasible and economically viable. Proper care should be taken so that the borrowers do not have any misunderstanding about the nationalised banks and their objectives. Further, banks also should educate the customers by providing information oriented publicity in turn with its changing concepts and objectives. Customers, at all types of areas should be provided with convenient banking hours suited to the needs of different places. Besides, banking offices should be kept open for long houses for transacting banking business. This is because banks in India are kept open for 22 hours a week, as against more than 42 hours a week in Zurich and 40 hours a week in New York[15]. The Courteous treatment of the customers from rural areas is another major relationship on the part of banks. As the commercial banks have certain responsibilities towards the customers, the customers are also required to extend full co-operation to the bank management. Giving proper accurate information, behaving with a sense of discipline and projecting rational behaviour are the expectations of the banks from the customers

Relationship with Society

Besides being an economic institutions, every economic enterprise is also a national and social institution. As the enterprise grows and attains prominence, its influence upon the society becomes important and hence its working should not be in any way detrimental to the interests of the society. The nationalised banks as centres of economic activity are called upon to solve many of the problems of the society such as abject poverty, unequal distribution of national income, chronic unemployment and under employment of natural, economic and human resources, lopsided economic development etc., Banks have been entrusted with the task of opening branches in unbaked centres, to evolve all-round development of those centres, commercial banks should also ensure that greater confidence of the society is inspired by providing efficient and regular services. This has been rightly stated by Edward W. Reed[16] that "the safety of commercial banks has always been of concern to stockholders, depositors and supervisory and regulatory authorities since bank failures have a more adverse effect on the economy than do failures in any other type of business". The commercial banks are supposed to see that evils like red-tapism, mis-utilisation, and misappropriation of funds do not creep in to the banking system which adversely affects the image of the banks. In turn, society should also extend its full co-operation to the banking industry by providing an amicable and legitimate environment for the banks to function more smoothly and responsibly.

Relationship with Government

The discharge of the social responsibilities enhances social welfare. A government committed to social welfare always strives to enhance the social welfare. The nationalisation of these banks is a step in that direction. As the sole owner of these banks, the objective of the government is not to make them unprofitable entities and philanthropic institutions but to ensure wider social service by maintaining their commercial nature. This requires that these banks are expected to give reasonable return to the government. There has been a spate of discussion over the issue of public enterprises are meant for discharging social responsibilities and hence profit making is not a major concern for them. But in a developing country like India,. The discharge of social responsibilities in inter-linked with earnings surplus and profit from operations. Besides, the major source of funds for commercial banks is the deposit of the customers. The increase in the deposits of commercial banks depends to a large extent upon the faith reposed in them by the depositors.[17] This faith *inter alia* is the outcome of profits, and continuous fall in the profits would mean loss of depositors and would hereby influence adversely then deposit resources

Further, the government as planning authority expects the management of these banks to ensure the functioning of these banks is in conformity with the plan strategy. The success of economic planning depends largely upon the co-operation from all sectors of the economy including the financial institutions the major part of which consists of these banks. The government has identified certain sector as priority sectors and timely and adequate credit should be extended to these sectors.

The commercial banks are expected to extend productive and employment oriented consultancy services with regard to technically feasible and economically viable projects. Further, commercial banks are expected to be responsible to the RBI, which is the monetary authority in our country[18]. It works in consultation with the government and is ultimately responsible for the sound banking system in the country. It has been assigned both primitive and regulatory functions. As a result, it also gives directions to the nationalised banks from time to time for a sound banking system with a view to serving the best interests of the society. In this connection all the commercial banks are expected to implement the several directions in respects of bills market, several schemes like lead bank, service area approach financing several farmers credit co-operative societies etc,., in turn RBI should also consider the nature of commercial banks and limitations of theses banks while exercising its regulatory and controlling powers.

Relationship with Financial Institutions

Nationalised commercial banks are a part of the organised financial infrastructure of the country. Apart from these banks, the financial infrastructure includes private banks, foreign banks, co-operative banks, Regional Rural banks as the constituents of the money market and LIC, IFC, SFC, ICICI, IDBI, UTI as institutions of the capital market. For a sound development, a co-ordinate approach between the various institutions of both money and capital markets is required. These institutions should act in an ethical, manner, properly guide the clientele, participate in their activities, provide consortium leadership to other institutions and agencies, resort to fair practices etc.[19]

Relationship with their Employees

As banking is a service industry, all types of services rendered by it are directly affected by the skill and attitude of employees who are in direct contact with customers. In addition to the handsome emoluments and other perquisites, many other aspects like security of job, human treatment for labour and adequate facilities for their promotions to higher status. Lack of cordial relations between the management and the employees of an enterprise leads to discontentment and dis-satisfaction which is visible through strikes, ghetto etc., which are the causes for the deterioration of profitability, efficiency and productivity of the banks which ultimately leads to poor customer services[20]. This discontentment and dissatisfaction can be reduced by paying fair and adequate remuneration, provision of proper working conditions, ensuring security to the job, resorting to fair Human resource development practices, positive motivation etc. As it has been rightly pointed out that a "strike bears a triple curse. It brings financial ruin upon both the employees and the employees. It victimises the public and the consumers. It may and often does hurt national interests when the public utility and defiance industries are involved." But these responsibilities are a two-way traffic, the employees have also many responsibilities towards the management of these banks. It can be remarked that " the harmonious industrial relations can develop only on the basis of mutual understanding and awareness of common responsibilities and obligations."

A stable and consistent growth in the banking industry is very much required for a developing country like India. This growth ensures the fulfilment of the different needs of the economy[21]. To ensure this growth banks should properly organised and efficiently managed. The administrative machinery should ensure easy location of responsibilities and accountability of its various employees besides it should ensure automatic growth of management executive necessary to cope up with the new tasks and challenges of the commercial banking. It should also ensure efficient and optimum utilisation of men and material resources of these banks.

Thus, the relationship between a banker and his customer begins with the opening an account by the former in the name of the latter. Initially all the accounts are opened with a deposit of money by the customer and hence these accounts are called deposits accounts. The banks have introduced different types of accounts which are classified into three categories: (1) The saving deposit account, (2) The fixcd deposit accounts, and (3) The current accounts. In recent years a few new types of accounts have also been introduced by banks. All these have changed the nature and scope of relationship among banker and customer. It is against this background, an empirical study has been taken up by the researcher.

REFERENCES

1. Shekar. K.C. & Shekar, Lekshmy. "*Banking Theory and Practice*", Vikas Publishing House Pvt. Ltd., New Delhi, 1998, pp. 167-169.
2. Tarapore, S.S., Chairman. "Report of the Committee on Fuller Capital Account Convertibility", Reserve Bank of India, July 2006, p. 66.
3. Sundharm, K.P.M. "*Money Banking–Trade and Finance*", Sultan Chand & Sons Publishers, New Delhi, 1998, p.78.
4. RBI Bulletin, "*Evolution of Central Banking in India,*" June 2006, p. 43.
5. Reddy, A. "Banking Sector Liberalisation and Efficiency of Indian Banks, *ICFAI Journal of Banking Management*, May 2004, pp.1-3.
6. Chitra Andrade, *Banking Products & Services*, 2nd edn., Taxmann Publications Private Limited, 2007, pp. 101-104.
7. Suryakant, B. "*The Indian Banking*", Palak Publications, Mumbai, 2004, p. 36.
8. RBI Bulletin, "*Monetary Policy and Exchange Rate Frameworks*", The Indian Experience, 2006.
9. Dale, Richard "*International Banking De-regulation*", "*The Great Banking Experiment*", Blackwell publishers, London, 1992, pp. 121-123.
10. Agarwal, B.P. "*Commercial Bank in India*", Classical Publishing Co., New Delhi, 1981, pp.23-28.
11. Sheth N.J. Mittal, B. and Newman, J.B. "*Customer Behaviour–Consumer Behaviour*", The Dryden Press, New York, 1999, pp.145-155.
12. Mohan Rao, P., Trilok Kumar Jain, "*Management of Banking and Financial Institutions*", Deep & Deep Publications Pvt. Ltd., New Delhi, 2002, p. 201.
13. Varughese, A.G. "Retail Banking in India", *Professional Banker,* The ICFAI University Press, Hyderabad, April 2005, p. 27.
14. Ranade, A., and G. Kapur, "Appreciating Rupee: Changing Paradigm", *Economic and Political Weekly*, February, 2003, pp. 1171-1179.
15. Narayana, M.S. "*Social Banking*", Ph.D. Thesis submitted to Nagarjuna University, Guntur District 2002, pp. 67-78.

16. Mahendra K, Goyath Shahadat Khan, "A comparative study of corporate disclosure issue in emerging economies', *The Journal of Accounting and Finance*, October 2006–March 2007, Vol.21, p . 21.
17. RBI Bulletin, "*Financial Stability: Indian Experience*", April-July 2004, p. 67.
18. RBI Bulletin, "*Monetary Policy and Exchange Rate Frameworks: The Indian Experience*", 2005.
19. RBI Bulletin, "*Reforms, Productivity and Efficiency in Banking: The Indian Experience.*" March, 2005, pp. 279-293..
20. Reddy, Y.V. "*Development of Money Market in India*", Address at the Fifth J.V. Somayajulu Memorial Lecture at Madras, February, 1999.
21. RBI Bulletin, *Report on Currency and Finance, 2003-04,* p. 23.

CHAPTER

Opinion Survey of Bankers on Banker-Customer Relationship

This Chapter is devoted to present the perceptions of bankers on the basis of an opinion survey on banker-customer relationship. The present analysis is done the basis of information collected from 180 bank officers with the help of a schedule distributed in the State Bank of India, the Andhra Bank, the ING Vysya Bank and the ICICI Bank Ltd. The empirical study has been taken up by the researcher in Visakhapatnam, Guntur and East Godavari district in the State of Andhra Pradesh. The three districts under the study represent an Urban, a semi-urban and a rural district respectively.

The opinions of the bank officers have been elicited by the researcher by administering the schedules to bank officers in the banks under study. The data have been collected from the bank officers on socio-economic variables like age, sex, education, designation, experience and nativity. The study takes into account the identification by bank officers as to reasons for opening account with the bank by the customers, the problems faced by the officers at the time of opening account, working hours and inconvenience caused by customers while opening accounts. The study covers the physical facilities such as seating arrangement, space for moving, problems faced by officers while collecting deposits, work load after computerisation, change in the attitude of customers, problems faced in cheque transactions, sanction of loans, technological services, job simplification procedures like ATM and their impact on the functioning. Finally an attempt is made to elicit the perception of officers as to their job. The study is supplemented by statistical tools — f-test, t-test, rank scoring, test of ANOVA and Chi-square to find out the significance level.

Socio-Economic Profile

The socio-economic factors of population sample indicate an important input in the organisation and functioning of any Bank. Therefore, an attempt is made to collect and interpret the socio-economic profile of 180 bank officers. The important factors covered under the present study are: 1. Age, 2. Sex, 3. Educational qualification, 4.Designation 5.Experience, and 6. Native place.

Age Group of Bank Officers

Age is an important socio-economic factor of any human group. It plays an important role in undertaking and pursuing any activity. Its impact is significant on the socio-economic activities of the population. Table 6.1 shows the age-wise and bank-wise classification of respondents under study.

Table 6.1: Age-wise and Bank-wise Classification of Respondents

Age (years)	State Bank of India		Andhra Bank		ING Vysya Bank		ICICI Bank		Total	
	No. of Respondents	Per cent	No. of Respondents	Per cent	No. of Respondents	Per cent	No. of Respondents	Per cent	No. of Respondents	Per cent
20-30	5	11.1	2	4.4	10	22.2	34	75.6	51	28.3
30-40	6	13.3	2	4.4	3	6.7	11	24.4	22	12.2
40-50	17	37.8	21	46.7	25	55.6	-	-	63	35.0
50 above	17	23.8	20	44.4	7	15.6	-	-	44	24.4
Total	**45**	**100**	**45**	**100**	**45**	**100**	**45**	**100**	**180**	**100.0**

Source: Primary Data.

The details relating to the age group of respondents are given in Table VI.1. The table indicates that the study is dominated by the respondents (35%) who are in the age groups of 40-50 years followed by (28.3%) 20-30 in the age group. Those who crossed 50 years of age and are nearing retirement constitute 24.4 per cent of the sample under the study. The bank–wise analysis also reveals that, the dominated age group is 40 to 50 years in the three banks under study (SBI 37.8%, AB 46.7% and ING Vysya Bank 55.6%). The total respondents of ICICI bank are distributed only in two age groups viz., 20–30 years (75.6%) and 30–40 years (24.4%). This indicates that all the three banks which are established and have been operating since a long time have more number of aged officers when compared to new generation private banks. This observation is useful to verify the influence of age on banker and customer relationship.

Sex-wise and Bank–wise classification of Respondents

Sex is an important socio-economic factor. Approximately 49 per cent of the total population in India indicates females. However, their representation in socio-economic activity is found to be less. Table 6.2 deals with the sex-wise classification of the respondents of various Banks respectively.

Table 6.2: Sex–Wise and Bank-wise Classification of Respondent

Sex	State Bank of India		Andhra Bank		ING Vysya Bank		ICICI Bank		Total	
	No. of Respon-dents	Per cent	No. of Respon-dents	Per cent	No. of Respon-dents	Per cent	No. of Respon-dents	Per cent	No. of Respon-dents	Per cent
Male	42	93.3	40	88.9	39	67.7	29	64.4	150	83.3
Female	3	6.7	5	11.1	6	13.3	16	35.6	30	16.7
Total	**45**	**100**	**45**	**100**	**45**	**100**	**45**	**100**	**180**	**100**

Source: Primary Data.

Table VI.2 revels that the male respondents are more (83.3%) while the female respondents are only of 16.7 per cent. The male respondents dominated the female respondents. The bank-wise analysis shows that the female is highly insignificant in SBI which is only (6.7%) out of 45 respondents. The female participation is equally insignificant in Andhra Bank (11.1%) and ING Vysya Bank (13.3%). The participation of female respondents is comparatively better in ICICI bank and it indicates that new generation private banks are employing comparatively a good number of female employees in their banks. It is also felt that the opinion of male and female employees may differ on banker and customer relationship.

Designation

Designation is an important factor that determines the level of income. It affects both the living and general conditions of life. It also determines the standards of life. Table VI.3 deals with the designation status of the bank officers respectively.

Table 6.3: Designation-wise and Bank-wise Classification of Respondents

Designation	State Bank of India		Andhra Bank		ING Vysya Bank		ICICI Bank		Total	
	No. of Respondents	Per cent	No. of Respondents	Per cent	No. of Respondents	Per cent	No. of Respondents	Per cent	No. of Respondents	Per cent
Branch Manager	13	28.9	13	28.9	8	17.8	7	15.6	41	22.8
Officers	32	71.1	32	71.1	37	82.2	38	84.4	139	77.2
Total	**45**	**100**	**45**	**100**	**45**	**100**	**45**	**100**	**180**	**100.0**

Source: Primary Data.

The distribution of respondents according to designation is shown in Table VI.3. According to the table, the respondents relating to officer cadre represent 77.2 per cent while the respondents relating to Branch manager cadre represent of 22.8 per cent. The table also indicates that there is a large variation in the cadres of respondents. The variation between the two cadres is much higher in the private banks when compared to the public sector banks. But the case of private bank ratio of officers and managers is just opposite the public sector banks. The respondents belonging to the Manager cadre in State Bank of India is 28.9 per cent while the respondents belonging to the Officer cadre is 71.1 per cent which is more than double. In the case of Andhra Bank, the percentage of manager and officers ratio remains the same as SBI. In case of ING Vysya and ICICI Banks, the managers constituted 17.8 and 15.6 per cent officers constituted 82.2 and 84.4 per cent respectively. As there are more number of officer cadre designations, in all these would help to promote banker-customer relationship.

Education

Education gives people a sense of independent judgement and power to distinguish between the good and the bad. Education is an instrument of socio-economic change. Lack of education is an obstacle to socio-economic development and Education is one of the important factor influencing human behaviour and qualities. Therefore, an attempt is made to identify the educational status of respondents belonging to the bank officers as well, as it may have its influence on the banker and customer relationship.

Table 6.4: Educational–wise and Bank-wise Classification of Respondents

Educational qualifications	State Bank of India		Andhra Bank		ING Vysya Bank		ICICI Bank		Total	
	No. of Respon-dents	Per cent	No. of Respon-dents	Per cent	No. of Respon-dents	Per cent	No. of Respon-dents	Per cent	No. of Respon-dents	Per cent
Degree	28	62.2	30	66.7	20	44.4	14	31.1	92	51.1
PG	17	37.8	15	33.3	25	56.6	31	68.9	88	48.9
Total	**45**	**100**	**45**	**100**	**45**	**100**	**45**	**100**	**180**	**100**

Source: Primary Data.

Table VI.4 provides information pertaining to educational qualification of the respondents. According to this, 48.9 per cent of the respondents are Post-Graduates. The remaining 51.1 per cent of the respondents' posses gradation as their qualification. The bank-wise analysis shows that there are more number of post-graduates in private sector banks when compared to public sector banks. As already noted education is one of the important factors that determine variations in human behaviour.

Experience

Experiences is an important factor that determines the level of an employee on the job. It affects both the living and general conditions of life. Experience determines satisfaction level. It also determines the standards of life. Table 6.5 presents data on the experience of the respondents in all the banks selected for study. The data on experience of respondents are collected with a view that experience has close relations with the satisfaction of the employees on the job. A satisfied employee on the job maintains good relations with his customers. Thus there is a close relationship between experience and customer relationship.

Table 6.5: Experience-wise and Bank-wise Distribution of Respondents

Experience years	State Bank of India		Andhra Bank		ING Vysya Bank		ICICI Bank		Total	
	No. of Respondents	Per cent	No. of Respondents	Per cent	No. of Respondents	Per cent	No. of Respondents	Per cent	No. of Respondents	Per cent
1-10	7	15.6	3	6.7	13	28.9	45	100	68	37.8
10-20	7	15.6	8	17.8	9	20.0	-	-	22	12.2
20-30	23	51.1	27	60.0	23	51.1	-	-	73	40.6
30 above	8	17.8	7	15.6	-	-	-	-	17	9.4
Total	**45**	**100**	**45**	**100**	**45**	**100**	**45**	**100**	**180**	**100**

Source: Primary Data.

According to the table, 40.6 per cent of the respondents have their experience ranging from 20 to 30 years. Interestingly, a significant number of respondents have experience ranging from 1 to 10 years. Only 9.4 per cent have 30 years and above experience in their service. The remaining respondents constituting 12.2 per cent have experience ranging from 10 to 20 years of service. An interesting observation is that in case the two public sector banks (State Bank of India and Andhra Bank), the majority of respondents have 20-30 years of experience, their per cent being (51.1% & 60%). All the respondents in ICICI Bank fall under a single group i.e., 1 to 10 years of experience. In the case of ING Vysya, a large majority (51.11%) also fall in the experience group of 20–30 years followed by 1–10 years and 10 to 20 years representing 28.9 per cent and 20 per cent respectively.

Native Place

Native place is an important factor to identify the local customer. It may influence the customer and banker relationship. The respondents are also identified on the basis of their nativity or residence. The details in this regard are furnished in Table 6.6.

Table 6.6: Nativity-wise and Bank–wise Distribution of Respondents

Native Place	State Bank of India		Andhra Bank		ING Vysya Bank		ICICI Bank		Total	
	No. of Respon-dents	Per cent	No. of Respon-dents	Per cent	No. of Respon-dents	Per cent	No. of Respon-dents	Per cent	No. of Respon-dents	Per cent
Local	17	37.8	11	24.4	5	11.1	10	22.2	43	23.9
Non local	28	62.2	34	75.6	40	88.9	35	77.8	137	76.1
Total	**45**	**100**	**45**	**100**	**45**	**100**	**45**	**100**	**180**	**100**

Source: Primary Data.

Table VI.6 shows that 76.1 per cent of the respondents belong to non-local category while the remaining 23.9 per cent belong to the local category. This shows that a large majority of employees belong to the non-local category. The percentage of non-locals is much higher in the case of private banks.

Reasons for Opening Account

Customers prefer to open their bank accounts basing on a number of considerations. The study has identified convenient location, suitable timings, image of the branch, regional affinity, image of the bank, size of the bank in terms of branches, staff attitude, systems of procedures, commercial affinity and so on. The responses in this regard by the bank officers have been presented in Table 6.7.

Table 6.7: Reasons for Opening Account Bank-wise Identification by Bank Officers

Reasons for opening account	State Bank of India		Andhra Bank		ING Vysya Bank		ICICI Bank		Total	
	No. of Respondents	Per cent	No. of Respondents	Per cent	No. of Respondents	Per cent	No. of Respondents	Per cent	No. of Respondents	Per cent
Convenient location	23	20.00	29	19.59	31	22.96	32	14.10	115	18.4
Suitable timings	18	15.65	22	14.86	16	11.85	28	12.33	84	13.44
Image of the branch	13	11.30	16	10.81	14	10.37	18	7.93	61	9.76
Regional affinity	3	2.61	4	2.7	1	.74	18	7.93	26	4.16
Image of the bank	0	17.39	22	14.86	15	11.11	32	14.10	89	14.24
Large no. of branches	14	12.17	15	10.14	6	4.95	23	10.13	58	9.28
Staff attitude	6	5.23	19	12.84	23	17.04	33	14.54	81	12.96
Systems and procedures	6	5.21	13	8.79	9	6.67	21	9.25	49	7.84
Commercial affinity	10	8.20	8	5.41	18	13.33	19	8.37	55	8.8
Others	2	1.74	-	-	2	1.48	3	1.32	7	1.12
Total	**115**	**100**	**148**	**100**	**135**	**100**	**227**	**100**	**625**	**100**

Source: Primary Data.

The table indicates that location of the bank, image of the bank, suitable timings of the bank and staff attitude are the four dominant factors responsible for opening a bank account. The four factors were followed by the image of the bank and the branches a bank possess. Bank-wise reasons identified show that officers felt that convenient location, suitable timings, branches and image of the branch are the reasons for opening account in the case of State Bank of India and Andhra Bank. The analysis across banks relating to reasons for opening their according in the branches revealed that:

1. Convenient location is the first important factor in case of State Bank India, Andhra Bank and ING Vysya banks. In case of ICICI bank this factor is secondary, while staff attitude is primary reason for opening an account.
2. The image of the bank is the second important factor in case of State Bank India, Andhra Bank and ICICI bank.
3. Suitable timings are the third important factor in case of State Bank India, ING Vysya bank and ICICI bank while in the case of Andhra Bank it was given second priority.
4. Large number of branches are the fourth important factor for State Bank India, Andhra Bank and ICICI bank.

Problems Faced by Officers at the time of Opening Account by the Customers

In the banks, bank officers face many problems at the time of opening accounts by the customers. These may vary in their size and complexity. Usually customers may not come in time. They may not observe the procedures but may insist on early completion. Introduction of customer opening account may cause another problem etc. These may have their bearing on banker customer relationship.

The respondents have been asked to give details of problems they experienced from customers in opening the accounts. The information furnished in Table VI.8 reveals that 60.29 per cent of the respondents did not face any problems in opening a bank account. However, introduction of a customer to a bank to open a bank account has been pointed out as the service bottleneck for opening an account.

The other two major problems are related to "customer without observing procedure" and customers "insistence on early completion". The analysis across sample banks reveals that In the case of ICICI Bank, ING Vysya Bank, Andhra Bank and State Bank of India, majority of the respondents did not have any problems. In case of Andhra Bank and State bank of India, the respondents have expressed difficulties in observing procedures. In case of Andhra Bank and ING Vysya bank, some of the respondents have faced difficulties like insistence on early completion. In the case of ING Vysya Bank, State Bank of India, Andhra Bank some of the respondents expressed difficulties like introduction of customers (KYC).

Table 6.8: Problems Faced by the Respondents at the Time of Opening Account by the Customers

Problem	State Bank of India		Andhra Bank		ING Vysya Bank		ICICI Bank		Total	
	No. of Respondents	Per cent	No. of Respondents	Per cent	No. of Respondents	Per cent	No. of Respondents	Per cent	No. of Respondents	Per cent
No problem	27	55.10	30	47.62	26	50.98	43	93.48	126	60.29
Customers do not come working hours	1	2.04	3	4.76	-	-	-	-	4	1.91
Customer without observing procedure	9	18.37	11	17.46	3	5.88	-	-	23	11.0
Insist on early completion	2	4.08	10	15.87	9	17.64	2	4.35	23	11.00
Introduction of customer	8	16.33	8	12.70	11	21.57	-	-	27	12.91
Others (KYC)	2	4.08	1	1.59	2	3.93	1	2.17	6	2.8
Total	**49**	**100**	**63**	**100**	**51**	**100**	**46**	**100**	**209**	**100**

Source: Primary data.

Procedure of Opening of Account after Computerisation

The Communication and Information Technology has its impact on all walks of life. Banks are no exception. Computerisation of Banks are expected to facilitate the banker customer relationship. Yet some problems are faced by the bankers as well as the customers. The opinion of officers as to procedure of opening of account after computerisation has been elicited and presented in Table VI.9.

Table 6.9: Bank-wise Distribution of Respondents as to Procedure of Opening of Account after Computerisation

Opinion of officers	State Bank of India		Andhra Bank		ING Vysya Bank		ICICI Bank		Total	
	No. of Respondents	Per cent	No. of Respondents	Per cent	No. of Respondents	Per cent	No. of Respondents	Per cent	No. of Respondents	Per cent
Simplified to large extent	17	37.78	13	28.89	19	42.22	24	53.33	73	40.55
Moderately simplified	16	35.56	12	26.67	14	31.11	11	24.44	53	29.44
Become complicated	4	8.88	11	24.44	5	11.11	-	-	20	11.12
No change	8	17.78	9	20.00	7	15.56	10	22.23	34	18.89
Total	**45**	**100**	**45**	**100**	**45**	**100**	**45**	**100**	**180**	**100.0**

Source: Primary Data.

The respondents were asked to give their opinion relating to any change that is being observed in opening an account after computerisation. A majority of respondents 40.55 per cent felt that there is simplification to a large extent in opening the account after computerisation. A large majority of respondents 29.44 per cent also felt that opening of an account was moderately simplified after computerisation. However, 18.89 per cent of respondents felt that there was no change even after computerisation. The remaining 11.12 per cent of respondents expressed that opening account became complicated even after computerisation. And the sample banks reveal that a majority of respondents of ICICI

Bank, State Bank India, Andhra Bank and ING Vysya bank observed that opening an account has been simplified to a large extent after computerisation. The majority of respondents 35.56 per cent in the case of State bank of India, 26.67 per cent in the case of Andhra Bank, 31.11 per cent in the case of ING Vysya bank and 24.44 per cent in the case of ICICI bank felt that there was moderate change in opening the accounts after computerisation. The same respondents (17.78% of SBI, 20% of AB, 15.56% of ING Vysya bank and 22.23% of ICICI bank) felt that there was no change in opening an account even after computerisation.

Inconvenience Caused by Customers to Banks by coming Late

Sometimes customers cause inconvenience to bank officers by coming late to banks. This adversely affects the banker customer relations. The responses of bank officers in this regard have been presented in Table VI.10.

Table 6.10: Bank-wise Distribution of Respondents as to the Inconvenience Caused by Customers by Coming Late

Educational qualifications	State Bank of India		Andhra Bank		ING Vysya Bank		ICICI Bank		Total	
	No. of Respon-dents	Per cent	No. of Respon-dents	Per cent	No. of Respon-dents	Per cent	No. of Respon-dents	Per cent	No. of Respon-dents	Per cent
Yes	8	17.8	9	20.00	8	17.8	8	17.8	33	18.3
No	37	82.2	36	80.0	37	82.2	37	82.2	147	81.7
Total	**45**	**100**	**45**	**100**	**45**	**100**	**45**	**100**	**180**	**100**

Source: Primary Data.

Table VI.10 indicates that a large majority of Bank Officers 81.7 per cent did not feel any inconvenience caused by the customers by coming late to branch during off hours. However, 18.3 per cent of respondents felt that majority of customers causing inconvenience by coming to the branch during off hours. The opinion of respondents of the banks under the study as to inconvenience caused by customers coming to the branch during off hours is presented in table

6.11. A large majority of the customers followed timings. This is confirmed by a majority of the respondents under the study. The parentage of respondents who did agree that customers do not cause inconvenience crossed 80 per cent in all banks. However, 17 to 20 percentages of respondents stated that customers cause inconvenience. This was even noticed by the researcher.

Punctuality of Opening Counters

Punctuality of bank officers plays a vital role in banker customer relations. Therefore, an attempt is made to find out the bank-wise opinion of officers on the punctuality of opening counters. The responses are shown in Table VI.11. Similarly, opinion regarding counters open for extra time is also elicited and the responses are recorded in Table VI.12.

Table 6.11: Bank-wise Opinion as to Punctuality of Opening Counters

Bank-wise opinion	State Bank of India		Andhra Bank		ING Vysya Bank		ICICI Bank		Total	
	No. of Respondents	Per cent	No. of Respondents	Per cent	No. of Respondents	Per cent	No. of Respondents	Per cent	No. of Respondents	Per cent
Yes	36	80.0	40	88.89	42	93.33	42	93.33	160	88.9
No	9	20.0	5	11.11	3	6.67	3	6.67	20	11.1
Total	45	100	45	100	45	100	45	100	180	100

Source: Primary Data.

The respondents were asked to furnish their views as to the punctuality in opening the counters of the bank. The details are given in Table VI.11. The table reveals that more than 88 per cent of the Bank officers agreed that all counters are kept open punctually for all the time. Nevertheless, the remaining 11.1 per cent of the respondents did not agree. They pointed out that of the staff are not punctual in opening their counters on time. This indicates that 80 per cent in SBI, 88.89 per cent in AB, 93.33 per cent in ING Vysya and 93.33 per cent in ICICI Bank have followed the principle of punctuality. The ICICI Bank and ING Vysya Bank officers have shown full confidence in punctuality. But in the State Bank of India, there is a significant number of respondents 20 per cent and in Andhra Bank there are respondents 11.11 per cent who stated that punctuality is not followed by the employees in opening the counters.

Table 6.12: Bank-wise Details of Pinion Regarding Counters open for Extra Time

Open for extra time	State Bank of India		Andhra Bank		ING Vysya Bank		ICICI Bank		Total	
	No. of Respon-dents	Per cent	No. of Respon-dents	Per cent	No. of Respon-dents	Per cent	No. of Respon-dents	Per cent	No. of Respon-dents	Per cent
No	6	13.33	7	15.56	4	8.9	4	8.9	21	11.67
Yes	39	86.67	38	84.44	41	91.1	41	91.1	159	88.33
Total	**45**	**100**	**45**	**100**	**45**	**100**	**45**	**100**	**180**	**100**

Source: Primary Data.

The respondents were asked to furnish their views whether the counters of the bank are kept open for extra hours, after business hours to clear off waiting customers. The analysis given in Table 6.12 reveals that more than 88 per cent of the officers observed that the counter was not kept open for extra hours, their percentage being (11.67%). A significant member of respondents 88.33 per cent stated that they keep open the counters for extra time for the convenience of the regular customers. Table 6.13 reveals that a large majority of respondents expressed the view that counters are kept open for extra hours. The percentage of response in this regard being 86.67 per cent, 84.44 per cent, 91.1 per cent and 91.1 per cent in State Bank of India, Andhra Bank, ING Vysya Bank, and ICICI Bank respectively. There are officers who admitted that the bank counters are not kept open for extra hours. The percentage of respondents in this regard being 13.33 per cent, 15.56 per cent, 8.9 per cent, and 8..9 per cent in SBI, AB, ING Vysya and ICICI bank respectively. The percentage is found much higher in Andhra Bank followed by State bank of India.

Bank-wise Physical Facilities

Bank-wise physical facilities play a vital role in banker-customer relations. Seating arrangement in banks, space for moving, interior decoration, air conditioning, drinking water facilities are the areas covered under physical facilities. Table 6.13 deals with bank-wise physical facilities.

Table 6.13 indicates that officers have agreed that almost all facilities are available in their banks. The banks have given top priority to drinking water 90 per cent. Equal importance has been given to seating arrangements (90.6%) respectively. The analysis reveals that 84.4 per cent to 88.9 per cent of facilities are with regard to seating and drinking water.

Table 6.13: Bankwise Physical Facilities

Facilities	SBI		Andhra Bank		ING Vysya		ICICI Bank		Total	
	Yes	No	Yes	No	Yes	No	Yes	No	Yes	No
Seating Arrangement	38 (84.4)	7 (15.6)	29 (64.4)	15 (33.3)	43 (95.1)	2 (4.4)	44 (97.7)	1 (2.23)	154 (86.7)	25 (13.3)
Space for moving	23 (51.1)	22 (48.9)	21 (46.7)	24 (53.3)	39 (86.7)	6 (13.3)	41 (91.1)	4 (8.9)	124 (68.4)	56 (31.6)
Interior decoration	23 (51.1)	22 (48.9)	25 (55.6)	20 (5144.4)	42 (83.3)	3 (6.7)	43 (95.1)	2 (4.43)	133 (73.4)	47 (26.6)
Air conditions	17 (37.8)	28 (62.3)	11 (24.4)	34 (375.6)	41 (91.1)	4 (8.9)	45 (100)	— (0.0)	114 (63.4)	66 (36.6)
Drinking water	37 (82.2)	8 (13.3)	40 (88.9)	5 (11.1)	45 (100)	— (—)	40 (88.9)	5 (11.1)	162 (90.0)	18 (10.0)

Source: Primary data.

Collecting Deposits and Withdrawals

Collection of deposits and withdrawals constitute the core functioning of banks officers often face problems in this regard. The general problems faced by the officers in this regard include customer bringing lower denominations, insisting on accepting soiled notes. It is also found that the customers visit branch after working hours and do not fill up vouchers. The opinion in this regard is presented in Table 6.14.

Table 6.14: Bank-wise Response as to Problems Faced by Bank Officers in Collecting Deposits and Withdrawals

Problems	State Bank of India		Andhra Bank		ING Vysya Bank		ICICI Bank		Total	
	No. of Respondents	Per cent	No. of Respondents	Per cent	No. of Respondents	Per cent	No. of Respondents	Per cent	No. of Respondents	Per cent
Customer bring lower denominations	20	44.4	23	51.1	18	40.0	11	24.4	72	40.0
Insist on Accepting soiled notes	8	17.8	6	13.3	6	13.3	-		20	11.1
Customers visit branch after working hours	9	20.0	8	17.8	-	-	-		17	9.4
Customer do not fill-up voucher properly	8	17.8	8	17.8	-	-	-	-	16	8.9
No Problem	-	-	-	-	21	46.7	34	75.6	55	30.6
Total	**45**	**100**	**45**	**100**	**45**	**100**	**45**	**100**	**180**	**100**

Source: Primary Data.

The problem faced by respondents in depositing cash is shown in Table VI.14. Apart from this, the respondents faced problems like 'customers do not fill up vouchers properly' 8.9 per cent, 'customers visit branch after working hours' 9.4 per cent and 'customer bring lower denomination' 40 per cent etc. Some of the respondents 30.6 per cent have expressed that they have not faced any problem. Bank-wise analysis of the problems faced by bank officer in collecting deposits and withdrawals reveals that the major problem is with regard to customers bringing lower denominations. Curiously, a huge majority 75.6 per cent in the case of ICICI and a large majority 46.7 per cent in the case of ING Vysya have been noticed under the head 'No problem'. This is significant when compared to the State Bank of India and Andhra Bank.

We did not find any response under this category. In between 'Customers visiting after working hours', Customers do not fill-up vouchers properly and insist on spoiled notes.

Reduction of Work Load after Computerisation

Computerisation of banks is expected in the reduction of workload to bank officers. The lesser the work the more leisure for maintaining better banker-customer relations. The data with regard to reduction of workload after computerisation in banks elicited with simple 'Yes', 'No' answers is presented in table 6.15. Similarly, job simplification is expected with the introduction of ATMs. Therefore, an attempt is made to know whether the introduction of ATMs resulted in job simplification or not. The responses are shown in table 6.16.

Table 6.15: Opinion Survey of Officers on Reduction of Work Load after Computerisation

Work load reduction	State Bank of India		Andhra Bank		ING Vysya Bank		ICICI Bank		Total	
	No. of Respon-dents	Per cent	No. of Respon-dents	Per cent	No. of Respon-dents	Per cent	No. of Respon-dents	Per cent	No. of Respon-dents	Per cent
Yes	17	37.8	16	35.6	21	46.7	16	35.6	70	38.9
No	28	62.2	29	64.4	24	53.3	29	64.4	110	61.1
Total	45	100	45	100	45	100	45	100	180	100

Source: Primary Data.

A large majority of the respondents 61.1 per cent have felt that there is no reduction in the work load after computerisation. However, 38.9 per cent of the respondents under study have perceived that there is reduction of workload after computerisation. The bank-wise perception of respondents as to reduction of work load after computerisation has differed. The table indicates that 37.8 per cent in the case of SBI, 35.6 per cent in the case of AB, 46.7 per cent in the case of ING and 35.6 in the case of ICICI have agreed that there is reduction in work load after computerisation. But a large majority of respondents perceived that computerisation has not made any difference in the case of reduction of work load. This could be seen from an increased percentage i.e., 62.2 per cent, 64.4 per cent, 53.3 per cent and 64.4 per cent in the case of SBI, AB, ING, and ICICI respectively. This could be seen from Table 6.15.

Table 6.16: Opinion Survey of Officerson Simplification of Job After Induction of Atms

Simplified	State Bank of India		Andhra Bank		ING Vysya Bank		ICICI Bank		Total	
	No. of Respon-dents	Per cent	No. of Respon-dents	Per cent	No. of Respon-dents	Per cent	No. of Respon-dents	Per cent	No. of Respon-dents	Per cent
Yes	39	86.7	28	62.2	29	64.4	40	88.9	136	75.6
No	6	13.3	17	37.8	16	35.6	5	11.1	44	24.4
Total	**45**	**100**	**45**	**100**	**45**	**100**	**45**	**100**	**180**	**100.00**

Source: Primary Data.

The researcher wanted to ascertain whether the officers' job is simplified with the introduction of ATM facilities. A majority of respondents of all banks agreed that their job was simplified by the introduction ATM centres. The responses have been indicated in Table VI.16. Nearly 75.6 per cent of officers have accepted that their job has been simplified with the introduction ofATMs. The remaining 24.4 per cent of respondents did not agree. The table makes it clear that 86.7 per cent of the SBI respondents and 88.9 per cent of the ICICI Bank respondents, 64.4 per cent of the ING Vysya Bank respondents, and 62.2 per cent of Andhra Bank respondents agreed that their Jobs were simplified after the introduction of ATMs. However, 13.3 per cent in SBI, 37.8 per cent in AB, 35.6 per cent in ING Vysya Bank and 11.1 per cent in ICICI Bank disagreed with remark that there was no correlation between Job simplification and ATMs.

Cheque Transactions

Bank officers face problems in cheque transactions. The problems generally associated are customers do not follow procedures, issue cheques without sufficient balance, insist on early clearance etc. The study attempt to find out the responses in this regard and presented the data in table VI.17.

Table 6.17: Bank-wise Details as to Problems Faced by Bank Officers in Cheque Transactions

Problems	State Bank of India		Andhra Bank		ING Vysya Bank		ICICI Bank		Total	
	No. of Respon-dents	Per cent	No. of Respon-dents	Per cent	No. of Respon-dents	Per cent	No. of Respon-dents	Per cent	No. of Respon-dents	Per cent
Customers do not follow procedures	20	44.5	14	31.1	11	24.5	9	20.0	54	30.0
Issue cheques with out sufficient balance	3	6.6	4	8.9	2	4.4	2	4.4	11	6.1
Insist on early clearance	20	44.5	18	40.0	22	48.9	12	26.7	72	40.0
No problem	2	4.4	9	20.0	10	22.2	22	48.9	43	23.9
Total	**45**	**100**	**45**	**100**	**45**	**100**	**45**	**100**	**180**	**100.00**

Source: Primary Data.

The table indicates that the bank officers to a large extent face the problems from customers. 40 per cent of the problems are related to customers' insistence on early clearance. 30 per cent of the customers do not follow the procedures. The problems relating to issue of cheques without sufficient balance constitute 6 per cent. However, nearly 24 per cent of the customers do not cause any problems to the bank officers in cheque transactions. The table also reveals that majority of problems from respondents are related to 'Insistence on early clearance' being faced by respondents. Regarding 'customers do not follow procedures' the problems faced by the officer is at 44.5 per cent in SBI, 31.1 per cent in AB, 24.5 in ING and 20 per cent in ICICI.. Regarding clearance, 44.5 per cent in SBI, 40.0 per cent in AB, 48.9 per cent ING Vysya and 26.7 per cent in ICICI of respondents have been facing problems.

Loans

Loans are provided to customers. They include crop loans, loans for SSI, business loans and personal loans. Provision for loans plays an important role in banker-customer relations. Bank-wise details of loans provided to customers are presented in Table VI.18. The problems faced with regard to sanction of loans also constitutes an important factor The problems faced with regard to sanction of loans are – customers do not apply for loan in time, customers do not comply with all procedures of loan sanction, customers insisting on early sanction and undue delay in repayment of loans by the customers. The data in this regard are presented in Table VI.19. It is not uncommon to press for loans to the customers by the political leaders. Therefore, political pressure in sanctioning of loans has its bearing on banker-customer relations. The perceptions of bank officers in this regard are presented in Table VI.20.

Table 6.18: Bank-wise Details of Loans Provided to Customers

Educational qualifications	State Bank of India		Andhra Bank		ING Vysya Bank		ICICI Bank		Total	
	No. of Respon-dents	Per cent	No. of Respon-dents	Per cent	No. of Respon-dents	Per cent	No. of Respon-dents	Per cent	No. of Respon-dents	Per cent
Crop Loan	19	12.93	21	15.56	22	17.19	26	19.55	88	16.21
Loan for SSI	34	23.13	31	22.96	30	23.44	26	19.55	121	22.28
Business Loan	37	25.17	31	22.96	35	27.34	31	23.31	134	24.68
Personal Loan	36	24.49	29	21.48	25	19.53	34	25.56	124	22.84
All the above	17	11.56	18	13.34	14	10.94	14	10.53	63	11.60
Education Loan	4	2.72	5	3.70	2	1.56	2	1.50	13	2.39
Total	147	100	135	100	128	100	133	100	543	100.0

Source: Primary Data.

The information relating to type of loan provided to customers is shown in the Table VI.18. A majority of respondents have provided business loan 24.68 per cent, personal loans 22.84 per cent, Loan for SSI 22.28 per cent, crop loan 16.21 per cent to customers. The analysis across sample banks reveals that in the case of SBI, AB & ING Vysya, a majority of respondents provided bank loans 25.17 per cent, 22.96 per cent and 27.34 per cent while in the case of ICICI, personal loans 35.56 per cent have been provided. Business loans were followed by personal loans 24.49 per cent in the case of SBI. In the case of AB along with business loans 22.96 per cent, SSI loans 22.96 per cent have also been equally provided followed by personal loans 21.48 per cent. Similarly ING also provides" for SSI loans 23.44 per cent next to business loans 27.34 per cent followed by personal loans. In the case of ICICI, the personal loans 25.56 per cent were followed by business loans 23.31 per cent and crop and SSI loans 19.55 per cent.

Table 6.19: Bank-wise Details of Problems Faced in Loans Provided to Customers

Problems	State Bank of India		Andhra Bank		ING Vysya Bank		ICICI Bank		Total	
	No. of Respon-dents	Per cent	No. of Respon-dents	Per cent	No. of Respon-dents	Per cent	No. of Respon-dents	Per cent	No. of Respon-dents	Per cent
Customers do not apply in time	11	12.50	10	11.63	7	10.14	2	14.28	30	11.67
They do not comply with all procedures	20	22.73	21	24.42	13	18.84	2	14.28	56	21.80
Insist on early sanction	23	26.14	17	19.77	17	24.64	2	14.28	59	22.96
Undue delay in repayment	19	21.57	18	20.93	19	27.54	3	21.43	59	22.96
Over dues	15	17.06	20	23.25	13	18.84	5	35.73	53	20.61
Total	**88**	**100**	**86**	**100**	**69**	**100**	**14**	**100**	**257**	**100.00**

Source: Primary Data.

The problems faced by respondents in the sanction of loan to customers is presented in Table VI.19. Majority of the respondents have faced problems like: (i) Insistence by the customers for early sanction, and (ii) Undue delay in repayment etc. The table indicates that a majority of respondents 22.96 per cent felt that customers insist on early sanction of loans. 21.80 per cent of the respondents expressed the view that customers do not comply with all procedures. Another problem identified by the officers is that customers do not apply for loan in time. The percentage in this respect is 11.67 per cent. The problem faced with customers regarding over dues constitute 16.34 per cent. The analysis across individual Bankers reveals different observations. In the case of SBI officers, the problem faced is insistence even on early loans sanction 26.14 per cent. In the case of AB the problem faced by respondents is highest in the case of complying procedures (24.42%). Undue delay in payment is the highest (27.54%) problem in the case of ING Vysya Bank respondents. In the case of ICICI Bank the respondents face maximum problems in over dues. However, in all the banks officers have been facing problems with customers with regard to 1, 2, 3, 4 and 5 though the intensity of the problems is different as perceived from the table.

Table 6.20: Bank-wise Perception on Political Pressure in Sanctioning of Loans

Perception	State Bank of India		Andhra Bank		ING Vysya Bank		ICICI Bank		Total	
	No. of Respondents	Per cent	No. of Respondents	Per cent	No. of Respondents	Per cent	No. of Respondents	Per cent	No. of Respondents	Per cent
Yes	5	11.1	6	11.3	-	-	-	-	11	6.1
No	40	88.9	39	88.7	45	100	45	100	165	93.9
Total	**45**	**100**	**45**	**100**	**45**	**100**	**45**	**100**	**180**	**100**

Source: Primary Data.

The problem faced by bank officers in the form of political pressure in the sanction of loan to customers is presented in Table VI.20. A majority of the respondents stated that they have not faced problems like political pressure. However, 6.1

per cent of the sample expressed that there is political pressure for sanctioning loans. The analysis across sample bankers reveals a similar observation as a great majority of respondents' opine that political pressure is very low in sanctioning a loan.

Technology

Technological upgradation is a sine qua non for banking sector reforms, particularly to achieve better customer service, internal control, house-keeping and augmenting productivity and profitability. Concerted efforts have been made to achieve bank mechanisation and computerisation both at macro and micro level.. the technological services offered by banks

Table 6.21: Bank-wise Details of Technological Services Offered

Service	State Bank of India		Andhra Bank		ING Vysya Bank		ICICI Bank		Total	
	No. of Respondents	Per cent	No. of Respondents	Per cent	No. of Respondents	Per cent	No. of Respondents	Per cent	No. of Respondents	Per cent
Debit card	28	16.87	41	19.43	43	21.72	33	15.00	145	18.26
Online banking	18	10.84	37	17.54	39	19.69	33	15.00	127	15.99
Inter-net banking	21	12.65	16	7.58	40	20.20	35	15.91	112	14.11
ATM	33	19.88	40	18.96	41	20.71	32	14.55	145	18.26
Electronic fund transfer	20	12.05	32	15.17	15	7.57	23	10.45	90	11.34
Travel cards	12	7.23	6	2.84	5	2.54	21	9.55	44	5.54
Credit card	17	10.24	30	14.22	15	7.57	29	13.18	91	11.46
All of the above	17	10.24	9	4.26	-	-	14	6.36	40	5.04
Total	**166**	**100**	**211**	**100**	**198**	**100**	**220**	**100**	**794**	**100.00**

Source: Primary Data

include Debit Card, Online Banking, Internet Banking, ATM, Electronic Fund Transfer, Travel Cards, and Credit Cards. The bank wise details of technological services offered by the banks under the study are shown in Table VI.21.

The services offered by the banks under the investigators' study have been shown in Table VI.21. It reveals that the respondent banks have been offering services ranging from Debit card to Credit card via On-line banking, Internet banking, besides ATM, EFT and TCs. ATMs and Debit cards with 18.26 per cent occupying the first place followed by On-line banking, Internet banking, Credit card EFT and TCs. Of all the banks under study, the State Bank of India ranks first in providing ATM service in public sector and ICICI in private sector with much higher percentage.

Providing Technological Services

While providing the aforesaid services, officers of the banks under the study identified some problems. They comprise of 'customers do not pay regularly on credit cards in time', customers complaining loss of cards, misuse of cards and forget pin numbers of the cards. These cause irritation in banker-customer relations. The data in this regard are provided in table VI.22.

The problems faced in providing services to customers are summarised in Table VI.22. The problems faced by majority of respondents include, 'Do not pay regularly on credit card in times 43.33 per cent, followed by 'Complaint on loss of cards frequently 30 per cent', 'Misuse of service' 20 per cent and 'Forget Pin numbers' 6.67 per cent. The analysis across individual bankers reveals that there are changes in the priority of problems as expressed by a majority of respondents. The priorities are:

1. In the case of SBI, AB & ICICI – do not pay regularly on Credit cards in time 48 per cent, 62.22 per cent, and 61.54 per cent respectively.
2. In the case of ING Vysya Bank, Cards Misuse in transfer of security related problems 40.54 per cent.

Table 6.22: Bank-wise Details with Regard to Problems Faced by Officer in Providing Technological Services

Educational qualifications	State Bank of India		Andhra Bank		ING Vysya Bank		ICICI Bank		Total	
	No. of Respondents	Per cent	No. of Respondents	Per cent	No. of Respondents	Per cent	No. of Respondents	Per cent	No. of Respondents	Per cent
Do not pay regularly on Credit Cards in time	12	48.00	28	62.22	4	10.81	8	61.54	52	43.33
Complain lost of cards frequently	10	40.00	9	20.00	13	35.14	4	30.77	36	30.00
Misuses	3	12.00	5	11.11	15	40.54	1	7.69	24	20.00
Forget Pin Numbers	-		3	6.67	5	1351	-		8	6.67
Total	25	100	45	100	37	100	13	100	120	100.00

Source: Primary Data.

3. In the case of all banks, the problem is complaint of loss of cards frequently

Totally, the problems faced by a majority of respondents include. They do not pay regularly on credit card in times (43.33%), followed by complaints of loss of cards frequently (30%), misuse of services (20.00%) and forgetfulness of Pin Numbers (6.67%). The analysis can be observed in Table VI.26.

Perception of Officers as to the Statements

In the changing scenario of bank functioning, some factors may affect the banker customer relationship. Such factors include insecurity of job, increase in pressure from customers, increase in pressure from government, increase in pressure from head office, and competition for fixed targets. Therefore, the perception of officers as to their job in the context of changing scenario is presented in Table VI.23.

Table 6.23: Bank-wise Perception of Officers as to their Job in the Context of Changing Scenario

Statements	State Bank of India		Andhra Bank		ING Vysya Bank		ICICI Bank		Total	
	No. of Respondents	Per cent	No. of Respondents	Per cent	No. of Respondents	Per cent	No. of Respondents	Per cent	No. of Respondents	Per cent
Insecurity of job	3	4.35	10	10.87	11	17.19	3	5.88	27	9.78
Increase in pressure from customers	21	30.34	23	25.00	14	21.88	24	47.06	82	29.71
Increase in pressure from Government/ RBI	3	4.35	12	13.04	11	17.18	6	11.75	32	11.60
Increase in pressure from Head office/ Higher official	13	18.84	17	18.48	12	18.75	7	13.75	49	17.75
Competition forces to increase target	19	27.53	26	28.26	16	25.00	9	17.64	70	25.36
All of the above	10	14.50	4	4.35	-	-	2	3.92	16	5.80
Total	69	100	92	100	64	100	51	100	276	100.00

Source: Primary Data.

Table VI.23 shows the perception of officers as to 6 statements. These include 'insecurity of job', 'increase in pressure from customers', 'increase in pressure from Government/RBI', 'increase in pressure from Head office/ Higher official, 'competition forces to increase target'. An attempt is also made to identify the overall responses. A majority of respondents stated that there is an increase in pressure from customers, their percentage being 29.71 per cent. 25.36 per cent of the respondents rated competition forces to increase target

The comparative mean scores of opinion on Customer service, Customer problems and Physical facilities by bank officers respondents' on different aspects related to customer and banker relationship in the changing scenario are presented in the ensuing analysis to show the significance under three groups viz., customer service, customer problems and physical facilities.

Table 6.24: Bank-wise Distribution of Mean Scores of Bank Officers on Different Aspects Regarding Customer Satisfactory Levels

Sl. No.		Type of Banks	N	Mean	Std. Deviation	Std. Error	Min	Max
1.	Customer service	SBI	45	9.00	2.78	.41	4	15
		AB	45	10.24	2.52	.37	4	16
		ING	45	9.80	3.55	.53	3	15
		ICICI	45	9.53	1.59	.24	7	13
		Total	**180**	**9.64**	**2.72**	**.20**	**3**	**16**
2.	Customer Problems	SBI	45	12.93	1.72	.26	8	15
		AB	45	12.67	2.16	.32	6	15
		ING	45	13.16	1.99	.30	9	15
		ICICI	45	13.49	1.70	.25	7	15
		Total	**180**	**13.06**	**1.91**	**.14**	**6**	**15**
3.	Physical Facilities	SBI	45	4.44	1.98	.30	0	7
		AB	45	4.44	2.38	.35	0	15
		ING	45	6.20	2.06	.31	0	7
		ICICI	45	6.60	1.16	.17	3	7
		Total	**180**	**5.42**	**2.17**	**.16**	**0**	**15**

Source: Primary Data.

The table analyses the statistical average and standard deviations of the banker from various banks and their performance in different aspects regarding the functioning of banks. It was observed that highest average found with ICICI Bank regarding "Customer problems", which is 13.49. Where as it is least in case of "Physical facilities" of SBI, which is 4.44. Standard deviation in case of ING Vysya Bank with regard to customer service is high 3.55 where as it is least in case of ICICI – Physical facilities 1.16.

Table 6.25: Anova-Table

		Sum of Squares	df	Mean Square	F	Sig.
Customer service	Between Groups	36.533	3	12.178	1.668	.176
	Within Groups	1284.711	176	7.299		
	Total	**1321.244**	**179**			
Customer Problems	Between Groups	16.372	3	5.457	1.506	.215
	Within Groups	637.956	176	3.625		
	Total	**654.328**	**179**			
Physical Facilities	Between Groups	175.689	3	58.563	15.425	.000
	Within Groups	668.222	176	3.797		
	Total	**843.911**	**179**			

Source: Primary Data.

The table explains the f-values of the variables customer service, customer problems and shows physical facilities among the bankers working in different banks as 1.668, 1.506 and 15.425 respectively. Among them, customer services, and customer problems variables are not significant, where as physical facilities variable is significant at 0.01 level. In the first two variables, the mean performance of the bankers working in different banks is not significantly different but in the case of physical facilities, the private banks mean is more than the nationalised banks. This shows that the private banks are providing more physical facilities to the customers than the nationalised banks.

The table analyses the means and standard deviations among four age-grouped bankers in their performance on different aspects like customer service, customer problems and physical facilities regarding the functioning of banks.

Table 6.26: Significance of Age-wise *vs* Bank Officer Satisfactory Levels

Sl. No.		Age group	N	Mean	Std. Deviation	Std. Error	Min	Max
1.	Customer service	20-30	51	9.57	3.34	.47	3	15
		30-40	22	10.09	2.79	.60	5	15
		40-50	63	9.44	2.35	.30	4	16
		50-60	44	9.80	2.40	.36	4	14
		Total	**180**	**9.64**	**2.72**	**.20**	**3**	**16**
2.	Customer Problems	20-30	51	13.20	1.93	.27	7	15
		30-40	22	12.23	2.39	.51	6	15
		40-50	63	13.17	1.77	.22	8	15
		50-60	44	13.16	1.78	.27	7	15
		Total	**180**	**13.06**	**1.91**	**.14**	**6**	**15**
3.	Physical Facilities	20-30	51	5.80	2.23	.31	0	7
		30-40	22	5.95	1.86	.40	0	7
		40-50	63	5.25	2.36	.30	1	15
		50-60	44	4.95	1.88	.28	0	7
		Total	**180**	**5.42**	**2.17**	**.16**	**0**	**15**

Source: Primary Data.

The results indicate that Bank Officers among 40-50 years age group are highly satisfied relating to customer problems as average in high with 13.17. Where as in case of 50-60 age group (officers) are not satisfied with reference to physical facilities as the average is 4.95.

The table explains the f-values of the variables i.e., customer service, customer problems and physical facilities among different age groups, which are 0.366, 1.608 and 1.796 respectively. Among them all variables are not significant. This shows that in all the variables the mean performance of the bankers with different age grouped is not significantly different.

Table 6.27: Anova of the Scores of Bank Officers Satisfactory Aspects Classified According to Age Groups Different Bank Officers

		Sum of Squares	df	Mean Square	F	Sig.
Customer service	Between Groups	8.202	3	2.734	.366	.777
	Within Groups	1313.043	176	7.460		
	Total	**1321.244**	**179**			
Customer Problems	Between Groups	17.459	3	5.820	1.608	.189
	Within Groups	636.869	176	3.619		
	Total	**654.328**	**179**			
Physical Facilities	Between Groups	25.072	3	8.357	1.796	.150
	Within Groups	818.839	176	4.652		
	Total	**843.911**	**179**			

Source: Primary Data.

The table analyses the means and standard deviations in their performance among male and female bank employees on different aspects regarding the functioning of banks. In the bank customer service, the means of male is 9.74 and the mean of female is 9.17 and standard deviations are 2.63 and 3.13 respectively. The obtained t-value is 1.055 is not significant. Regarding the customers' problems, the

Table 6.28: Distribution of Mean Score Significance of Gender-wise Officer Satisfactory Level

	Sex	N	Mean	Std. Deviation	t-value
Customer service	Male	150	9.74	2.63	1.055
	Female	30	9.17	3.13	
Customer Problems	Malc	150	13.08	1.85	0.296
	Female	30	12.97	2.22	
Physical Facilities	Male	150	5.37	2.13	0.674
	Female	30	5.67	2.37	

Source: Primary Data.

means of bank managers is 13.08 and the mean of other bank officers is 12.97 and the standard deviations are 1.85 and 2.22 respectively. The generated t-value is 0.296 which is not significant. Regarding the physical facilities of the bank, the performance means of male is 5.37 and the mean of female is 5.67 and the standard deviations are 2.13 and 2.37 respectively. The calculated t-value is 0.674 which is not significant. This shows that in all the variables there is no significant difference in the mean performance of male and female bank employees.

Table 6.29: Designation-wise Distribution of Mean Scores of Bank Officers on Different Aspects Regarding Customer Satisfactory Levels

	Designation	N	Mean	Std. Deviation	t-value
Customer service	Bank Manager	41	9.29	2.36	0.943
	Other Employees	139	9.75	2.81	
Customer Problems	Bank Manager	41	12.98	1.75	0.325
	Other Employees	139	13.09	1.96	
Physical Facilities	Bank Manager	41	4.93	2.11	1.671
	Other Employees	139	5.57	2.17	

Source: Primary Data.

The table analyses the means and standard deviations in their performance among bank managers and other bank employees on different aspects regarding the functioning of banks. In the bank customer service the means of bank managers is 9.29 and the mean of other bank employees is 9.75 and standard deviations are 2.36 and 2.81 respectively. The obtained t-value is 0.943 is not significant. Regarding the customers' problems, the means of bank managers is 12.98 and the mean of other bank officers is 13.09 and the standard deviations are 1.75 and 1.96 respectively. The generated t-value is 0.325 which is not significant. In the physical facilities of the bank the performance means of bank managers is 4.93 and the mean of other bank officers is 5.57 and the standard deviations are 2.11 and 2.17 respectively.

The calculated t-value is 1.671 which is not significant. This shows that in all the variables there is no significant difference in the mean performance of bank managers and other bank employees.

Table 6.30: Education-wise Distribution of Mean Scores of Bank Officers on Different Aspects Regarding Customer Satisfactory Levels

	Educational Qualification	N	Mean	Std. Deviation	t-value
Customer service	Degree	92	9.91	2.43	1.359
	Post Graduation	88	9.36	2.98	
Customer Problems	Degree	92	12.98	1.77	0.593
	Post Graduation	88	13.15	2.05	
Physical Facilities	Degree	92	5.16	2.25	1.645
	Post Graduation	88	5.69	2.06	

Source: Primary Data.

The table analyses the means and standard deviations in their performance among degree and post graduation bankers' performance on different aspects regarding the functioning of banks. In the bank customer service the means of degree-qualified bankers is 9.91 and the mean of PG qualified bankers is 9.36 and standard deviations are 2.43 and 2.98 respectively. The obtained t-value is 1.359 is not significant. Regarding the customers' problems, the means of degree-qualified bankers is 12.98, and the mean of PG qualified bankers is 13.15, and the standard deviations are 1.77 and 2.05 respectively. The generated t-value is 0.593 which is not significant. As regards the physical facilities of the banks, the performance means of local bankers is 5.16 and the mean of non-local bankers is 5.69 and the standard deviations are 2.25 and 2.06 respectively. The calculated t-value is 1.645 which is not significant. This shows that in all the variables the mean performance of the degree qualified bankers and PG qualified bankers are found to be different but not at significant level.

Table 6.31: Significance of Experience *vs* Bank Officers Satisfactory Levels

Sl. No.		Experience	N	Mean	Std. Deviation	Std. Error	Min	Max
1.	Customer service	1-10 years	68	9.79	3.19	.39	3	15
		10-20 years	22	9.18	1.82	.39	5	12
		20-30 years	73	9.55	2.43	.28	4	16
		30-40 years	17	10.06	2.90	.70	4	14
		Total	**180**	**9.64**	**2.72**	**.20**	**3**	**16**
2.	Customer Problems	1-10 years	68	12.85	2.02	.24	7	15
		10-20 years	22	12.77	2.11	.45	6	15
		20-30 years	73	13.40	1.74	.20	7	15
		30-40 years	17	12.82	1.88	.46	8	15
		Total	**180**	**13.06**	**1.91**	**.14**	**6**	**15**
3.	Physical Facilities	1-10 years	68	6.01	2.07	.25	0	7
		10-20 years	22	5.50	1.65	.35	3	7
		20-30 years	73	5.04	2.24	.26	0	15
		30-40 years	17	4.59	2.40	.58	0	7
		Total	**180**	**5.42**	**2.17**	**.16**	**0**	**15**

Source: Primary Data.

The table analyses the means and standard deviations in their performance among experience with banker of customers of banks depending on the experience in the performance of banks on different aspects regarding the functioning of banks. The above table focuses that the experience of 20–30 years gives highest satisfaction of customer problems with 13.40 average, where as it is least in case of 30–40 year experienced people with regard to physical facilities (4.59).

The table explains the f-values of the variables customer service, customer problems and physical facilities among different age groups are 0.44, 1.281 and 3.416 respectively. Among them, physical facilities variable is significant at 0.05 level and the remaining two variables are not significant.

Table 6.32: Anova of the Scores of Bank Officers Satisfactory Aspects Classified According to Experience of Different Bank Officers

		Sum of Squares	df	Mean Square	F	Sig.
Customer service	Between Groups	9.831	3	3.277	.440	.725
	Within Groups	1311.414	176	7.451		
	Total	**1321.244**	**179**			
Customer Problems	Between Groups	13.985	3	4.662	1.281	.282
	Within Groups	640.343	176	3.638		
	Total	**654.328**	**179**			
Physical Facilities	Between Groups	46.431	3	15.477	3.416*	.019
	Within Groups	797.480	176	4.531		
	Total	**843.911**	**179**			

Source: Primary Data.

This shows that in all the variables, the mean performance of the bankers with different experienced grouped is not significantly difference. The less experienced bankers' performance is more at physical facilities and more experienced bankers performance is less.

Table 6.33: Native Place-wise Distribution of Mean Scores of Bank Officers on Different Aspects Regarding Customer Satisfactory Levels

	Native place	N	Mean	Std. Devia-tion	t-value
Customer service	Local	43	8.81	2.95	2.326*
	Non-Local	137	9.91	2.59	
Customer Problems	Local	43	12.98	1.95	0.331
	Non-Local	137	13.09	1.91	
Physical Facilities	Local	43	4.63	2.16	2.802**
	Non-Local	137	5.67	2.12	

Source: Primary Data.

The table analyses the means and standard deviations in their performance among native place of bankers' performance on different aspects regarding the functioning of banks. As regards the bank customer service, the means of local bankers is 8.81 and the mean of non-local bankers is 9.91 and standard deviations are 2.95 and 2.59 respectively. The obtained t-value is 2.346 is significant at 0.05 level. Regarding the customers' problems the means of local bankers is 12.98, and the mean of non-local bankers is 13.09, and the standard deviations are 1.95 and 1.91 respectively. The generated t-value is 0.331 which is not significant. As regards the physical facilities of the bank, the performance means of local bankers is 4.63 and the mean of non-local bankers is 5.67 and the standard deviations are 2.16 and 2.12 respectively. The calculated t-value is 2.802 which is significant at 0.01 level. This shows that in all the variables, the mean performance of the non-local bankers is more than the local bankers. This is because non local bankers are more facilitating than the local bankers.

CHAPTER

Perception of Customers on Customer–Banker Relationship

This Chapter aims at to presenting the perception of customer on customer–banker relationship. It is based on the opinions collected from 300 customers with the help of a schedule. Occupational significance made the researcher to take into account equal number of respondents from small scale industries, micro creditors, business, farmers and others each constituting 20 per cent each because each occupational category influences the customer banker relations in its own way. This has been done for the convenience of the study. The sample is shown in Table 7.1.

Table 7.1: Respondents Distribution

Occupation	State Bank of India		Andhra Bank		ING Vysya Bank		ICICI Bank		Total	
	No. of Respondents	Per cent	No. of Respondents	Per cent	No. of Respondents	Per cent	No. of Respondents	Per cent	No. of Respondents	Per cent
S S I	30	28.6	30	28.6	-	-	-	-	60	20.0
Micro Creditors	30	28.6	30	28.6	-	-	-	-	60	20.0
Business	15	14.3	15	14.3	15	33.3	15	33.3	60	20.0
Farmers	15	14.3	15	14.3	15	33.3	15	33.3	60	20.0
Others	15	14.3	15	14.3	15	33.3	15	33.3	60	20.0
Total	**105**	**100.00**	**105**	**100.00**	**45**	**100.00**	**45**	**100.00**	**300**	**100.00**

Source: Primary data.

The chapter deals with the independent variables of the study like sex, age, education, annual income and occupation of the customers undue the study and the length of their relationship with banker etc. The data have been collected from the customers selected for the present study from the State Bank of India, the Andhra Bank, the ING Vysya Bank and the ICICI Bank Ltd, as one of the primary objectives of this research study is to analyses the perception of the customers as to the attitude of the Bankers undue the study. The researcher has applied statistical tools – Chi-square test, "f" and "t" tests and Test of ANOVA and the result to measure the table values so as to find out the significance level. .

Socio-economic Attributes

The socio-economic attributes of population sample indicate an important input in the organisation and functioning of any Bank. Therefore, an attempt is made to collect and interpret the socio-economic attributes of three hundred bank Customers' selected for the purpose of this study. Four banks namely State Bank of India, Andhra Bank ING Vysya Bank and ICICI Bank and their respective customers are considered for the study. The important attributes covered under the present study are 1.Age, 2.Sex, 3.Education, 4.Occupation, 5.Annual income, 6.Length of relationship with banker and 7. Type of bank account

Age

Age Group of Customers of the study banks

As stated earlier, age is an important socio-economic attribute of any human group. It plays an important role in undertaking and pursuing any activity. Its impact is found on the socio-economic activities of the population. The population for the purpose of this study indicates the customer's sample of the study.

Bank-wise age wise distribution of customers is presented in Table 7.2. The table indicates that on the whole a large majority of the respondents on an average in the form banks under the study are in the age group of 40-50 years constituting 36.33 per cent. The next significant age groups constituted 30-40 years: 50-60 years; and 20-30 years with 22 per cent; 21.67 per cent; and 16.67 per cent respectively. The respondents belonging to the age group of 60 and above constituted only 3.33 per cent. Therefore, the potential age groups to the banks are 20-30 years to 50-60 years with productive sources of income.

Table 7.2: Classification of Respondents on the Basis of Age Group

Age Group	State Bank of India		Andhra Bank		ING Vysya Bank		ICICI Bank		Total	
	No. of Respondents	Per cent	No. of Respondents	Per cent	No. of Respondents	Per cent	No. of Respondents	Per cent	No. of Respondents	Per cent
20-30	19	18.1	14	13.3	09	20.0	08	17.8	50	16.67
30-40	20	20.0	25	23.8	10	22.2	10	22.2	66	22.00
40-50	36	34.3	39	37.1	17	37.8	17	37.8	109	36.33
50-60	25	23.8	22	21.0	08	17.8	10	22.2	65	21.67
60 Above	04	3.8	05	4.8	01	2.2	-	-	10	3.33
Total	**105**	**100.00**	**105**	**100.0**	**45**	**100.00**	**45**	**100.00**	**300**	**100.00**

Source: Primary Data.

SEX

Sex wise classification of Respondents

Sex is an important socio-economic attribute. Approximately 49 per cent of the total population indicates females. However, their representation in socio-economic activity is found to be less. Table 7.3 deals with the sex wise classification of the respondents.

Table 7.3 indicates that on an average the customers belonging to male category constitute 71.7 per cent while the Females constitute 28.3 per cent. The study shows that though females constitute approximately 50 per cent of the population, their interaction with the banks constitutes nearly 30 per cent. The reasons are that most of the females are house wives with less productive work.

Table 7.3: Bank-wise Customers Classification of Respondents on the Basis of Sex

Age Group	State Bank of India		Andhra Bank		ING Vysya Bank		ICICI Bank		Total	
	No. of Respondents	Per cent	No. of Respondents	Per cent	No. of Respondents	Per cent	No. of Respondents	Per cent	No. of Respondents	Per cent
Male	67	63.8	67	63.8	42	93.3	39	86.7	215	71.7
Female	38	36.2	38	36.2	3	6.7	6	13.3	85	28.3
Total	105	100.0	105	100.0	45	100.0	45	100.0	300	100.00

Source: Primary Data.

Income

Income of population is an important variable of any socio-economic activity. It decides the consumption capacity of the population. Table 7.4 indicates the data relating to the household income of the different bank customers. For the purpose of identifying income levels, the study has identified 5 levels of income per year ranging from Rs. <50,000 to Rs.>2,00,000.

Table 7.4: Distribution of Customers on the Basis of Their Income

Year-wise Income (in rupees)	State Bank of India		Andhra Bank		ING Vysya Bank		ICICI Bank		Total	
	No. of Respondents	Per cent	No. of Respondents	Per cent	No. of Respondents	Per cent	No. of Respondents	Per cent	No. of Respondents	Per cent
<-50,000	38	36.2	38	36.2	8	17.8	4	8.9	88	29.3
50,000 to 1,00,000	25	23.8	30	28.6	19	42.2	22	48.9	96	32.0
1,00,000 to 1,50,000	28	26.7	29	27.6	15	33.3	19	42.2	91	30.3
1,50,000 to 2,00,000	12	11.4	8	7.6	3	6.7	-	-	23	7.7
2,00,000 above	2	1.9	-	-	-	-	-	-	2	0.7
Total	105	100.00	105	100.00	45	100.00	45	100.00	300	100.00

Source: Primary Data.

Table 7.4 shows that on an average, a large majority of customers belonging to the income groups of Rs.50,000 to Rs.1,50,000, 32 per cent of the sample represents the income group of Rs.50,000 to Rs.1,00,000 followed by the income levels of Rs.1,00,000 – Rs.1,50,000 and Rs.<50,000 constituting approximately 30 per cent each. The higher income groups of Rs.1,50,000 to Rs.2,00,000 and Rs.2,00,000 and above constitute 7.7 per cent and 0.7 per cent only. Therefore, the customer–banker relationship effort should focus on the income levels that range between < Rs.50,000 to Rs.1,50,000 as indicated from the study.

Education

Among different qualities of a population, education perhaps is the most important attribute. Education gives people a sense of independent judgement and power to distinguish between the good and the bad. It may have its impact on the customer–banker relationship. As such, this is considered to be an important variable with its impact on saving power of the investors. The information pertaining to the educational qualifications of the respondents is presented in Table 7.5.

Table 7.5: Classification of Respondents on the Basis of Education

Education Qualification	State Bank of India		Andhra Bank		ING Vysya Bank		ICICI Bank		Total	
	No. of Respondents	Per cent	No. of Respondents	Per cent	No. of Respondents	Per cent	No. of Respondents	Per cent	No. of Respondents	Per cent
Primary	32	30.5	28	26.7	8	17.8	5	11.1	73	24.3
Secondary	21	20.0	23	21.9	10	22.2	10	22.2	64	21.3
Higher	26	24.8	35	33.3	19	42.2	20	44.4	100	33.3
Technical	26	24.8	19	18.1	8	17.8	10	22.2	63	21.0
Total	105	100.00	105	100.00	45	100.0	45	100	300	100.0

Source: Primary Data

According to the table 54.4 per cent of the respondents have higher and technical qualifications. On an average the respondents whose education qualifications are primary and secondary constitute 45.6 per cent on an average. An interesting observation from Table 7.5 is that in the case of SBI, 50.5 per cent of the respondents have primary and secondary education and in the case of all other banks, the respondents whose educational qualification are higher and technical dominated the study.

Occupation

Occupation is an important factor that determines the level of income. It not only affects both the living and general conditions of life, but also determines the income. It also determines the standards of life. It is an important variable for the understanding of the customer–banker relationship.

Table 7.6: Classification of Respondents on the Basis of Occupation

Occupation	State Bank of India		Andhra Bank		ING Vysya Bank		ICICI Bank		Total	
	No. of Respondents	Per cent	No. of Respondents	Per cent	No. of Respondents	Per cent	No. of Respondents	Per cent	No. of Respondents	Per cent
S.S.I.	30	28.6	30	28.6	-	-	-	-	60	20.0
Micro Creditors	30	28.6	30	28.6	-	-	-	-	60	20.0
Business	15	14.3	15	14.3	15	33.3	15	33.3	60	20.0
Farmers	15	14.3	15	14.3	15	33.3	15	33.3	60	20.0
Others	15	14.3	15	14.3	15	33.3	15	33.3	60	20.0
Total	105	100.00	105	100.00	45	100.00	45	100.00	300	100.00

Source: Primary Data.

Occupational significance has made the researcher take into account equal number of respondents from small scale industries, micro creditors, business, farmers and others each constituting 20 per cent each because each occupational category influences the customer banker relations in its own way. This has been done for the convenience of the study.

Classification of Respondents on the Basis of Relationship with Banker

The relationship between the customers and bankers plays a very pivotal role for the successful operation of the banking sector. The relationship between the two parties may vary in time. For the purpose of the study, the length of relationship is put on a four point scale comprising 1-10years, 10-20 years, 20-30 years, and above 30 years. The length shows the affinity between the customer and banker. The information relating to the period of relationship of customer with banks is shown in Table 7.7.

Table 11.7: Distribution of Respondents on the Basis of their Length of Relationship with Banker

Length	State Bank of India		Andhra Bank		ING Vysya Bank		ICICI Bank		Total	
	No. of Respondents	Per cent	No. of Respondents	Per cent	No. of Respondents	Per cent	No. of Respondents	Per cent	No. of Respondents	Per cent
1 to 10 Years	51	49.3	47	44.8	28	62.2	45	100.0	166	55.3
10 to 20 Years	44	41.3	54	51.4	14	31.1	-	-	117	39.0
20 to 30 Years	9	8.5	2	1.9	3	4.4	-	-	14	4.7
Above 30 years	1	0.9	2	1.9	-	-	-	-	3	1.0
Total	105	100.00	105	100.00	45	100.00	45	100.00	300	100.00

Source: Primary Data.

Table 7.7 shows that on an average 55.3 per cent of the respondents under study fall under the category of 1-10 years followed by the respondents under 10-20 years category constituting 39 per cent. A very few have 20-30 years and above 30 years of affinity representing 4.7 per cent and 1 per cent respectively. Curiously the relationship between customers and bankers in the case of all banks is higher with shorter length of 1-20 years.

The relationship between the customers and bankers depends on a number of factors such as opening of accounts, cash deposits, withdrawal of cash, issue of cheques books, issue of loans, recovery of loans, interest rates, debit credit card services, technology based facilities like ATM cards etc., provision for complaints, mutual interactions, and customer satisfaction.

Reasons for Preference in Opening a Bank Account

The present study also focuses on the reasons for opening the account. The respondents are asked to furnish reasons. The parameters identified for this purpose include convenient location of the bank, timings of the branch, image of the branch, regional affinity, image of bank, number of branches, staff attitude, systems and procedures, and commercial affinity. The responses in this regard are presented in Table 7.8.

Table 7.8: Bank-wise Identification of Customer's Preference Related to Opening a Bank Account

Reasons	State Bank of India		Andhra Bank		ING Vysya Bank		ICICI Bank		Total	
	No. of Respondents	Per cent	No. of Respondents	Per cent	No. of Respondents	Per cent	No. of Respondents	Per cent	No. of Respondents	Per cent
Convenient Location	50	29.76	39	27.86	22	23.91	16	17.39	127	28.0
Suitable timings	24	14.29	18	12..86	11	11.96	10	10.87	63	13.9
Image of the branch	6	3.57	6	4.29	4	4.35	5	5.43	21	4.6
Regional affinity	4	2.38	3	2.14	1	1.09	1	1.87	09	1.9
Image of the Bank	14	8.33	13	9.29	21	22.83	19	20.65	67	14.7
Large No. of Branches	9	5.36	12	8.57	1	1.09	4	4.35	26	5.7
Staff attitude	7	4.17	3	2.14	9	9.78	11	11.96	30	6.6
Systems & Procedures	7	4.17	10	7.14	13	14.13	19	20.65	49	10.8
Commercial affinity	15	8.93	8	5.71	9	9.78	7	7.61	39	8.6
Other (loans & salaries)	32	19.05	28	20.00	1	1.09	-	-	61	13.4
Total	168	100	140	100	92	100	92	100	453	100.00

Source: Primary data

The analysis across banks relating to reasons for opening their accounts with the branches revealed that the convenient location is the first important factor in the case of State Bank of India, Andhra Bank and ING Vysya Bank. Suitable timings is the second important factor in the case of State Bank of India and Andhra Bank. In the case of ING Vysya bank and ICICI bank this factor received fourth priority. The image of the bank is the next important factor for Andhra Bank and ING Vysya Bank. While for State Bank of India, it was given fourth priority and in case of ICICI bank, it was given second priority. Systems and Procedures, has been the first important factor for ICICI Bank, where as it received third priority in the case of ING Vysya Bank. On the whole, it can be said that convenient location and image of the bank are the two dominant factors for opening of an account by the customers in the bank.

Satisfaction Level for opening a Bank Account

An attempt has been made to find the perceptions of the respondents as to their satisfaction for opening an account in their respective banks. Table 7.9 shows this information.

Table 7.9: Satisfaction of the Customers Regarding Opening A Bank Account

Satisfaction	State Bank of India		Andhra Bank		ING Vysya Bank		ICICI Bank		Total	
	No. of Respon-dents	Per cent	No. of Respon-dents	Per cent	No. of Respon-dents	Per cent	No. of Respon-dents	Per cent	No. of Respon-dents	Per cent
Very much	27	25.7	17	16.2	9	20.0	15	22.7	67	22.33
Much	33	31.4	33	31.4	19	42.2	18	34.3	96	32
Average	38	36.2	47	44.8	17	37.8	12	38.0	113	37.67
Less	6	5.7	6	5.7	-		-		21	7
Very Less	1	1.0	2	1.9	-		-		3	1
Total	105	100	105	100	45	100	45	100	300	100

Source: Primary Data.

It is evident from the table that 37.67 per cent of the sample under the study on an average stated that their satisfaction is 'Average'. 22.33 per cent of the customers under study indicated 'Very much satisfied'. Less than 1 per cent feels that they are less satisfied in opening an account. The analysis across individual banks reveals that in case of SBI and AB, the majority of respondents felt that their Satisfaction is 'Average'. The majority of respondents of ING Vysya and ICICI show mixed reactions. The respondents of ICICI have 'Average' satisfaction level. In the case of customers belonging to ING Vysya, the satisfaction level is 'Much'.

Opening of Bank Account after Computerisation

The respondents are asked to give details of problems experienced in opening a Bank Account after computerisation. The details are furnished in Table 7.10.

Table 7.10

Problems	State Bank of India		Andhra Bank		ING Vysya Bank		ICICI Bank		Total	
	No. of Respon-dents	Per cent	No. of Respon-dents	Per cent	No. of Respon-dents	Per cent	No. of Respon-dents	Per cent	No. of Respon-dents	Per cent
No problem	46	40.35	45	40.54	13	27.27	17	37.78	121	38.2
Took more than 20 minutes	13	11.40	22	19.82	7	15.91	5	11.11	47	14.9
Difficulty in getting introduction	16	14.04	9	8.00	13	29.55	10	22.22	48	15.2
Delay in giving Cheque Book	4	3.51	6	5.41	1	2.27	1	2.22	12	3.8
Too many procedures	22	19.30	19	17.12	9	20.45	11	24.44	61	19.4
Delay in giving Pass Book	13	11.40	10	9.01	2	4.55	1	2.22	26	8.2
Total	**114**	**100**	**111**	**100**	**45**	**100**	**45**	**100**	**315**	**100**

Source: Primary Data.

Problems as to Opening of Account after computerisation

The table reveals that 38.2 per cent of the respondents did not face any problem in opening a bank account after computerisation. However, some of the respondents (19.4%) commented that the problem is with 'too many procedures', while others (15.12%) identified 'difficulty in getting introduction' as a problem in opening a account after computerisation. 14.9 per cent of the sample identified 'more than 20 minutes to open an account' as another problem in opening an account. The analysis across sample (bank-wise) reveals that in the case of the State Bank of India, the ICICI Bank and the Andhra Bank, majority of the respondents did not encounter any problem. Some of the respondents of ING Vysya Bank expressed major difficulties such as introduction and the respondents of State Bank of India and Andhra Bank, faced difficulties like complicated procedures like taking more than 20mts to open the account.

Problems Faced by Customers in Depositing Cash

Depositing cash by the customers in the banks and obtaining receipt influences customer and banker relations. The details of data relating to problems faced by the customers with regard to depositing cash in various banks are shown in Table 7.11.

The table reveals that, majority of the customers (32.44%) expressed 'No problems' in cash deposit and 25.55 pr cent of customers complained of problems like 'Soiled notes not being accepted by the banks'. 'Insistence on higher denominations' is another problem faced by 18.67 per cent of the customers, even when the banks are fully computerised, 11.90 per cent of customers waste their time due to slow and sluggish operations of the staff. The delay in checking entries by the officers (11.33%) is also pointed out by the customers under the study as another problem.

In the case of sample banks, the views of the customers have differed in the case of SBI and AB. Similar reasons were highlighted by majority of respondents. While in case of ING Vysya and ICICI banks Majority of respondents felt that the banks insisted on higher denomination and soiled notes are not accepted, slow operations of staff are the major problems, as stated by the majority of the respondents of all banks.

Table 7.11: Problems Faced by Customer in Depositing Cash

Problems	State Bank of India		Andhra Bank		ING Vysya Bank		ICICI Bank		Total	
	No. of Respondents	Per cent	No. of Respondents	Per cent	No. of Respondents	Per cent	No. of Respondents	Per cent	No. of Respondents	Per cent
Insisting on higher Denomination	19	18.09	24	22.86	7	15.56	6	13.33	56	18.67
Slow and lazy operations of Staff	12	11.43	12	11.43	6	13.33	4	8.89	34	11.33
Delay in checking entries by Officers	16	15.24	12	11.43	4	8.89	3	6.67	35	11.90
Soiled notes not accepted	20	19.05	28	26.66	14	31.11	15	33.33	77	25.55
No problem	38	36.19	29	27.62	14	31.11	17	37.78	98	32.55
Total	**105**	**100**	**105**	**100**	**45**	**100**	**45**	**100**	**300**	**100**

Source: Primary Data

Obtaining Cash Deposit Receipt

The opinions of respondents on time taken to obtain cash deposit receipt is collected and presented in Table 7.12.

Table 7.12 indicates that on an average, 31 per cent of respondents stated that it takes 6-10 minutes of time for taking cash deposit receipt, 26.3 per cent of the sample stated that it takes 11 to 20 minutes to obtain receipts. Of the remaining sample 17.7 per cent, 13.7 per cent, and 11.3 per cent stated that it takes above 10 minutes, 11-20 minutes, and above 30 minutes respectively. About 50-60 per cent of the respondents of SBI, AB and ING Vysya have expressed the view that it has taken 6-10 mts. to deposit cash. In the case of the ICICI, the respondents differed. For some of the respondents (31.1%) it took 30 minutes and for some 26.6 per cent of respondents, the transaction was completed in 5 minutes.

Table 7.12: Details of Respondents Relating to Taken Time for Obtain Cash Deposit Receipt

Distribution	State Bank of India		Andhra Bank		ING Vysya Bank		ICICI Bank		Total	
	No. of Respondents	Per cent	No. of Respondents	Per cent	No. of Respondents	Per cent	No. of Respondents	Per cent	No. of Respondents	Per cent
Above 5 Minutes	16	15.2	16	15.2	9	20.07	12	26.6	53	17.7
6–10 Minutes	35	33.3	32	30.5	12	26.7	14	31.31	93	31.0
11-20 Minutes	30	28.6	30	28.6	10	22.2	9	20.00	79	26.3
21-30 Minutes	14	13.3	12	11.5	8	17.8	7	15.6	41	13.7
Above 30 minutes	10	9.5	15	14.3	6	13.3	3	6.7	34	11.3
Total	**105**	**100**	**105**	**100**	**45**	**100**	**45**	**100**	**300**	**100**

Source: Primary Data.

Deposits Related Transactions

Deposit related transactions play a vital role in customer banker relations. The respondents, therefore, have been asked to express their views on improvement in the deposit related transactions. The data collected in this regard are interpreted in Table 7.13.

The table reveals that 37.7 per cent of the respondents on an average in the banks under study expressed concern for improvement in the deposit related transactions and 28.3 per cent of the respondents responded positively stating that there is a "definite improvement in the transactions".

However, 33.7 per cent of respondents stated that there is 'no change' regarding improvement in the deposit related transactions. The table reveals that there has been an improvement in the deposit related services of the banks as mentioned by majority of respondents of all select banks. Bank wise perception shows that there is improvement (36.2%), (32.4%) , (42.2%) and (48.2%) in the case of State Bank of India, Andhra Bank, ING Vysya bank and ICICI Bank respectively. The respondents percentage as to "Definite improvement' is 26.7 per cent, 27.6 per cent, 33.3 per cent, and 31.11 per cent in the case of SBI, Andhra Bank, ING Vysa Bank, and ICICI Bank respectively. However, a significant percentage of respondents in the case of SBI, Andhra Bank, ING Vysya, and ICICI Banks constitutes 37.1 per cent, 40.0 per cent 24.4 per cent, and 20 per cent respectively. The finding is that the positive perception is more in the case of the two corporate banks when compared to the public sector banks.

Table 7.13: Customer Perception as to Improvement in the Deposit Related Transactions

Occupation	State Bank of India		Andhra Bank		ING Vysya Bank		ICICI Bank		Total	
	No. of Respondents	Per cent	No. of Respondents	Per cent	No. of Respondents	Per cent	No. of Respondents	Per cent	No. of Respondents	Per cent
Definite improvement	28	26.7	29	27.6	15	33.3	14	31.1	86	28.3
Improved	38	36.2	34	32.4	19	42.2	22	48.9	113	37.7
No change	39	37.1	42	40.0	11	24.4	8	20.0	101	33.7
Total	**105**	**100**	**105**	**100**	**45**	**100**	**45**	**100**	**300**	**100**

Source: Primary Data.

Withdrawal of Cash

The perception as to time taken to withdraw cash and the problems associated with it may influence the nature of customer-banker relations. The opinions 'on time taken' to withdraw cash and problems experienced in withdrawing cash are presented in Table 7.14 and 7.15.

Table 7.14: Customers Perception as to Time Taken to Withdrawal of Cash

Withdrawn Time	State Bank of India		Andhra Bank		ING Vysya Bank		ICICI Bank		Total	
	No. of Respondents	Per cent	No. of Respondents	Per cent	No. of Respondents	Per cent	No. of Respondents	Per cent	No. of Respondents	Per cent
Less than 5 Minutes	39	37.0	29	27.6	11	24.4	14	31.1	93	31.0
6–10 minutes	11	10.5	23	21.9	11	24.4	10	22.2	55	18.3
10-20 minutes	26	24.8	22	21.0	10	22.2	9	20.0	67	22.3
20-30 minutes	18	17.1	17	16.2	9	20.0	6	13.3	50	16.7
Above 30 Minutes	11	10.5	14	13.3	4	8.9	6	13.3	35	11.7
Total	105	100	105	100	45	100	45	100	300	100

Source: Primary Data.

Table 7.14 shows that on an average in the banks under study, 31 per cent of the respondents spent less than 5 minutes of time to withdraw cash and about 11.7 per cent of the respondents spent more than 30 minutes. Regarding the individual banks, in the case of SBI and AB, a similar observation was noticed, while in the case of ING Vysya and ICICI 60-75 per cent of the respondents could withdraw cash with in 20 minutes. Almost all the banks are clearing the withdrawals in 20 minutes of time in most of the cases.

The details relating to problems faced by the customers in withdrawing cash from various banks are shown in Table 7.15. The table reveals that, majority of the customers (25.33%) expressed the view that the banks are not making payments in required denominations, 19 per cent of the customers stated that the banks are giving soiled notes. A good number of respondents constituting 15 per cent of the sample pointed to the slow and lazy operations of staff, while the transactions are going, particularly in the case of withdrawals. The Slow operation of the staff is another problem. Delay in payment by the bank employees is another reason attributed by 12.67 per cent of the customers while

8.67 per cent of the customers under the study stated that there is delay caused by the bank employees in checking entries. There is inconvenience caused to the customers in withdrawal transactions on the whole as pointed by the customers as the total percentage is as high as 80 per cent.

Table 7.15: Distribution of Respondents as to Problems Experienced in Withdrawing Cash

Problems	State Bank of India		Andhra Bank		ING Vysya Bank		ICICI Bank		Total	
	No. of Respondents	Per cent	No. of Respondents	Per cent	No. of Respondents	Per cent	No. of Respondents	Per cent	No. of Respondents	Per cent
Delay in Payment	14	13.30	14	13.33	6	13.33	4	8.89	38	12.67
Not making payment in Required denominations	25	23.81	28	26.67	12	26.67	11	24.45	76	25.33
Slow and lazy operations of staff	22	20.95	18	17.14	3	6.67	2	4.44	45	15.00
Delay in checking entries by officers	14	13.33	8	7.62	2	4.44	2	4.44	26	8.67
Soiled notes are given	18	17.15	28	26.67	5	11.11	6	13.33	57	19.00
No problems	12	11.43	9	8.57	17	37.78	20	44.45	58	19.33
Total	**105**	**100**	**105**	**100**	**45**	**100**	**45**	**100**	**300**	**100**

Source: Primary Data.

ATMs

The networking of compurterised branches enables customers to operate their account through any branch of the bank once they become the account holder of any branch. The introduction of Automated Teller Machines facilitates the customers to transact with the bank all through the 24 hours. At Present ATMs are city-oriented in our country. Gradually the facilities of ATMs are to be introduced in other parts of the country also.

Business from the Internet, ATMs and other electronic channels now comprises 50 per cent of all transactions, up from 5 per cent just two years ago. The ATMs are now playing a very important role in customer banker relationship as they are providing speedy disposal of withdrawal transactions. The study takes into account the perceptions (of the customers under the study as to) the factors of the customers concerning the functioning of the ATMs. The details relating to problems faced by the customers with ATMs of various banks is shown in Table 7.16.

Table 7.16: Bank-wise Classification of Respondents with Regard to Problems Faced with Atms

Occupation	State Bank of India		Andhra Bank		ING Vysya Bank		ICICI Bank		Total	
	No. of Respondents	Per cent	No. of Respondents	Per cent	No. of Respondents	Per cent	No. of Respondents	Per cent	No. of Respondents	Per cent
Cash not available	12	5	-	-	4	14.29	3	13.04	9	7.38
No proper working	7	17.5	2	6.45	4	14.29	3	13.04	16	13.11
Not located in important Centres	13	32.5	8	25.80	6	21.43	4	17.39	31	25.41
Receipt not available	-	-	3	9.68	3	10.71	-	-	6	4.92
Required denomination not available	14	35.0	15	48.39	8	28.57	8	34.78	45	36.89
Soiled/fake notes are inserted	4	10.00	3	9.68	3	10.71	5	21.75	15	12.30
Total	**40**	**100**	**31**	**100**	**28**	**100**	**23**	**100**	**122**	**100**

Source: Primary Data.

Table 7.16 reveals that, a majority of the customers (36.89%) expressed the view that the 'required denomination is not available' in the ATMs. 25.41 per cent of the customers opined that the ATMs are 'not located at important centres'. Non–functioning of ATMs is a problem faced by 13.11 per cent of the customers. Complaints of 'a soiled/fake notes through the ATMs' is another problem faced by 12.30 per cent of the customers. About 7.38 per cent of the customers opined that 'cash is not available' at times in spite of computerisation of the banking system. The same observation has been made in the case of customers' perception across the banks under the study.

Impact of Technology on Withdrawal Service

The enormous challenges in this new era can be met effectively only when the banking institutions also make knowledge an engine for growth. Technological upgradation is a sine qua non for banking sector reforms, particularly to achieve better customer service. Concerted efforts have been made to achieve bank mechanisation and computerisation both at macro and micro level on the lines recommended by Dr. Rangarajan committee. The respondents are asked to give their views regarding improvement in the withdrawal related transactions to find out the impact of technology based services. This is interpreted in Table 7.17.

Table 7.17: The Impact of Technology on Withdrawal Services

Occupation	State Bank of India		Andhra Bank		ING Vysya Bank		ICICI Bank		Total	
	No. of Respon-dents	Per cent	No. of Respon-dents	Per cent	No. of Respon-dents	Per cent	No. of Respon-dents	Per cent	No. of Respon-dents	Per cent
Definitely improved	72	54.2	52	49.5	25	55.6	26	53.3	160	53.3
Improved	30	28.6	23	21.9	16	35.6	15	33.3	84	28.0
No change	18	17.1	30	21.86	4	8.9	4	8.9	56	18.7
Total	**105**	**100**	**105**	**100**	**45**	**100**	**45**	**100**	**300**	**100**

Source: Primary Data.

Table 7.17 reveals that 53.3 per cent of the respondents on an average felt that there is a definite improvement in the withdrawal related transactions followed by 28.0 per cent of the respondents who responded that there is an improvement in transactions. About 18.7 per cent of respondents stated that there is 'no change'. Among the banks, statement by Definite improvement is witnessed by

54.2 per cent, 49.5 per cent , 55.6 per cent and 53.3 per cent of the respondents in the case of the State Bank of India, the Andhra Bank, the ING Vysya bank and the ICICI Bank respectively. However, 17.1 per cent, 21.86 per cent, 8.9 per cent and 8.9 per cent respectively of the sample belongs to the response 'no change'.

Technology Management

With the operation of central computers, it is now possible to access the entire chain of accounts for a customer. India has made to the first transition from physical cash to "anytime money and anywhere money". Technology has now become 'market differentiated' and is clearly used as a competitive edge. As a result a number of related services such as debit card, online banking, electronic fund transfer, travel cards, and credit card. The details of response as to utilising technology related services of the banks are incorporated in Table 7.18. An attempt is also made here to find out the time utilisation of the technology related services. The details of are provided in Table 7.19.

Table 7.18: Details as to Utilising Technology Related Services of the Banks

Occupation	State Bank of India		Andhra Bank		ING Vysya Bank		ICICI Bank		Total	
	No. of Respondents	Per cent	No. of Respondents	Per cent	No. of Respondents	Per cent	No. of Respondents	Per cent	No. of Respondents	Per cent
Debit card	40	43.01	31	48.44	28	41.79	23	28.05	122	39.87
Any where Banking	14	15.05	6	9.38	11	16.42	18	21.95	49	16.01
Internet Banking	9	9.68	5	7.81	10	14.93	15	18.29	39	12.75
Electronic fund transfer	4	4.30	1	1.56	2	2.99	7	8.54	14	4.58
Travel cards	7	7.53	1	1.56	1	1.49	1	1.22	10	3.27
Credit card	19	20.43	20	31.25	15	22.39	18	21.95	72	23.53
Not utilising	—	—	—	—	—	—	—	—	—	—
Total	93	100	64	100	67	100	82	100	306	100

Source: Primary Data.

Table 7.18 reveals that all the customers are utilising the technology based services like debit card, Any where Banking, internet banking, electronic fund transfer, travel cards, and credit card. Curiously there is no single negative answer. Of the total sample, on an average, a large majority of respondents are utilising debit card (39.87%), and debit card (23.53%). Of the remaining respondents, the consumers are using online banking (16.01%), internet banking (12.75%), electronic fund transfer (4.58%), and travel cards (3.27%).

Table 7.19: Respondents as to Time Utilisation for the Technology Related Services

Occupation	State Bank of India		Andhra Bank		ING Vysya Bank		ICICI Bank		Total	
	No. of Respon-dents	Per cent	No. of Respon-dents	Per cent	No. of Respon-dents	Per cent	No. of Respon-dents	Per cent	No. of Respon-dents	Per cent
Weekly once	25	62.5	26	70.27	21	72.41	22	78.57	94	70.15
Monthly once	13	32.5	9	24.32	7	24.14	6	21.43	35	26.12
Once in quarterly	1	2.5	2	5.41	1	3.45	-	-	4	2.99
Once in half yearly	1	2.5	-	-	-	-	-	-	1	0.75
Total	40	100	37	100	29	100	28	100	134	100

Source: Primary Data.

Table 7.19 shows that a large majority of respondents (70.15 per cent) are using the technology based services frequently i.e., weekly once. Of the remaining, the respondents using the services monthly once constitute 26.12 per cent, once in quarterly constitute 2.99 per cent and once in half yearly constitute 0.75 per cent. Curiously, in the private sector banks, the respondents are utilising the services regularly either weekly once or monthly once.

Cheques

An attempt is made to find out the perception of the respondents under study regarding the time taken to get a new cheque book and the impact of computerisation on the collection of cheques as an aspect of customer-banker relationship. The data with regard to the time taken to get a new cheque book is presented in Table 7.20 and the data on the impact of computerisation on the collection of cheques are presented in Table 7.21.

Table 7.20: Time Taken to Get A New Cheque Book

Occupation	State Bank of India		Andhra Bank		ING Vysya Bank		ICICI Bank		Total	
	No. of Respondents	Per cent	No. of Respondents	Per cent	No. of Respondents	Per cent	No. of Respondents	Per cent	No. of Respondents	Per cent
5-10	18	29.51	7	11.48	2	7.41	5	20	34	19.54
11-20	12	19.67	20	32.79	9	33.33	11	44	52	29.89
21-30	27	44.26	26	42.62	13	48.15	8	32	74	42.53
30 More	4	6.56	8	13.11	3	11.11	1	4	14	8.05
Total	**61**	**100**	**61**	**100**	**27**	**100**	**25**	**100**	**174**	**100**

Source: Primary Data.

Table 7.20 shows that nearly 43 per cent of respondents spent 20–30 minutes of time to take the cheque book. Some of the respondents stated that it takes 11-20 minutes (29.89%), while others stated the period as 5-10 minutes (19.54%). A few respondents (8.05%) opined that it takes more than 30 minutes. The study shows that there are variations causing inconvenience to customers which may undermine the morale of the customers.

Table 7.21: The Impact of Computerisation in Collection of Cheques

Response	State Bank of India		Andhra Bank		ING Vysya Bank		ICICI Bank		Total	
	No. of Respondents	Per cent	No. of Respondents	Per cent	No. of Respondents	Per cent	No. of Respondents	Per cent	No. of Respondents	Per cent
Definitely improves	6	11.54	10	18.52	4	19.05	6	30	26	17.69
Improved	19	36.54	14	25.93	10	47.62	7	40	50	34.01
No Change	27	51.92	30	55.57	7	33.33	7	40	71	48.30
Total	**52**	**100**	**54**	**100**	**21**	**100**	**20**	**100**	**147**	**100**

Source: Primary Data

Table 7.21 reveals that a large percentage of 48.30 per cent of the respondents felt that there is no change in the attitude of the bankers even after computerisation in collection of cheques despite online banking services. The customers have been facing problems in this regard with regard to the attitude of the bank staff. However, almost identical percentages state that 17.69 per cent of respondents responded that there is definite improvement in transactions.

Loans

Recently, owing to the impact of rationalisation and heavy competition in the banking sector, the activities of the banks have been undergoing changes in all aspects like customer services including loans, withdrawal of money, interaction with customers, change in interest rates etc. Loans constitute an important segment in the customer-banker relationship. There are different types of loans such as crop loan, working capital loan for the SSIs, Education loans for children, personal loan for domestic purpose and such as SHG loans. The problems in this regard are often encountered by the customers in relation to time taken to get the sanction of the loan, recovery and interests. Therefore, an attempt is made to identify the perceptions of the customers as to availing loans, time taken to get sanction for the loans, problems faced by the customers to get the sanction of loans, recovery of loans and interests on loans. The data relating to the perceptions of the customers under the study relating to availing the type of loan is presented in Table 7.22; the data relating to time taken for the sanction of loan is presented in Table 7.23, and the data relating to the problems faced to get the sanction of loan is presented in Table 7.24. Perceptions of the loan recovery methods and interest rates are presented in Table 7.25 and 7.26.

Table 7.22 provides the information relating to type of loan availed by the respondents. Basing on the source of field data, Crop loan and Self Help Group loans are availed by 22.73 per cent of the respondents and about 14.39 per cent

Table 7.22: Particulars of Various Loans Availed by Sample Respondents of Various Banks during the Study Period

Type of loans	State Bank of India		Andhra Bank		ING Vysya Bank		ICICI Bank		Total	
	No. of Respondents	Per cent	No. of Respondents	Per cent	No. of Respondents	Per cent	No. of Respondents	Per cent	No. of Respondents	Per cent
Crop Loan	15	15.79	15	15.62	15	40.58	15	41.67	60	22.73
Working capital for SSI	30	31.59	30	31.25	-	-	-	-	60	22.73
Business Loan	10	10.53	9	9.38	9	24.32	10	27.78	38	14.39
Education Loan for children	1	1.05	3	3.13	3	8.11	2	5.56	09	3.41
Personal loan for domestic purpose	9	9.47	9	9.38	10	27.3	9	25.00	37	14.06
Others (SHG loans)	30	31.59	30	31.24	-	-			60	22.73
Total	95	100	96	100	37	100	36	100	264	100

Source: Primary Data

and 14.06 per cent of respondents got loans for business and personal loans respectively. The ING Vysya and ICICI banks do not offer the working capital for Small Scale Industries and Self Help Group loans. These two banks are at present providing Business and Personal loans. The other two banks give loans for the purpose of Crop and Self Help Group in the study area.

Table 7.23 provides the opinions of the customers on time taken for sanction of loan. Nearly 40.15 per cent of respondents took 2 3 weeks of time for sanction of loan and about 11.36 per cent of the customers have loans sanctioned within a period of one week. The remaining sample stated that it takes one to two weeks (26014) and above three weeks (22.35) to get the sanction for a loan. The analysis across sample banks reveals that in the case of majority of

Table 7.23: Time Taken for Sanction of the Loan

Time pattern	State Bank of India		Andhra Bank		ING Vysya Bank		ICICI Bank		Total	
	No. of Respon-dents	Per cent	No. of Respon-dents	Per cent	No. of Respon-dents	Per cent	No. of Respon-dents	Per cent	No. of Respon-dents	Per cent
Below 1 week	13	13.67	6	6.25	7	18.92	4	11.11	30	11.36
1 – 2 weeks	16	16.84	19	19.79	16	43.24	18	50	69	26.14
2 – 3 weeks	41	43.16	49	51.04	8	21.62	8	22.22	106	40.15
Above 3 weeks	25	26.36	22	22.92	6	16.22	6	16.66	59	22.35
Total	**95**	**100**	**96**	**100**	**37**	**100**	**36**	**100**	**274**	**100**

Source: Primary Data

respondents of SBI and AB, it took 2 to 3 weeks, while in case of ING Vysya and ICICI, it took less than 2 weeks for sanction of loan.

Table 7.24: Problems Faced by Customers in Sanction Of Loan

Problems	State Bank of India		Andhra Bank		ING Vysya Bank		ICICI Bank		Total	
	No. of Respon-dents	Per cent	No. of Respon-dents	Per cent	No. of Respon-dents	Per cent	No. of Respon-dents	Per cent	No. of Respon-dents	Per cent
Insisting on heavy Documen-tation	18	18.95	21	21.88	7	18.92	13	36.11	59	22.35
Under delay in sanction of Loan	34	35.79	27	28.12	6	16.22	4	11.11	71	26.89
Not for sanction of the amount applied	21	22.11	28	29.17	16	43.24	11	30.56	76	28.79
Problem regarding surety, Guaranteed	22	23.16	20	20.83	8	21.62	8	22.22	58	21.97
Total	95	100	96	100	37	100	36	100	264	100

Source: Primary Data

The details relating to problems faced by the customers in sanction of loans of various banks is shown in Table 7.24. The table reveals that, a majority of the customers (28.79%) expressed the view that they are not sanctioned the amount applied for the loan, and some of the customers faced problems like delay in sanction of loan (26.89%). Insistence on heavy documentation is another problem faced by 22.35 per cent of the customers, even after the banks are fully computerised, and the remaining 21.97 per cent of customers faced problems regarding surety and guarantee. The analysis across individual banks reveals different observations. In the case of SBI, undue delay has been seen. In the case of Andhra Bank and ING Vysya, 'non–sanction of the amount applied for' has been high lighted and in the case of ICICI insistence on heavy documentation has been understood as a major problem.

Table 7.25: Perceptions on Loan Recovery Methods by the Banks

Occupation	State Bank of India		Andhra Bank		ING Vysya Bank		ICICI Bank		Total	
	No. of Respon-dents	Per cent	No. of Respon-dents	Per cent	No. of Respon-dents	Per cent	No. of Respon-dents	Per cent	No. of Respon-dents	Per cent
Reasonable	50	52.63	41	42.71	17	45.95	16	44.44	124	46.97
Unfair	18	35.99	17	17.71	8	21.62	10	27.78	53	20.08
Very Strict	22	23.16	34	35.42	9	24.32	9	25.00	74	28.03
Too liberal	5	5.26	4	4.17	3	8.11	1	2.78	13	4.92
Total	**95**	**100**	**96**	**100**	**37**	**100**	**36**	**100**	**264**	**100**

Source: Primary Data.

The respondents are asked to give their views regarding perceptions as to loan recovery method. They are interpreted in Table 7.25. The table reveals that 46.7 per cent of the respondents felt that the recovery method adopted by banks is reasonable and 28.3 per cent of respondents stated that the banks are very strict in recovering the loans. About 20.08 per cent of respondents called loan recovery unfair, and 4.92 per cent of respondent said that the banks are 'too liberal' in loan recovery. The analysis across individual banks reveals that a similar observation has been made by a majority of respondents.

Table 7.26: Reasonability of Interest Rates Charged on Loans by the Banks

Reasonable	State Bank of India		Andhra Bank		ING Vysya Bank		ICICI Bank		Total	
	No. of Respondents	Per cent	No. of Respondents	Per cent	No. of Respondents	Per cent	No. of Respondents	Per cent	No. of Respondents	Per cent
Yes	68	71.58	55	57.29	23	62.16	20	55.56	166	62.88
No	27	28.42	41	42.71	14	37.84	16	44.44	98	37.12
Total	95	100	96	100	37	100	36	100	264	100

Source: Primary Data

Table 7.26 gives the information regarding the reasonability of interest rates. A very large majority of respondents under the study (62.88%) observed that the interest rates are reasonable. At the same time, 37.12 per cent of the customers expressed the view that high interest charges have been levied on loan services. The analysis across individual banks also reveals a similar trend.

Mutual Interaction

There must always room for proper interaction of the customers and bankers to meet the end objectives of the banks. Mutual interaction plays a very important role in customer-banker relationship. Therefore, an attempt is made to perceive the customers perception as to the customer-banker interaction. The responses have been presented in Table 7.27. And the frequent allegations that adversely affect the mutual interaction have been also identified by the present study. The factors of allegation include – misbehaviour of staff, delaying transactions, and errors in transactions. The perceptions in this regard are shown in Table 7.28.

The respondents have been asked to express whether they would interact with various authorities of the banks under the study. Table 7.27 reveals that on the whole 50.67 per cent of the respondents have stated that there has been

Table 7.27: Customer-banker Interaction

Interaction	State Bank of India		Andhra Bank		ING Vysya Bank		ICICI Bank		Total	
	No. of Respon-dents	Per cent	No. of Respon-dents	Per cent	No. of Respon-dents	Per cent	No. of Respon-dents	Per cent	No. of Respon-dents	Per cent
Yes	63	60.0	38	36.2	28	62.2	23	51.1	152	50.67
No	42	40.0	67	63.8	17	37.8	22	489	148	49.33
Total	105	100	105	100	45	100	45	100	300	100

Source: Primary Data

better interaction between them and the bankers while the remaining 49.33 per cent stated that they have not. The derivation is the banks in terms of mutual interaction have been lagging behind as the percentages of responses are identical in positive as well as negative responses.

Table 7.28: Factors Affecting Mutual Interaction between the Customers and the Bankers

Factors	State Bank of India		Andhra Bank		ING Vysya Bank		ICICI Bank		Total	
	No. of Respon-dents	Per cent	No. of Respon-dents	Per cent	No. of Respon-dents	Per cent	No. of Respon-dents	Per cent	No. of Respon-dents	Per cent
Misbeha-viour of staff	9	16.98	8	14.29	2	13.33	2	11.76	21	14.89
Delay in transa-ctions	38	71.70	29	51.79	13	86.67	12	70.59	92	65.25
Errors in transa-ctions	6	11.32	19	33.92	-	-	3	17.65	28	19.86
Total	53	100	56	100	15	100	17	100	141	100

Source: Primary Data

Table 7.28 shows the factors that affect the mutual interactions as per the study. A large majority of respondents (65.25%) expressed that they have filed complaints relating to delay in transactions. The complaints relating to errors in transactions and behaviour of staff are lodged by 19.86 per cent and 14.89 per cent respondents respectively.

The study shows that there is delay in transactions and it is a major cause that affects the customer-banker relations.

Customer Satisfaction

Customer satisfaction is the primary objective of any business organisation. The current banking sector either in public or private sector is not an exception. Therefore, the present study attempts to know the perception of customer satisfaction of the banks under the study. The opinions of customer satisfaction as to the overall performance of the banks under the study have been provided in Table 7.29.

Table 7.29: Customer Satisfaction with the Services

Consumer satisfaction	State Bank of India		Andhra Bank		ING Vysya Bank		ICICI Bank		Total	
	No. of Respondents	Per cent	No. of Respondents	Per cent	No. of Respondents	Per cent	No. of Respondents	Per cent	No. of Respondents	Per cent
Yes	70	66.07	77	73.3	33	73.3	34	75.6	214	71.33
No	34	33.3	28	26.7	12	26.7	11	24.4	86	28.67
Total	105	100	105	100	45	100	45	100	300	100

Source: Primary Data.

Table 7.29 makes it clear that the over all performance of the banks under the study comes to 71.33 per cent. A significant number of respondents constituting 28.67 per cent have expressed their dissatisfaction with the banking sector. This reveals a negative trend in the banking sector as to customer satisfaction to that extent. The bank wise perception shows that the difference between the positive and negative perception is more and similar with more or less variations whether they are public sector banks like the State Bank of India with 66.07 per cent and 33.03 per cent of positive and negative perceptions; the Andhra Bank and the ING Vysya Bank with around 73.03 per cent and 26.07 per cent of positive and negative perceptions each; and the ICICI Bank with 75.06 and 24.04 per cent of positive and negative perceptions.

Physical Facilities available in Banks

Physical facilities like availability of vouchers, enquiry and assistance, seating arrangement, space for queuing, air conditioning water coolers and parking place come under infrastructure facilities available with the banks. Modern banking institutions have been paying much attention to the physical facilities in the context of the evolving corporate culture. Hence, an attempt is made to gauge the perception of the customers as to the availability of physical facilities of the banks under the study. The data relating to the physical facilities are provided in Table 7.30.

Table 7.30 indicates that the physical facilities have been identified under three conditions labelled as 'poor', 'good', and 'better'. Regarding the availability of vouchers, 55.02 per cent of respondents and 43.09 per cent of respondents rated as good and better respectively. Similar trend is seen in the case of Andhra bank and ING Vysya Bank and ICICI Bank, however with varying percentages. Regarding enquiry and assistance14.03 per cent in the case of State Bank of India, 7.06 per cent in the case of Andhra Bank, 8.08 per cent in the case of ING Vysya Bank 2.02 per cent of respondents in the case of ICICI Bank rated the facility as poor. However, the percentages of good and better in the case of these banks are much higher. Regarding seating arrangement a very large number of respondents rated them as good and better. The percentages being 58.01 and 31.05 in the case of SBI; 57.02 and34.03 in the case of Andhra bank, 71.02 and 26.06 in the case of ING Vysya; and 68.09 and 28.09 in the case of ICICI bank as good and better respectively. Regarding space for queuing, it can be said that the percentages of responses with good and better are higher in all the banks. However, the corporate banks score higher as the percentages in this regard are 71.01 and 26.06 in the case of ING Vysya and 68.09 and 28.09 in the case of ICICI as against 56.02 and 38.01 in the case of SBI and 60.09 and 35.03 in the case of Andhra bank. Regarding air conditioning, the public sector banks are lagging behind as the rating of poor is very much higher in the case of SBI and Andhra Bank with 61.00 per cent and 57.01 per cent respectively as against 6.07 and 4.01 per cent of the ING Vysya and ICICI banks respectively. Regarding water facilities also the private sector banks are in a much better position. With regard to parking facilities, the banks in both the sectors are yet to pay much attention as the rating of poor in all the banks is higher.

The comparative mean scores of opinion on different aspects relating to customer and banker relationship in the changing scenario are presented in the ensuing analysis to

Table 7.30 : Perception of Customers as to the Physical Facilities Available in Banks

	State Bank of India			Andhra bank			ING Vysya bank			ICICI Bank		
	Poor	Good	Better	Poor	Good	Better	Poor	Good	Better	Poor	Good	Better
Availability of vouchers	1 (1.00)	58 (55.02)	46 (43.09)	2 (1.09)	42 (40.00)	61 (58.01)	—	19 (42.02)	26 (57.08)	—	17 (37.08)	28 (62.02)
Enquiry and assistance	15 (14.03)	63 (60.00)	27 (25.07)	8 (7.06)	56 (53.03)	41 (39.01)	4 (8.08)	20 (44.05)	21 (46.06)	1 (2.02)	21 (46.07)	23 (51.01)
Seating arrangement	11 (10.05)	61 (58.01)	33 (31.05)	9 (7.06)	60 (57.02)	36 (34.03)	2 (4.04)	26 (57.07)	17 (37.07)	4 (8.08)	24 (53.03)	17 (37.08)
Space for queuing	6 (5.07)	59 (56.02)	40 (38.01)	4 (3.09)	64 (60.09)	37 (35.03)	1 (2.02)	32 (71.01)	12 (26.06)	1 (2.02)	31 (68.09)	13 (28.09)
Air-conditioning	64 (61.00)	17 (16.03)	24 (22.08)	60 (57.01)	25 (23.08)	20 (19.01)	3 (6.07)	19 (42.02)	23 (51.01)	2 (4.01)	24 (53.04)	19 (42.02)
Water coolers	19 (18.01)	51 (48.06)	34 (33.03)	15 (14.03)	61 (58.01)	29 (27.07)	1 (2.02)	30 (66.07)	14 (31.01)	—	29 (64.04)	16 (35.06)
Parking place	25 (23.08)	51 (48.06)	19 (27.06)	30 (28.06)	48 (41.07)	27 (25.07)	8 (17.08)	25 (55.06)	12 (26.06)	5 (11.01)	28 (62.02)	12 (26.06)

Source: Primary data.
Note: Figures in parentheses are shown percentage to total

Table 7.31: Bank-wise Distribution of Mean Scores of Customers on Different Aspects Regarding Customer Satisfactory Levels

Sl. No.	Customer Satisfactory Variables	Type of Banks	N	Mean	Std. Deviation	Std. Error	Minimum	Maximum
1.	Bank Physical Facilities	SBI	105	19.73	5.33	.52	8	35
		AB	105	20.34	4.97	.48	9	35
		ING	45	22.73	5.49	.60	16	35
		ICICI	45	23.67	3.99	.82	17	35
		Total	300	20.98	5.24	.30	8	35
2.	Services of the bank	SBI	105	14.11	6.25	.55	0	25
		AB	105	14.70	6.30	.61	0	59
		ING	45	16.57	5.77	.87	0	25
		ICICI	45	16.82	5.66	.93	0	25
		Total	300	15.09	6.06	.35	0	59
3.	Technological Services of Banks	SBI	105	3.75	5.69	.55	0	26
		AB	105	3.20	4.79	.46	0	26
		ING	45	6.95	7.84	1.18	0	24
		ICICI	45	9.73	8.11	1.21	0	25
		Total	300	4.92	6.59	.38	0	26
4.	Customers agreed statement	SBI	105	13.28	2.83	.28	0	18
		AB	105	13.53	2.81	.27	4	18
		ING	45	15.00	3.73	.56	8	33
		ICICI	45	14.78	3.88	.58	8	33
		Total	300	13.84	3.20	.18	0	33
5.	Improvement in opening an account	SBI	105	8.62	2.47	.24	4	15
		AB	105	8.31	2.53	.25	4	14
		ING	45	9.30	2.31	.35	4	15
		ICICI	45	9.64	2.00	.30	6	13
		Total	300	8.76	2.44	.14	4	15
6.	Satisfaction with Complaint deal	SBI	105	5.79	3.12	.30	1	13
		AB	105	5.41	2.94	.29	1	14
		ING	45	5.89	3.56	.54	0	13
		ICICI	45	4.91	3.25	.48	1	12
		Total	300	5.54	3.15	.18	0	14

Source: Primary data.

show the significance level under six groups viz., customer service, customer problems, physical facilities, customers agreed statements and improvement in opening accounts, satisfaction with complaint deal.

The above table considers the mean values. The ICICI Bank mean score value are high in bank Technological services, Services of the bank, Physical facilities of the bank and improvement in opening an account. The ICICI Bank gives more importance to the bank physical facilities, services of the bank, technological service of the bank and improvement in opening an account.

The ING Vysya bank mean score values is high in customer agreed statement and satisfaction with complaint deal than the remaining banks mean score values. The ING Vysya Bank gives importance to the customer agreed statement and satisfaction with complaint deal.

If we consider the standard deviation, ICICI Bank of India standard deviation values are least in Bank technological services of the bank and improvement in opening an account than the remaining banks standard deviation values. The ICICI Bank is more efficient Bank in Technological, services of the Bank and improvement in opening an account than the remaining banks.

Table 7.32: Anova of the Scores of Customer Satisfactory Aspects Classified According to Different Bank Customers

		Sum of Squares	df	Mean Square	F	Sig.
Bank Physical Facilities	Between Groups	665.802	3	221.934	8.693	.000
	Within Groups	7557.034	296	25.531		
	Total	**8222.837**	**299**			
Services of the bank	Between Groups	347.405	3	115.802	3.218	.023
	Within Groups	10650.341	296	35.981		
	Total	**10997.747**	**299**			
Technological Services of Banks	Between Groups	1682.126	3	560.709	14.681	.000
	Within Groups	11305.111	296	38.193		
	Total	**12987.237**	**299**			
Customers agreed statement	Between Groups	142.453	3	47.484	4.808	.003
	Within Groups	2923.183	296	9.876		
	Total	**3065.637**	**299**			
Improvement in opening an account	Between Groups	71.238	3	23.746	4.108	.007
	Within Groups	1710.959	296	5.780		
	Total	**1782.197**	**299**			
Satisfaction with Complaint deal	Between Groups	31.573	3	10.524	1.063	.365
	Within Groups	2931.023	296	9.902		
	Total	**2962.597**	**299**			

Source: Primary data

Andhra Bank and State Bank of India standard deviation values are least in Physical facilities of banks, Customer agreed statement and satisfaction with complaint deal, than the remaining Banks standard deviation values. So Andhra Bank is more efficient in physical facilities the of banks, customer agree statements and satisfaction with complaint deal than the remaining banks.

After analysing the whole table the conclusion is that, all banks are commonly giving more importance to physical facilities. Especially ICICI bank gives much importance to technological services.

According to the above table, the f-values for Bank Physical Facilities, Services of the bank, Technological Services of Banks, Customers agreed statement, Improvement in opening an account and Satisfaction with Complaint deal of the above four different bank customers (SBI, AB, ING Vysya and ICICI) are 8.693, 3.218, 14.681, 8.808, 4.108 and 1.063 respectively. Among them, Bank Physical Facilities, Technological Services of Banks, Customers agreed statement and Improvement in opening an account variables are found to be significant at 0.01 level, the variable Services of the bank is significant at 0.05 level of significance and the variable Satisfaction with Complaint deal is not significant. This shows that there is significant difference in the mean performance of the customers of different banks. The analysis shows that the performance of customers of private banks is significantly higher than those of the nationalised banks. This is because the private banks are providing considerable facilities to their customers than the nationalised banks

The table shows that 40-50 years age group customers, mean score values are high in Bank Physical facilities, Services of the bank, Technological service of the bank, Improvement in opening an account and satisfaction with compliant deal. So 40–50 years age group customers are more satisfied than the remaining age group customer in Bank Physical facilities, Bank Technological service of the Bank, Improvement in Opening an account and satisfaction with compliant deal.

Table 7.33: Age-wise Distribution of Mean Scores of Customers on Different Aspects Regarding Customer Satisfactory Levels

Sl. No.		Age Group	N	Mean	Std. Deviation	Std. Error	Min.	Max.
1	2	3	4	5	6	7	8	9
1.	Bank Physical Facilities	20-30 years	49	20.76	6.60	.94	8	35
		30-40 years	66	20.86	5.66	.70	9	35
		40-50 years	110	21.62	5.03	.48	9	35
		50-60 years	65	20.08	3.89	.48	12	33
		Above 60 years	10	21.60	4.88	1.54	17	28
		Total	**300**	**20.98**	**5.24**	**.30**	**8**	**35**
2.	Services of the bank	20-30 years	49	11.86	6.92	.99	0	25
		30-40 years	66	15.26	5.97	.73	0	24
		40-50 years	110	16.12	4.79	.46	0	25
		50-60 years	65	16.05	6.59	.82	0	59
		Above 60 years	10	12.20	6.03	1.91	0	20
		Total	**300**	**15.09**	**6.06**	**.35**	**0**	**59**
3.	Techno-logical Services of Banks	20-30 years	49	5.61	7.84	1.12	0	25
		30-40 years	66	5.86	7.11	.88	0	26
		40-50 years	110	5.91	6.36	.61	0	26
		50-60 years	65	2.54	4.90	.61	0	20
		Above 60 years	10	.00	.00	.00	0	0
		Total	**300**	**4.92**	**6.59**	**.38**	**0**	**26**
4.	Customers agreed statement	20-30 years	49	13.49	2.55	.36	8	20
		30-40 years	66	13.41	2.92	.36	0	18
		40-50 years	110	14.04	2.82	.27	5	19
		50-60 years	65	14.08	4.41	.55	4	33
		Above 60 years	10	14.80	2.35	.74	11	18
		Total	**300**	**13.84**	**3.20**	**.18**	**0**	**33**

1	2	3	4	5	6	7	8	9
5	Improvement in opening an account	20-30 years	49	8.84	2.58	.37	4	14
		30-40 years	66	8.86	2.58	.32	4	14
		40-50 years	110	9.08	2.26	.22	5	15
		50-60 years	65	8.12	2.45	.30	4	15
		Above 60 years	10	8.40	2.22	.70	6	12
		Total	300	8.76	2.44	.14	4	15
6.	Satisfaction with Complaint deal	20-30 years	49	5.43	3.27	.47	0	13
		30-40 years	66	5.47	3.23	.37	1	12
		40-50 years	110	5.85	3.02	.31	1	14
		50-60 years	65	5.38	3.06	.38	1	12
		Above 60 years	10	4.00	3.16	1.00	1	9
		Total	300	5.54	3.15	.18	0	14

The above 60 years age group customers mean value is high than the remaining age group customers in customer agreed statement. So above 60 years age group customers more satisfied than the reaming age group customers in customers agreed statement.

If we consider standard deviation, 50-60 years age group customers standard deviation values are least than the remaining age group customers in Bank Physical facilities and Technological service of the Bank. So 50-60 years age group customers are more satisfied with bank physical facilities and technological service of banks.

40-50 years age group customers standard deviation value are least in service of the bank and satisfaction with compliant deal. So 40–50 years age group customer are more satisfied than the remaining age group customers in the services offered by the bank and satisfaction with complaint deal.

Above 60 years age group customers standard deviation value, are least in customer agreed statement and improvement in opening an account. So above 60 years age group customers are more satisfied than the remaining age group customer in customer agreed statement and improvement in opening an account.

Table 7.34: Anova of the Scores of Customer Satisfactory Aspects Classified According to Age of Customers

		Sum of Square	df	Mean Squares	F	Sig
Bank Physical Facilities	Between Groups	105.024	4	26.256	.954	.433
	Within Groups	8117.813	295	27.518		
	Total	**8222.837**	**299**			
Services of the bank	Between Groups	773.200	4	193.300	5.577**	.000
	Within Groups	10224.546	295	34.659		
	Total	**10997.747**	**299**			
Technological Services of Banks	Between Groups	800.587	4	200.147	4.845**	.001
	Within Groups	12186.650	295	41.311		
	Total	**12987.237**	**299**			
Customers agreed statement	Between Groups	35.367	4	8.842	.861	.488
	Within Groups	3030.269	295	10.272		
	Total	**3065.637**	**299**			
Improvement in opening an account	Between Groups	40.051	4	10.013	1.695	.151
	Within Groups	1742.146	295	5.906		
	Total	**1782.197**	**299**			
Satisfaction with Complaint deal	Between Groups	37.100	4	9.275	.935	.444
	Within Groups	2925.497	295	9.917		
	Total	**2962.597**	**299**			

Source: Primary data.

According to the above table the f-values for Bank Physical Facilities, Services of the bank, Technological Services of Banks, Customers agreed statement, Improvement in opening an account and Satisfaction with Complaint deal of the above five different aged customers are 0.954, 5.577, 4.845, 0.861, 1.695 and 0.935 respectively. Among them Services of the bank and Technological Services of Banks variables are significant at 0.01 level and the remaining all variables are not significant. This shows that there is significant difference in the mean performance of the customers on Services of the bank and Technological Services of Banks variables because the middle age grouped customers are getting more satisfaction in these variable. The analysis shows that the performance of customers of the banks are almost close to one and another age group. Where as the middle age grouped customers (between 30 to 60 years) are more satisfied with the general and technical services of the banks.

Table 7.35: Gender-Wise Distribution of Mean Scores of Customers on Different Aspects Regarding Customer Satisfactory Levels

	Sex	N	Mean	Std. Deviation	t-value
Bank Physical Facilities	Male	215	21.77	4.82	4.272
	Female	85	18.98	5.75	
Services of the bank	Male	215	15.97	5.82	4.105
	Female	85	12.86	6.15	
Technological Services of Banks	Male	215	5.55	6.81	2.661
	Female	85	3.33	5.75	
Customers agreed statement	Male	215	13.96	3.44	0.988
	Female	85	13.55	2.51	
Improvement in opening an account	Male	215	8.90	2.46	1.572
	Female	85	8.41	2.37	
Satisfaction with Complaint deal	Male	215	5.64	3.18	0.880
	Female	85	5.28	3.07	

Source: Primary data.

The above table analyses the significance of difference levels of means and standard deviations in their satisfaction of customers of the banks among sex wise with banker services on Bank Physical Facilities, Services of the bank, Technological Services of Banks, Customers agreed statement, Improvement in opening an account and Satisfaction with Complaint deal of the banks. In the bank physical facilities, the means of male is 8.81, female is 18.98 and the standard deviations are 4.82 and 5.75 respectively. The obtained t-value is 4.272, which is significant at 0.01 levels. Regarding the services of the bank, the means of male is 15.97 and the mean of female is 12.86 and the standard deviations are 5.82 and 6.15 respectively. The derived t-value is 4.105, which is significant at 0.01 level. In the technological services of the bank, the performance of means of male is 5.55, the mean of female is 3.33 and the standard deviations are 6.81 and 5.75 respectively. The calculated t-value 2.661 is significant at 0.01 level. In the customers agreed statement of the bank, the performance of means of male 13.96 and the mean of female is 13.55 and standard deviations are 3.44 and 2.51 respectively. The computed t-value is 0.988 which is not significant. In the improvement of opening an account of the bank, the performance of means of male is 8.90 and the mean of female is 8.41 and the standard deviations is 2.46, 2.37 respectively. The generated t-value is 1.572 is not significant. Regarding the satisfaction with the complaints the mean of male 5.64, the mean of female is 5.28 and the standard deviations are 3.18 and 3.07 respectively. The calculated t-value 0.880 which is not significant.

This shows that Bank Physical Facilities, Services of the bank, and Technological Services of Banks are significance in their performance between male and female customers where as in Customers agreed statement, Improvement in opening an account and Satisfaction with Complaint deal variables the male and female performance of satisfaction is not significantly different.

If we consider the mean between 50,000 to 1,00,000 annual income, customers mean value are high in bank physical facilities and customers agreed statement than the remaining annual income customers. So 50,000 to 1,00,000 annul income customers are more satisfied with bank physical facilities and customer agreed statements.

Table 7.36: Income Level-wise Distribution of Mean Scores of Customers on Different Aspects Regarding Customer Satisfactory Levels

Sl. No.		Annual income (approximately)	N	Mean	Std. Deviation	Std. Error	Min.	Max.
1.	Bank Physical Facilities	Below 50 thousands	87	19.51	6.10	.65	8	35
		50 thousands to 1 lakh	96	21.66	3.97	.49	12	35
		between 1-2 lakhs	92	21.52	4.90	.51	13	35
		Above 2 Lakhs	25	21.48	4.80	.79	14	29
		Total	**300**	**20.98**	**5.24**	**.30**	**8**	**35**
2.	Services of the bank	Below 50 thousands	87	12.34	6.42	.69	0	25
		50 thousands to 1 lakh	96	15.57	5.21	.53	0	25
		between 1-2 lakhs	92	17.22	5.76	.60	0	59
		Above 2 Lakhs	25	14.92	5.63	1.13	0	21
		Total	**300**	**15.09**	**6.06**	**.35**	**0**	**59**
3.	Technological Services of Banks	Below 50 thousands	87	2.82	6.11	.65	0	26
		50 thousands to 1 lakh	96	6.03	6.98	.71	0	25
		between 1-2 lakhs	92	6.04	6.25	.65	0	20
		Above 2 Lakhs	25	3.88	6.25	1.25	0	21
		Total	**300**	**4.92**	**6.59**	**.38**	**0**	**26**
4.	Customers agreed statement	Below 50 thousands	87	13.61	2.40	.26	8	19
		50 thousands to 1 lakh	96	14.42	3.92	.40	5	33
		between 1-2 lakhs	92	13.66	2.89	.30	0	19
		Above 2 Lakhs	25	13.12	3.52	.70	5	18
		Total	**300**	**13.84**	**3.20**	**.18**	**0**	**33**
5.	Improvement in opening an account	Below 50 thousands	87	8.00	2.39	.26	4	14
		50 thousands to 1 lakh	96	8.91	2.28	.23	4	15
		between 1-2 lakhs	92	9.33	2.55	.27	5	15
		Above 2 Lakhs	25	8.80	2.31	.46	4	13
		Total	**300**	**8.76**	**2.44**	**.14**	**4**	**15**
6.	Satisfaction with Complaint deal	Below 50 thousands	87	5.10	2.99	.32	1	13
		50 thousands to 1 lakh	96	5.30	3.27	.33	0	14
		between 1-2 lakhs	92	5.87	3.13	.33	1	12
		Above 2 Lakhs	25	6.72	3.02	.60	2	12
		Total	**300**	**5.54**	**3.15**	**.18**	**0**	**14**

Source: Primary data.

Between 1–2 lakhs annual income customers the mean values are high in services provided by the bank, technological services of banks, improvement in opening an account and satisfaction with complaint deal. So between 1–2 lakhs annual income customers are more satisfied in service of the banks, technological service of bank, improvement in opening an account and satisfaction with complaint deal than the remaining customers.

Table 7.37: Anova of the Scores of Customer Satisfactory Aspects Classified According to Income Levels of Customers

		Sum of Squares	df	Mean Square	F	Sig.
Bank Physical Facilities	Between Groups	266.237	3	88.746	3.301	.021
	Within Groups	7956.600	296	26.880		
	Total	**8222.837**	**299**			
Services of the bank	Between Groups	1095.110	3	365.037	10.911	.000
	Within Groups	9902.637	296	33.455		
	Total	**10997.747**	**299**			
Technological Services of Banks	Between Groups	646.807	3	215.602	5.171	.002
	Within Groups	12340.430	296	41.691		
	Total	**12987.237**	**299**			
Customers agreed statement	Between Groups	52.396	3	17.465	1.716	.164
	Within Groups	3013.240	296	10.180		
	Total	**3065.637**	**299**			
Improvement in opening an account	Between Groups	81.823	3	27.274	4.748	.003
	Within Groups	1700.374	296	5.745		
	Total	**1782.197**	**299**			
Satisfaction with Complaint deal	Between Groups	66.813	3	22.271	2.276	.080
	Within Groups	2895.783	296	9.783		
	Total	**2962.597**	**299**			

Source: Primary data.

If we consider the standard deviation between 50,000 to 1,00,000 annual income customer's, the standard deviation values are least in bank physical facilities, services of the bank and improvement in opening an account. So 50,000 to

1,00,000 annual income customer are more satisfied with bank physical facilities service of the bank and improvement in opening an account then the remain annual income customers.

Below 50 thousand annual income customers standard deviation values are lest in technological services of the bank, customers agreed statement and satisfaction with complaint deal. So below 50 thousand annual income customer are more satisfied in Technological services, the bank customers agreed statesmen and satisfaction with compliant deal than the reaming annual income customers.

According to the above table the f-values for Bank Physical Facilities, Services of the bank, Technological Services of Banks, Customers agreed statement, Improvement in opening an account and Satisfaction with Complaint deal of the above, four different income levels of customers are 3.301, 10.911, 5.171, 1.716, 4.748 and 2.276 respectively. Among them Services of the bank and Satisfaction with Complaint deal variables are significant at 0.05 level and Services of the bank, Technological Services of Banks and Improvement in opening an account variable are significant at 0.01 level. The remaining customer agreed statement variable is not significant. This shows that there is significant difference in the mean performance of the customers on all services provided by the banks are varied in the income levels of the customers. The more of income grouped customers are getting more of satisfaction from the banker. This is because the higher income grouped customers are attracted by the banker through their better services. So they are enjoying all facilities by the bankers.

If we consider the mean (Table 7.38), the Technical education customers mean values are high in bank physical facilities, Technological services of the banks and improvement in opening an account. So Technical education customers are more satisfied with bank physical facilities, Technological service of the bank and improvement in opening an account than the reaming education qualification

Table 7.38: Education Level-wise Distribution of Mean Scores of Customers on Different Aspects Regarding Customer Satisfactory Levels

	Educational Qualification	N	Mean	Std. Devia-tion	Std. Error	Min	Max
Bank Physical Facilities	Primary	73	19.12	4.82	.56	8	32
	Secondary	65	20.09	5.15	.64	9	35
	Higher	99	22.10	5.16	.52	12	35
	Technical	63	22.27	5.26	.66	14	35
	Total	**300**	**20.98**	**5.24**	**.30**	**8**	**35**
Services of the bank	Primary	73	13.16	5.49	.64	0	20
	Secondary	65	13.92	4.90	.61	0	23
	Higher	99	16.57	6.58	.66	0	59
	Technical	63	16.19	6.21	.78	0	25
	Total	**300**	**15.09**	**6.06**	**.35**	**0**	**59**
Technological Services of Banks	Primary	73	2.05	5.63	.66	0	26
	Secondary	65	2.80	5.90	.73	0	24
	Higher	99	7.00	6.05	.61	0	25
	Technical	63	7.17	7.24	.91	0	20
	Total	**300**	**4.92**	**6.59**	**.38**	**0**	**26**
Customers agreed statement	Primary	73	14.27	3.85	.45	8	33
	Secondary	65	13.69	2.68	.33	7	18
	Higher	99	13.94	3.11	.31	0	20
	Technical	63	13.35	3.01	.38	5	18
	Total	**300**	**13.84**	**3.20**	**.18**	**0**	**33**
Improvement in opening an account	Primary	73	7.60	2.19	.26	4	14
	Secondary	65	8.42	2.16	.27	4	14
	Higher	99	9.42	2.50	.25	5	15
	Technical	63	9.43	2.36	.30	4	15
	Total	**300**	**8.76**	**2.44**	**.14**	**4**	**15**
Satisfaction with Complaint deal	Primary	73	4.45	2.97	.34	1	13
	Secondary	65	5.45	2.87	.37	1	12
	Higher	99	6.20	3.41	.34	0	14
	Technical	63	5.84	2.91	.37	1	11
	Total	**300**	**5.54**	**3.15**	**.18**	**0**	**14**

Source: Primary data.

customers. Higher education customer mean values are high in services of the bank, customers agreed statement and satisfaction with compliant deal. So higher education customers are more satisfied with the services of the bank, customer agreed statement and satisfaction with complaint deal.

If we consider the standard deviation, the secondary education customers standard deviation values are least in all facilities. So secondary education customer are more satisfied with all the facilities.

Table 7.39: Anova of the Scores of Customer Satisfactory Aspects Classified According to Education Levels of Customers

		Sum of Squares	df	Mean Square	F	Sig.
Bank Physical Facilities	Between Groups	532.098	3	177.366	6.826	.000
	Within Groups	7690.739	296	25.982		
	Total	**8222.837**	**299**			
Services of the bank	Between Groups	651.066	3	217.022	6.209	.000
	Within Groups	10346.680	296	34.955		
	Total	**10997.747**	**299**			
Technological Services of Banks	Between Groups	1639.976	3	546.659	14.260	.000
	Within Groups	11347.260	296	38.335		
	Total	**12987.237**	**299**			
Customers agreed statement	Between Groups	31.316	3	10.439	1.018	.385
	Within Groups	3034.321	296	10.251		
	Total	**3065.637**	**299**			
Improvement in opening an account	Between Groups	177.322	3	59.107	10.902	.000
	Within Groups	1604.874	296	5.422		
	Total	**1782.197**	**299**			
Satisfaction with Complaint deal	Between Groups	136.081	3	45.360	4.750	.003
	Within Groups	2826.516	296	9.549		
	Total	**2962.597**	**299**			

Source: Primary data.

According to the above table, the f-values for Bank Physical Facilities, Services of the bank, Technological Services of Banks, Customers agreed statement, Improvement in opening an account and Satisfaction with Complaint deal of the above, four different income levels of customers are 6.826, 6.209, 4.260, 1.018, 10.902 and 4.750 respectively. Among them, Bank's Physical Facilities, Services of the bank, Technological Services of Banks, Improvement in opening an account and Satisfaction with Complaint deal variables are significant at 0.01 level and customer agreed statement variable is not significant. This shows that there is significant difference in the mean performance of the customers on all services provided by the banks. It is varied at the education levels of the customers. The more of educated customers are getting more satisfaction from the banker. This is because the higher educated group of customers are getting better services with the help of their education skills.

If we consider the mean (Table 7.40), other occupation customers mean values are high in physical facilities, Technological services of the bank and improvement in opening an account than the remaining occupation customers. So other occupation customer are more satisfied in physical facilities, Technological service and improvement in opening an account. Business professional customers' mean score values are high in the services of the bank and satisfaction with complaint deal than the remaining occupation customers. So business professional customers have minimum satisfaction in the services of the bank, and satisfaction with complaint deal. Farmers mean score values is high in customers agreed statement. So farmers are the minimum satisfied group in customer agreed statement than the reaming occupation.

If we consider the standard deviation, farmers standard deviation values are least in bank physical facilities, services of the bank, technological services of bank, customers agreed statement, improvement in opening an account and satisfaction with compliant deal. So farm sector customers

Table 7.40: Occupation-wise Distribution of Mean Scores of Customers on Different Aspects Regarding Customer Satisfactory Levels

Sl. No.		Occupation	N	Mean	Std. Deviation	Std. Error	Min	Max
1	2	3	4	5	6	7	8	9
1.	Bank Physical Facilities	Industrialist	61	21.56	4.36	.56	12	31
		Micro-business	60	18.17	6.10	.79	8	35
		Business	62	21.23	4.55	.58	15	35
		Farmers	60	20.70	3.05	.39	15	26
		Others	57	23.33	6.35	.84	13	35
		Total	**300**	**20.98**	**5.24**	**.30**	**8**	**35**
2.	Services of the bank	Industrialist	61	16.25	4.51	.58	0	25
		Micro- business	60	10.88	6.14	.79	0	22
		Business	62	17.32	6.63	.84	0	59
		Farmers	60	15.32	3.22	.42	10	22
		Others	57	15.60	7.06	.93	0	25
		Total	**300**	**15.09**	**6.06**	**.35**	**0**	**59**
3.	Technological Services of Banks	Industrialist	61	2.02	4.13	.53	0	20
		Micro- business	60	2.00	5.20	.67	0	26
		Business	62	8.19	5.91	.75	0	25
		Farmers	60	1.88	5.83	.75	0	24
		Others	57	10.75	6.05	.80	0	20
		Total	**300**	**4.92**	**6.59**	**.38**	**0**	**26**
4.	Customers agreed statement	Industrialist	61	13.93	3.53	.45	0	18
		Micro- business	60	13.22	3.87	.29	8	18
		Business	62	13.69	2.39	.30	7	20
		Farmers	60	15.10	2.26	.50	9	33
		Others	57	13.25	3.39	.45	5	19
		Total	**300**	**13.84**	**3.20**	**.18**	**0**	**33**
5.	Improvement in opening an account	Industrialist	61	9.33	2.32	.30	5	15
		Micro- business	60	8.07	2.53	.33	4	14
		Business	62	8.76	2.71	.34	5	14

1	2	3	4	5	6	7	8	9
		Farmers	60	7.55	1.60	.21	4	11
		Others	57	10.18	2.03	.27	4	15
		Total	**300**	**8.76**	**2.44**	**.14**	**4**	**15**
6.	Satisfaction with Complaint deal	Industrialist	61	6.52	2.84	.36	1	12
		Micro- business	60	4.92	2.94	.38	1	13
		Business	62	6.40	3.37	.43	1	14
		Farmers	60	4.12	2.57	.33	1	10
		Others	57	5.68	3.38	.45	0	13
		Total	**300**	**5.54**	**3.15**	**.18**	**0**	**14**

are more satisfied with bank physical facilities, services of the bank, Technological services of the bank, customer agreed statement, improvement in opening an account and satisfaction with complaint deal than the remaining occupation customers i.e., all those with farmer occupation. These customers have consistence satisfaction to the all facilities.

According to the above table, the f-values for the variables Bank Physical Facilities, Services of the bank, Technological Services of Banks, Customers agreed statement, Improvement in opening an account and Satisfaction with Complaint deal of the above five different occupational groups of the customers are 8.162, 11.379, 35.050, 3.544, 12.064 and 6.838 respectively. Among them, all the variables i.e., Bank Physical Facilities, Services of the bank, Technological Services of Banks, customer agreed statement, Improvement in opening an account and Satisfaction with Complaint deal variables are significant at 0.01 level. This shows that there is significant difference in the mean performance of different occupation customers on all services provided by the banks. It is varied at the education levels of the customers. The analysis explains that the mean performance on the above variables at industrialists and business people is more than other customers because the business and industrialist customers are used to utilising more

Table 7.41: Anova of the Scores of Customer Satisfactory Aspects Classified According to Occupation of Customers

		Sum of Squares	df	Mean Square	F	Sig.
Bank Physical Facilities	Between Groups	819.349	4	204.837	8.162	.000
	Within Groups	7403.488	295	25.097		
	Total	**8222.837**	**299**			
Services of the bank	Between Groups	1470.001	4	367.500	11.379	.000
	Within Groups	9527.746	295	32.297		
	Total	**10997.747**	**299**			
Technological Services of Banks	Between Groups	4183.831	4	1045.958	35.050	.000
	Within Groups	8803.406	295	29.842		
	Total	**12987.237**	**299**			
Customers agreed statement	Between Groups	140.577	4	35.144	3.544	.008
	Within Groups	2925.060	295	9.915		
	Total	**3065.637**	**299**			
Improvement in opening an account	Between Groups	250.554	4	62.639	12.064	.000
	Within Groups	1531.643	295	5.192		
	Total	**1782.197**	**299**			
Satisfaction with Complaint deal	Between Groups	251.382	4	62.845	6.838	.000
	Within Groups	2711.215	295	9.191		
	Total	**2962.597**	**299**			

and more transactions than other customers. So in general, the bankers provide more facilities to those people who have more and heavy transaction.

If we consider mean (Table 7.42), above 30 years banker-customers' relationship mean score values are high in bank physical facilities, service of the bank and satisfaction with complaint deal. So customers above 30 years relationship with bank are more satisfied in bank physical facilities, service of the bank and satisfaction with complaint deal than the remaining, customers.1-10 year relationship with bank customers mean values is high in Technological services of the bank. So 1–10 years relationship customers are more

Table 7.42: Length of Relationship with Bank Wise Distribution of Mean Scores of Customers on Different Aspects Regarding Customer Satisfactory Levels

Sl. No.		Length of Relationship with Banker	N	Mean	Std. Deviation	Std. Error	Min	Max
1.	Bank Physical Facilities	1-10 years	165	21.15	6.13	.48	8	35
		10-20 years	118	20.84	3.96	.36	12	32
		20-30 years	14	20.00	3.11	.83	15	25
		Above 30 years	3	21.67	6.03	3.48	16	28
		Total	**300**	**20.98**	**5.24**	**.30**	**8**	**35**
2.	Services of the bank	1-10 years	165	14.36	6.37	.50	0	25
		10-20 years	118	15.56	4.20	.37	0	23
		20-30 years	14	17.50	3.99	1.12	9	25
		Above 30 years	3	25.33	29.50	17.03	4	59
		Total	**300**	**15.09**	**6.06**	**.35**	**0**	**59**
3.	Technological Services of Banks	1-10 years	165	5.87	7.29	.57	0	26
		10-20 years	118	3.87	5.64	.52	0	21
		20-30 years	14	2.79	3.36	.90	0	9
		Above 30 years	3	4.33	5.13	2.96	0	10
		Total	**300**	**4.92**	**6.59**	**.38**	**0**	**26**
4.	Customers agreed statement	1-10 years	165	13.82	2.39	.19	8	20
		10-20 years	118	14.09	3.87	.36	0	33
		20-30 years	14	12.21	4.59	1.23	5	17
		Above 30 years	3	13.00	5.00	2.89	8	18
		Total	**300**	**13.84**	**3.20**	**.18**	**0**	**33**
5.	Improvement in opening an account	1-10 years	165	8.98	2.37	.18	4	15
		10-20 years	118	8.45	2.47	.23	4	14
		20-30 years	14	9.21	2.67	.71	5	15
		Above 30 years	3	7.00	3.46	2.00	5	11
		Total	**300**	**8.76**	**2.44**	**.14**	**4**	**15**
6.	Satisfaction with Complaint deal	1-10 years	165	5.27	3.18	.24	0	13
		10-20 years	118	5.83	3.13	.29	1	14
		20-30 years	14	5.93	3.20	.85	1	10
		Above 30 years	3	6.67	4.93	2.85	1	10
		Total	**300**	**5.54**	**3.15**	**.18**	**0**	**14**

Source: Primary data.

satisfied in technological services of the bank. 10–20 years relationship customers mean value is high in customer agreed statement. So customers with 10–20 years relationship with bank are more satisfied in customer agreed statement. According to those with 20-30 years relationship with bank the mean value is high in improvement in opening an account. So customers with 10-20 year relationship with bank are more satisfied in improvement in opening an account.

Table 7.43: Anova of the Scores of Customer Satisfactory Aspects Classified According to Length of Service with Bank to Customers

		Sum of Squares	df	Mean Square	F	Sig.
Bank Physical Facilities	Between Groups	21.720	3	7.240	.261	.853
	Within Groups	8201.116	296	27.706		
	Total	**8222.837**	**299**			
Services of the bank	Between Groups	510.592	3	170.197	4.804	.003
	Within Groups	10487.154	296	35.430		
	Total	**10997.747**	**299**			
Technological Services of Banks	Between Groups	342.053	3	114.018	2.669	.048
	Within Groups	12645.184	296	42.720		
	Total	**12987.237**	**299**			
Customers agreed statement	Between Groups	46.759	3	15.586	1.528	.207
	Within Groups	3018.877	296	10.199		
	Total	**3065.637**	**299**			
Improvement in opening an account	Between Groups	31.699	3	10.566	1.787	.150
	Within Groups	1750.498	296	5.914		
	Total	**1782.197**	**299**			
Satisfaction with Complaint deal	Between Groups	27.664	3	9.221	.930	.427
	Within Groups	2934.933	296	9.915		
	Total	**2962.597**	**299**			

Source: Primary data.

If we consider the standard deviation, customers with 20–30 years of bank relationship standard deviation values are least in bank physical facilities, services of the bank and technological services of the bank. So customers with 20–30 years relationship with bank are more satisfied with bank physical facilities, services of the bank and technological services of the bank. The standard deviation value of customers with 1–10 years relationship with bank are least in customers' agreed statement, improvement in opening an account and satisfaction with complaint deal. So customers with 1-10 years relationship with bank are more satisfied in customer agreed statement, improvement in opening an account, and satisfaction with complaint deal.

The above table explains the f-values of the variables Bank Physical Facilities, Services of the bank, Technological Services of Banks, Customers agreed statement, Improvement in opening an account and Satisfaction with Complaint deal of the above five different levels of customers depending on the length of relation with the banker are 0.261, 4.804, 2.669, 1.528, 1.787 and 0.930 respectively. Among them, all the variables Services of the bank is significant at 0.01 level and the variable Technological Services of Banks is significant at 0.05 level. All the remaining variables are not significant. This shows that in general and technical services of the bank the senior customers are enjoying more benefits than the junior customers.

If we consider the mean values (Table 7.44), the mean score values of customers' having saving bank account are high in bank physical facilities, technological services of the bank and improvement in opening an account. So saving bank account customers are minimum satisfied with bank physical facilities, technological services of the bank and improvement in opening an account.

Current account customers' mean values are high in the services of the bank and satisfaction with compliant deal. So current account customers are maximum satisfied in the services of the bank, and satisfaction with compliant deal. As loan account customers mean score value are high in customer agreed statement, loan account customer are more satisfied in bank customers' agreed statements.

Table 7.44: Type of Account-wise Distribution of Mean Scores of Customers on Different Aspects Regarding Customer Satisfactory Levels

Sl. No.		Type of Account	N	Mean	Std. Deviation	Std. Error	Min	Max
1.	Bank Physical Facilities	SB A/c	220	21.19	5.63	.38	8	35
		Current A/c	46	20.74	4.17	.61	13	31
		Loan A/c	34	19.94	3.70	.63	15	26
		Total	**300**	**20.98**	**5.24**	**.30**	**8**	**35**
2.	Services of the bank	SB A/c	220	14.60	5.97	.40	0	25
		Current A/c	46	17.22	7.60	1.12	0	59
		Loan A/C	34	15.38	3.22	.55	11	21
		Total	**300**	**15.09**	**6.06**	**.35**	**0**	**59**
3.	Technological Services of Banks	SB A/c	220	5.82	7.04	.47	0	26
		Current A/c	46	3.80	4.69	.69	0	20
		Loan A/c	34	.62	2.85	.49	0	16
		Total	**300**	**4.92**	**6.59**	**.38**	**0**	**26**
4.	Customers agreed statement	SB A/c	220	13.97	3.35	.23	4	33
		Current A/c	46	12.98	3.15	.46	0	18
		Loan A/c	34	14.21	1.95	.33	9	18
		Total	**300**	**13.84**	**3.20**	**.18**	**0**	**33**
5.	Improvement in opening an account	SB A/c	220	8.94	2.45	.17	4	15
		Current A/c	46	8.89	2.72	.40	5	15
		Loan A/c	34	7.47	1.48	.25	4	10
		Total	**300**	**8.76**	**2.44**	**.14**	**4**	**15**
6.	Satisfaction with Complaint deal	SB A/C	220	5.29	3.10	.21	0	13
		Current A/C	46	7.02	3.10	.46	1	14
		Loan A/C	34	5.12	3.02	.52	1	10
		Total	**300**	**5.54**	**3.15**	**.18**	**0**	**14**

Source: Primary data.

If we consider the standard deviation, the loan account customers' standard deviation values are least in all banks in providing facilities. So loan account customers are more satisfied in all the banks in providing facilities.

Table 7.45: Anova of the Scores of Customer Satisfactory Aspects Classified According to Type of Account of Customers

		Sum of Squares	df	Mean Square	F	Sig.
Bank Physical Facilities	Between Groups	48.726	2	24.363	.885	.414
	Within Groups	8174.111	297	27.522		
	Total	**8222.837**	**299**			
Services of the bank	Between Groups	264.896	2	132.448	3.665	.027
	Within Groups	10732.851	297	36.138		
	Total	**10997.747**	**299**			
Technological Services of Banks	Between Groups	865.882	2	432.941	10.608	.000
	Within Groups	12121.355	297	40.813		
	Total	**12987.237**	**299**			
Customers agreed statement	Between Groups	42.322	2	21.161	2.079	.127
	Within Groups	3023.314	297	10.180		
	Total	**3065.637**	**299**			
Improvement in opening an account	Between Groups	64.160	2	32.080	5.546	.004
	Within Groups	1718.036	297	5.785		
	Total	**1782.197**	**299**			
Satisfaction with Complaint deal	Between Groups	120.707	2	60.354	6.307	.002
	Within Groups	2841.889	297	9.569		
	Total	**2962.597**	**299**			

Source: Primary data.

The above table explains the f-values of the variables Bank Physical Facilities, Services of the bank, Technological Services of Banks, Customers agreed statement, Improvement in opening an account and Satisfaction with Complaint deal of the above three different types of account holder customers of the bank are 0.885, 3.665, 10.608, 2.079, 5.546 and 6.307 respectively. Among them Technological Services of Banks, Improvement in opening an account and Satisfaction with

Complaint deal variables are significant at 0.01 level, services of the bank variable are significant at 0.05 level and Services of Banks and customers agreed statement are not significant. This shows that in general in all the variables the current account holders get more services than the other customers and the mean performance also more the same customers.

CHAPTER

Summary of Findings, Conclusion and Suggestions

Banking is a service-oriented industry. Its survival depends on its ability to provide sustainable service to its customers. This function of banking system is at micro-level. At the macro-level, banking system contributes immediately to economic development. The present study postulates that the expansion and utility of banking system in the Indian economy depends on the banker-customer relationship. Its existence is due to its quality of service to the society. The survival and growth of a bank depend not only on its size of fund but also on its ability to provide qualitative services to its customers on a sustainable basis. In order to compete, the bankers need to understand the various needs of different customers so as to provide customised services, which will not only satisfy the customers but also enlighten them.

Banking sector is basically a service sector in the present day competitive service sector. The Customer plays a very significant role in achieving the objectives of business. The banking sector always displays a statement on customer relationship in every branch of the Bank. In this context, it is appropriate to quote Mahatma Gandhi who stated that, *"Customer is the most important person ever in this office- in person or by mail. A customer is not dependent on us. We are dependent on him. A customer is not an interruption of our work ... he is the purpose of it. We are not doing a favour by serving him ... he is doing us a favour by giving us the opportunity to do so. A Customer is not someone to argue or match wits with. Nobody ever won an argument with a customer. A customer is a person who brings us his wants. It is our job to handle them profitability to him and to ourselves."*

This statement indicates the importance of Customer relationship in the banking sector. The service sector today is emphasising the importance of People, Process and Physical evidence to impress upon the customer and build relationship through these three P's. Hence, the present study (aims at the study of Banker-Customer relationship in both public and private sector banks).

In view of the significance of the banking sector, an attempt has been made to examine some major developments, particularly in terms of technology up gradations and banker-customer relationship. The study makes an earnest attempt to seek answers to the following issues:

The perception of the customers as to the services provided to them by the banks under the study *vis-a-vis* the perception of bankers as to their customers whose transactions with their banks are deemed significant.

The problems faced by the customers and bankers in relation to each other in the context of providing services are dealt with and analysed.

The study considered the fact that customer retention has been one of the cost-effective mechanisms for revenue and profitability growth vis-à-vis new customer acquisition.

The foremost contention of the thesis as stated in the introductory chapter is that there is a large database of knowledge about existing customers, which is seldom effectively used by banks and other financial institutions. For example, apart from demographic profile, personal and family income details and a host of other background information influence banks. Similarly, the second contention of the thesis proceeded on the assumption that the real-time customer segmentation is a key benefit provided by Customer Relationship

The focus of the study has been on banker-customer relations and customer banker relations. Chapter-VI is devoted to banker customer relations while Chapter-VII is devoted to customer-banker relations. The opinions of bank officers and customers as to customer service provided by the banks under the study have been collected and analysed.

Need of the Study

From the survey of literature, it is evident that there are very few studies with their direct focus on customer-banker relationship. The research on Banker-Customer relationship in the changing scenario is inevitable as is suggested from the recent studies reviewed so far. There are no doubt umpteen studies on banking sector, but they have focused little on the relationship aspect between the banks and the customers. Hence a need was felt to study the attitudes of the customers of banks and the bankers as well.

In fact, there is abundant literature on banking sector. The study has made use of the relevant literature. A review of literature has been made from the context of policy, performance, customer orientation and service, social responsibility and banking concerns. From the survey of the relevant literature, it is evident that there is need to study the customer and banker relationship from specific banks' point of view and from the viewpoint of the attitude of customers towards the specific banks under study. The purpose of the study as has been stated is to fill the gap at micro-level study in the customer-banker relationship, and to identify the problems faced by both the customers and bankers point of view. For this purpose, the study has taken into account the banks such as the State Bank of India, the Andhra Bank, the ING Vysya Bank Ltd., and the ICICI Bank Ltd., in Coastal Andhra. The study is primarily empirical, though secondary data on banks have been extensively used for the purpose of theory.

Based on the secondary data, an attempt has been made to identify and analyse the changing trends in banking sector in India.

Objectives of the Study

The main objective of the study is to study the relationship between the banks and their customers. The study has aimed at analysing the service rendered by the select banks, the relations maintained by the banks with their customers and identifying the degree of satisfaction among customers.

The detailed objectives of the research study are:

1. To understand various services provided by the selected banks under the study to society in general and to their customers in particular.
2. To examine the nature and scope of relationship between the banks and customers in the light of changing competitive scenario in the banking sector.
3. To elicit the opinions of bankers on customer requirements, customer services, customer care, and customer satisfaction.
4. To examine the feelings of customers on the services received from their respective banks.
5. To highlight the challenges and problems faced by both the bankers and the customers in the light of the changing scenario in the banking sector and thereby.
6. To suggest suitable strategies and measures that would help to build up a strong relationship between the bankers and the customers.

Hypotheses

The study has examined the following hypotheses:

- The relationship between banker and customer is being affected during the post reform period, because of various developments, changes and challenges that have taken place in the banking sector in the recent past.

- There has been a significant change in the banker and customer relationship in the select districts in the recent past i.e., after reforms were introduced.
- There has been no significant difference in the views of customers and Bank officers of both Public and Private sector banks in the districts.

In order to test the Hypotheses, one hundred eighty Bankers and three hundred Customers are taken as sample for the present study at random basis. The primary data are collected with the help of a structured schedule through personal interviews, observations and discussions with bank officers concerned and bank customers. The schedule was administered to different categories of customers like Agricultural, Self Help Groups, Business Customers, Small scale industries and other customers (Household, salaried employees, educational loan holders etc.). Apart from this information, the researcher has verified Annual reports, Booklets, Periodically publications of all the four Banks to get information about the profile of the Banks under study.

Data Analysis

The acquired data have been subjected to simple statistical treatment and presented in the form of cross tables. The interpretations of tables (SPSS package has used for tabulation) are given under each table with Chi-square values. The succeeding chapters of the study contain the tabulations of data with f-test (ANOVA) and t-test analysis and their interpretation was constructed below the tables percentages are also calculated at appropriate places.

Findings and Conclusions

1. The study shows that despite six decades of economic planning, India continues to exhibit the basic characteristics of an underdeveloped country. Its central problem is mass poverty indicated by a low level of per capita income. An underdeveloped economy can have good potential prospects for using material and human resources towards achieving

a higher rate of economic growth in terms of per capita income. The economy also exhibits lack of suitable economic organisation, which is necessary for adequate capital formation. Landlords, moneylenders, and indigenous bankers have acted as blood suckers and appropriated a major share of production (which was spent an extravagance). Consequently, the significance of a better financial institutional infrastructure of credit is felt necessary.

2. The study makes it clear that the Indian money market has both the organised and unorganised sectors. The organised sector comprises formal financial institutions while the unorganised sector comprises moneylenders. Before the emergence of banking sector in India, most of the rural population depended heavily on moneylenders to meet their needs including agricultural activities. The agricultural farmers, a majority segment of the rural population used to fall in the debt traps of moneylenders. As they are proverbially described as helpless and helpless farmers born in debt grown in debt and dead in debt. This has made the government recognise the significance of the role of banks in the as saviours and samaritans.

3. In the system of banks, credit occupies a significant place. Bank credit has a dynamic role to play for the development of consumers, may be small – farmers or entrepreneurs of small-scale enterprises. In the organised sector, the commercial banks are the oldest institutions. They have a wide network of branches attracting public confidence in the form of deposits, savings and other schemes in urban areas in particular.

Thus, the banking system in India is credit based and savings oriented. It undoubtedly contributes to increase the pace of economic development. Therefore, the study underlined the contribution of banking sector towards the process of economic development.

4. It is an established fact that the development of financial infrastructure is an important aspect of economic development. The growth of commercial banks signifies the

development of financial infrastructure. The analysis shows that the commercial banks provide both 'saving intermediation' and 'money-market intermediations'. Further, banks play pivotal role as intermediaries by bridging the gap between savings and investments through capital formations. These banks also provide for entrepreneurial development, stabilising the price mechanisms, and activation of government for economic development. Thus, banks play different roles in the transformation of the development process.

5. The study established that over a period of time one could witness the conversion of class banking into mass-banking. The present study, which has been initiated by the researcher in this context, emphasises the banker-customer relations in two public sector banks – State Bank of India and Andhra Bank, and two corporate sector banks – ICICI and ING Vysya Bank. Mass-banking has ups and downs, because of recovery problems,

6. A review of the trends in banking in India shows that significantly one can notice their changing trends in the growth of banking sector in India. The reference has been made to the pre-nationalisation, post-nationalisation and post-reform periods. In the pre-nationalisation period the study established that the formal commercial banking in India could be traced back to the 18th century. The banks acted as bankers to government under the British Government during 1770-1862. The most significant development during this period was the establishment of the Reserve Bank of India as a central bank of the country. By the time, India got Independence, there were 640 banks of which 96 were scheduled banks as seen from the study. The banking sector was in favour of industry and trading sectors confining its operations to metropolitan areas.

7. The Banking Companies Act, 1949 changed the structural and functional aspects of the banking sector, as ascertained by the study. There are regulations of banking sector to protect the interests of depositors. Another

significant change was that banks were involved in the development of rural India. During the First Five Year Plan period, the State Bank of India was established. This marked emergence of State – controlled banking system in India.

8. The second period witnessed social control of bank credit with the nationalisation of banks in India in 1969. Since then, one can witness a sea change in the Indian banking system. However by 1980s, the operational efficiency of banks in India showed a downtrend. The quality of customer service did not keep pace with the increasing expectations. This paved the way for further nationalisation of banking sector in 1980s. The study shows that this governmental effort raised the public sector banks share of deposits from 86 per cent in 1969 to 92 per cent in 1980. The study also analysed the post-nationalisation trends. It shows that the banks achieved remarkable progress during the post-reform period. The study also focused on the financing role of banks in India in agricultural, industry, education and exports and the changes that took place in banking industry in India. This shows how there has been a gradual shift from national banking to universal banking.

9. The central concern of this thesis on the customer-banker relationship. Therefore, an attempt has been made to analyse the essential requisites of a customer and the general relationship between the bankers and the customers under the study. In fact, a banker renders a number of services to his customers. The primary relationship between a banker and a customer is that of a creditor and debtor.

10. The study attempts to present profiles of banks under study. The study has covered the State Bank of India, the Andhra Bank, the ING Vysya Bank Ltd., and the ICICI Bank Ltd., The State Bank of India is the earliest of all the banks in India. The Imperial Bank was transformed into the State Bank of India based on the recommendations of the All India Rural Credit Survey Committee (Gorwala Committee). It was established with the objective of taking banking to the interior and remote parts of India. Its

corporate centre is in Mumbai. It has 14 local Head Offices and 57 Zonal Offices. It has the corporate accounts group to meet the needs of top corporate. Besides, the bank has 52 foreign offices in 34 countries across the global.

11. The ICICI Bank in India is the second largest bank, which is under the corporate sector. It was originally promoted in 1994 by ICICI Limited. It has a network of 614 branches and extension counters and over 2,200 ATMs. It offers a wide range of banking products and financial services to corporate and retail customers. It has an inter-cross boarder need of its clients. The Bank disseminates information on its operations and initiatives on a regular basis, and thus maintains customer relations. In October 2001, the Boards of Directors of ICICI and ICICI bank approved the merger of ICICI and its retail finance subsidiaries, ICICI personal financial services limited and ICICI capital service limited, with ICICI Bank. The merger was approved of shareholders of ICICI and ICICI Bank in January 2002.

12. Regarding customer relations of ICICI Bank, it is understood that the Bank disseminates information on its operations and initiatives on a regular basis. The Bank has investor relations' personnel. These personnel play a proactive role in disseminating information to analysts and investors as well. The Banks' focus on customer relations is a beacon to other public sector banks. The bank today is a technology and retail-banking leader as revealed from the study.

13. Another Bank under the study is the Andhra Bank. The Andhra Bank was founded by Dr. Bhogaraju Pattabhi Sitaramayya. It was registered and subsequently commenced business in 1923 with a paid up capital of Rs 1.00 lakhs and an authorised capital of Rs.10.00 lakhs. The bank has grown up in tune with the needs of the society. The bank is rendering service under the public sector through a wide network comprising 1811 business delivery channels covering 21 States and 2 Union Territories.

14. Regarding customer relations, the Andhra Bank attempts to provide value added services. To provide these,

the bank has set up its own 425 ATMs (2006) and ATM sharing arrangements with several banks like SBI, ICICI, IDBI and UTI. Indian Bank, HFDC and so on. The study reveals that Andhra Bank is credited with being a pioneer in introducing credit cards as early as 1981. It has been promoting banking in Gulf countries.

15. The ING Vysya Bank under study is an entity formed combining the erstwhile Vysya Bank Ltd., and ING of Dutch Origin in 2002. It has gained recognition for its integrated approach of banking insurance and asset management in the corporate sector. It has established life insurance companies across the nations. It has become a global financial services giant with an asset base of 1159 billions Euros with a net profit of 7.21 billions euros by the end of 2011 March.

16. The study as to the perceptions of the bank officers shows that the banks under study have been competing with one another in meeting the needs of all sections of people with emphasis on regional, national and international banking, however, with their primary focus on customer relations for their survival. The study is distinct as it attempts an 'opinion survey' on customer service to elicit perceptions of the customers and the bankers as well under study.

17. The opinion survey on the customer service of the banks through bank officers who constitute the respondents under study reveals the following aspects.

The bank-wise classification of respondents on the basis of age reveals that a large majority of respondents in SBI, AB and ING Vysya Bank represent the 40–50 age group while the ICICI bank has the largest percentage (75.6%) in the age group of 20–30 years. This may be due to the latest origin of the bank followed by another bank of recent origin ING Vysya with 22.2 per cent of employees in the age group 20–30 years.

Sex-wise details reveal that in all the banks under study, the males dominate. Even then ICICI bank represents the highest per cent (35.6%) of females followed by ING Vysya 13.3 per cent.

Regarding educational qualifications also, the ICICI bank has the largest number of post-graduates (68.9%) followed by ING Vysya with 56.6 per cent. The Public sector banks have on the other hand been dominated by the graduates i.e., 62.2 per cent in the case of SBI and 66.7 per cent in the case of Andhra Bank. The bank-wise analysis as to education shows that there is more number of post-graduates in private sector banks when compared to public sector banks.

The study indicates that of all the banks under study the old generation public sector banks have greater number of aged officers when compared to new generation private banks.

18. The study shows that the participation of female respondents is comparatively better in ICICI bank and it indicates that new generation private banks are employing comparatively good number of female employees in their banks.

19. Respondents on the basis of experience show that in all the banks under the study, the highest percentage of respondents with 20–30 years of experience are found in all the banks. Similarly non-locals dominates the banks.

20. The analysis across banks relating to reasons for opening their accounts revealed that convenient location is the first important factor in case of State Bank India, Andhra Bank and ING Vysya banks but this is secondary in case of ICICI as staff attitude is primary reason for opening an account in this case.

21. With regard to problems faced as to opening account, the study reveals that in the case of the ICICI Bank, ING Vysya Bank, Andhra Bank and State Bank of India, majority of the respondents did not have any problems. In the case of Andhra Bank and State Bank of India, the respondents expressed difficulties in observing procedures. In the case of Andhra Bank and ING Vysya bank, some of the respondents faced difficulties like insistence on early completion. In the case of ING Vysya bank, State Bank of India, Andhra Bank,

some of the respondents faced difficulties like introduction of customers (KYC).

22. Regarding the procedure for opening an account, a majority of the customers felt that the procedures are simplified. The impact of computerisation on opening bank account has been measured. The largest number of respondents in all the banks under study pointed out the positive impact of computerisation. The positive response is highest in ICICI and ING Vysya banks, while it is found to be higher in the case of SBI and AB.

23. That the customers cause inconvenience now and then to the bank officials is an established fact as revealed in this study. They constitute nearly 20 per cent. The punctuality of opening counters is much higher in the private sector banks (ICICI and ING Vysya) when compared to the public sector banks. Similarly, counter are kept open for extra time in the private banks for the benefit of customers when compared to the public sector banks.

24. Bank-wise physical facilities are also rated higher in the private sector in such spheres as the availability of vouchers, enquiry and assistance, seating arrangements, space for moving, interior decoration, air-conditioning and even in respect of drinking water, the rating is higher in the ICICI and ING Vysya banks. These will have their bearing on customer satisfaction also.

25. In collecting deposits and in the case of withdrawals the problems faced by the public sector banks are greater. The positive impact of computerisation on reduction of workload is higher in ING Vysya Bank, but equal in ICICI Bank and SBI. Nevertheless, respondents believe that to a large extent there is reduction of workload after computerisation.

26. Regarding the problems faced by Bank Officers in cheque transactions, the study makes it clear that the percentage of problems is higher with regard to customers who do not follow procedures and issue cheques without sufficient balance in SBI and AB when compared to ING

Vysya and ICICI Banks. Job simplification after the introduction of ATMs has been felt varyingly in the banks under the study.

27. Providing loans to customers is an important aspect of customer-banker relations. The variables identified by the study are Crop loan, loan for SSI, Business loans, Personal loans and educational loans. The percentage of crop loans provided by ICICI & ING Vysya is higher when compared to public sector banks. The percentage of loans provided to SSI is higher in ING, SBI and AB when compared to ICICI. The percentage of business loans is higher in ING Vysya and SBI. The percentage of personal loans is higher in ICICI and SBI.

28. Regarding educational loans, the percentage of public sector banks is almost doubled when compared to the private sector banks. Thus, we find a mixed trend with regard to bank loans provided to customers. The banks experience it convenience to sanction personal and retail loans. Political pressure is less in sanctioning loans in all the banks as revealed from the study. It can be deduced that the banks to a large extent are insulated from political pressures.

29. The banks offer a wide variety of services as part of customer–banker relations. The services provided include debit cards, on line banking, Inter-net banking, ATMs, Electronic fund transfers, Travel cards and Credit cards. All these services are offered by these banks with regard to debit cards, on line banking, and ATMs. The percentage of services offered by AB and ING Vysya is higher. Similarly the services used by the customers are rated higher. The customers are not paying regularly on credit cards. The percentage of non-payment on regular basis is higher in Andhra Bank and ICICI banks'. Customers often complained loss of cards. The percentage is higher in SBI and ING Vysya. This is a hurdle in customer-banker relations.

30. The study also shows that the banks have not given priority to drinking water and to seating arrangements as part of their infrastructure facilities. Through Air

conditioning, interior decoration and space for moving have been provided currency, the focus should be primarily on seating arrangements and drinking water facilities.

31. Employee perception as to their job, customers and policies of the Government and the organisation in which they work has been studied as these factors play a very important role in promoting or undermining customer-banker relations. The study identified that the insecurity feeling of employees in the case of the corporate bank ING Vysya and also Andhra Bank in the public sector is high and almost identical.

The employees in all the banks under study have been feeling pressure of the customers. When compared to customer pressure, there is pressure from government side and the organisational side, but the pressure is less. The study however shows that the customer pressure and the pressure for meeting managements target achievements are identical in the case of all banks under study. The application of statistical tools establishes the facts.

32. The focus of the study is on customer banker relationship. Therefore, opinion survey based on the responses of 300 customers with the help of a schedule has been conducted. Occupational significance made the researcher take into account equal number of respondents from small scale industries, micro creditors, business, farmers and others each constituting 20 per cent because each occupational category influences the customer banker relations in its own way. This has been done for the convenience of the study as stated earlier.

33. First of all, the socio-economic aspects of the customers under study reveal that the potential age groups of the customers that transact with the banks are 20-30 years to 50-60 years with productive sources of income. Sex-wise analysis shows that though females constitute approximately 50 per cent of the population, their interaction with the banks constitutes nearly 30 per cent. The reasons are that most of the females are housewives with less productive work.

Income-wise analysis shows that, the customer–banker relationship effort should focus on the income levels that range between <Rs.50,000 and Rs.1,50,000 as indicated from the study.

34. The study shows that the relationship between the customers and bankers is dependent on a number of factors such as opening of accounts, cash deposits, withdrawal of cash, issue of cheques books, issue of loans, recovery of loans, interest rates, debit credit card services, technology based facilities like ATM cards etc., provision for complaints, mutual interactions, and customer satisfaction.

35. The study focused on the reasons for opening the account. The parameters identified for this purpose include convenient location of the bank, timings of the branch, image of the branch, regional affinity, image of bank, number of branches, staff attitude, systems and procedures, and commercial affinity.

On the whole, the study showed that convenient location and image of the bank are the two dominant factors for opening of an account by the customers in the bank.

As to satisfaction of opening an account, the study reveals that the majority of respondents of ING Vysya and ICICI have mixed reaction. The respondents of ICICI have 'Average' satisfaction level. In the case of customers belonging to ING Vysya, the satisfaction level is 'Much' when compared to other banks. As to the problems faced with regard to opening an account, the study reveals that in the case of the State Bank of India, the ICICI Bank and the Andhra Bank, majority of the respondents did not encounter any problem. Some of the respondents of ING Vysya Bank expressed major difficulties such as introduction and the respondents of State Bank of India and Andhra Bank, faced complicated procedures more than 20 mts to open the account.

36. Regarding deposits of cash, majority of respondents felt that the banks insist on higher denomination and soiled notes are not accepted. Slow operations of staff are the major

problems, as stated by the majority of the respondents of all banks.

There is improvement in deposit related transaction in the two corporate banks when compared to the public sector banks. Almost all the banks are clearing the withdrawals before 20 minutes of time in most of the cases. Nevertheless, inconvenience is caused to the customers in withdrawal transactions on the whole as pointed by the customers as the total percentage is as high as 80 per cent.

37. Regarding ATMs, the study reveals that, 'required denomination is not available' in the ATMs. Further, ATMs are 'not located at important centres' and non–functioning of ATMs, 'soiled/fake notes through the ATMs', 'cash is not available' at times in spite of computerisation of the banking system are some other problems faced by the customers which need to be rectified.

38. With the operation of central computers, it is now possible to access the entire chain of accounts for a customer. India has made to the first transition from physical cash to "anytime money and anywhere money". Technology has now become 'market differentiated' and is clearly used as a competitive edge. As a result, a number of related services such as debit card, online banking, electronic fund transfer, travel cards, and credit card.

39. The study reveals that all the customers are utilising the technology-based services like debit card, online banking, Internet banking, electronic fund transfer, travel cards, and credit card. Curiously there is no single negative answer.

40. The study shows that there are variations causing inconvenience to customers, which may undermine the morale of the customers. The ING Vysya and ICICI banks are not offering the working capital for small scale Industries and Self Help Group loans. These two banks are providing Business and Personal loans. The other two banks are giving loans for the purpose of Crop and Self Help Group in the study area.

41. The analysis across sample banks reveals that in the case of majority of respondents of SBI and AB, it took 2 to 3 weeks, while in case of ING Vysya and ICICI, it took less than 2 weeks for sanction of loan. Insistence on heavy documentation has been seen as a major problem in this regard. Added to this, the customers expressed the view that high interest charges have been levied on loan services. The analysis across individual banks also reveals a similar trend. The derivation is the banks, in terms of mutual interaction have been lagging behind, as the percentages of responses are identical in positive as well as negative responses.

The study further shows that there is delay in transactions and it is a major cause that affects the customer-banker relations. With regard to physical facilities like availability of vouchers, enquiry and assistance, seating arrangement, space for queuing, air conditioning water coolers and parking place that come under infrastructure facilities available with the banks the responses are satisfactory. Modern banking institutions have been paying much attention to the physical facilities in the context of the evolving corporate culture.

Suggestions

1. In the transformation of economy, banks have to assert their role positively. For this purpose, banks have to focus on customers and make them free from the clutches of landlords and moneylenders by encouraging all types of customers to approach the banks. This also requires a further policy shift.
2. To make the statement that 'the farmers' born in debt grow in debt and die in debt unreal, the government has recognised the significance of banks and their role in poverty eradication. Therefore, banks need to enhance their role of social responsibility by meeting the needs of rural customers like farmers'.
3. The significant place of banks is commendable in the development of customers. However, banks should

focus their attention on rural areas to make their role more dynamic in the context of rural development.

4. Though there is a significant development of financial infrastructure, the banks in the public and private sector should expand the infrastructure facilities to the nook and corner of the country.
5. Though there is conversion of banking sector from class – banking to mass-banking, mass-banking has its limitations such as collateral security and the problems of recovery. For this, it is suggested that the Reserve Bank of India and NABARD need to initiate measures for strengthening the methods of collateral security.
6. The banking sector is at present focusing on industry and trading sectors, confining its operations to metropolitan cities. This study suggests the need for the banks to focus on extending banking activity to non-metropolitan and semi-urban areas. There is also a need for extension of banking activity.
7. The emergence of state – controlled banking system in India no doubt provided for protecting the interests of the depositors. But some banks in the private sector like Krishi Bank, Prudential Banks etc., have to take up effective measures and proper controls to protect the interests of the depositors.
8. By 1980s, the operational efficiency of the banks decreased. Fortunately, the post-nationalisation of banking sector, further, (after 1968) achieved remarkable progress. This resulted a shift from national–banking to universal banking. This suggests the need for reforms in improving the operational efficiency of public banking sector.
9. The utility of banking system depends on Banker-Customer relationship. Therefore, banks need to provide qualitative services to its customers.

10. To achieve its objectives, the State Bank of India has to put in concerted efforts to take the banking activities to remote and interior parts of India. For this, the State Bank of India still has to extend its extension counters.
11. Though the ICICI Bank officers a wide range of services to corporate and retail customers, the emphasis of the bank is on service sector only. Therefore, it is suggested that the ICICI Bank has to cover the primary sector with emphasis on agriculture and Micro credit.
12. The ICICI bank has to focus on the mass–banking concept besides its emphasis on technology and retail banking.
13. There are 28 States and 7 Union Territories in India. The Andhra Bank is covering only 21 States at present. It is suggested that there is large scope for the Andhra Bank in the remaining seven States and 5 Union Territories to carry on its banking operations.
14. As a pioneer in the introduction of ATMs, the Andhra Bank could provide more ATM service counters for the benefit of the bank and its customers.
15. The ING Vysya Bank can make introduce in the Indian Banking scene, it progresses in the retail counters. It is, therefore, suggested that the ING Vysya Bank has to operate greater number of branches in the coastal districts to attract customers.
16. The bank employees have been positive in perception with regard to their banks. This attitude is to be maintained for longer periods. For this, it is suggested that the banks have to conduct attitudinal surveys to know the perceptions of their employees always.
17. The Public sector banks need to attract the youth in the age group of 20-30 years to make their organisations young, energetic and dynamic. At the same time, all the banks are neglecting women, who

account for approximately 50 per cent of the total population. They need to reorient their policy of recruitment to attract women.

18. It is suggested that the other banks under the study like the ING Vysya Bank, State bank of India and Andhra Bank have to employ good number of female employees like the ICICI. All Banks, however, have to focus on this issue to attract female customers.
19. The Banks are flooded with middle and old age people. It is suggested that the banks need to attract young talented person with software background for speedy disposal of bank transactions.
20. The Banks for their focus on Customer relations need to locate their branches at convenient and accessible locations. This would help the customers to operate their accounts comfortably.
21. Attitude training to the bank staff at all levels is the need of the hour to improve customer-banker relations.
22. Regarding customer mobility, the bank should focus on productive income groups. Further, women potential is to be tapped by the banks, as the mobility of women is only 30 per cent at present. The banks need to provide required denominations to the customers through ATMs.
23. The Bank officers are feeling not only customer pressure and but also pressure in meeting the targets set by the management. The respective banks whether in public or private sector, should focus on enlightened Human Resources Management practices. Dress code maintenance, as in the case of ICICI and ING Vysya by the public sector banks, would enhance the morale of the workforce.
24. The bankers need to make use of the services of the gold checking machines instead of getting the gold loans appraised by the appraisers so as to improve customer belief and cost effectiveness.

25. In collecting deposits and in case of withdrawals, the public sector banks have to modify the procedures to avoid facing adverse banker–customer relationship.
26. Regarding customers who do not follow procedures and issue cheques without proper balance, it is suggested that the bank should exhibit placards at strategic locations so as to enlight the customer with the consequences of such practices.
27. To avoid hurdles in customer–banker relations, customers are to be pursued at regular intervals to repay the amounts on loans and credit cards and for this open houses need to be conducted.
28. Regarding educational loans, it is suggested that the banks, in particular the ICICI and ING Vysya Banks have to introduce new schemes as these would result in profits in the current software employment boom.
29. To avoid facing hurdles in customer–banker relations with regard to irregular payments on credit cards and complaints on loss of cards, it is suggested that the personal banking divisions need to be strengthened.
30. The public sector banks have to provide physical facilities on par with those of private sector banks.
31. To avoid the sense of 'insecurity' on the part of employees, the banks are suggested that they should take appropriate measures to boost up the morale of their employees through occasional counselling.
32. The banking sector was in favour of metropolitan cities, focusing rather highly on trade and industry. For its survival, it should keenly focus further on customers in semi–urban and rural areas which approximates to 72 per cent of the entire country's population.
33. Banks should focus on their potential customers in the age groups of 20–30 years and 50–60 years by keeping in constant touch with them through information and communication technology.

34. Banks need to carefully understand the different needs of customers and focus on them to satisfy the customers.
35. The private sector and the so-called corporate banks have been making headway when compared to the public sector banks like the State Bank of India and Andhra Bank. These public sector banks also must involve in fair competition with private sector banks like ICICI and ING Vysya Banks in terms of effectively reaching customers.
36. In depositing cash, banks have to find out the means for speedy disposal of customers through simplification of procedures.
37. ATM centres need to be established in the rural centres as these areas are potential centres of bank transactions.
38. The public sector banks have to find out means and ways to simplify the procedures as simplification of procedures by private sector banks are attracting greater number of customers (Similarly, the procedures for introduction for opening accounts need the attention of all banks). Regarding cheques transactions, it is suggested that the banks need to arrange for cheques and demand draft collections through collection boxes at ATM and other Institutions of reputation. The procedure for cheques collections by filling the details can be avoided to save time to the customer and cost to the banker.
39. Banks must have a clear procedure for maintaining punctuality in opening counters so to avoid causing inconvenience to customers, and the customers are to be enlightened as to the same.
40. Regarding sanction of loans, customers should not experience inconvenience. This definitely undermines the morale of the customers in relation to Banks. Banks have to initiate measures to provide working

loans to small-scale industries and self help groups as per the guidelines of the SIDBI, Reserve Bank of India and NABARD.

41. With regard to sanction of loans, it is also suggested that the documentation procedures are to be simplified and the time for examination of documents should be reduced to a maximum span of one week.
42. Now-a-days, the corporate sectors are promoting basic educational and health facilities as part of their social responsibility programmes. The software companies are an example in this respect. Therefore, it is suggested that the banking sector should also take up such responsibility, besides its profit-making activities, as it is a major service sector in the society.

Customer satisfaction is the primary objective of any business organisation. The current banking sector whether in public or private sector is not an exception. The present study makes it clear that the over all performance of the banks under the study comes to 71.33 per cent in the existing scenario. Banks have to exploit changing and widening markets and concentrate on a customer centric approach. An insight into the growth of banking sector reveals that bankers will have to face competitive forces in the coming years. Therefore, for their survival in the competitive market, banks should focus on customers, niche competitors and a new work force. In particular, banking business has to be customer centric for its survival. Market changes will pose growing challenges for conventional banks, particularly in the public sector. The solution lies in customer integration with banks by promoting effective e—banker-customer relations and satisfaction.

Bibliography

Books

Agarwal, B.P. "*Commercial Bank in India*", Classical Publishing Co., New Delhi, 1981.

Agarwal, O.P., Oberoi, S.P., Mallya, K.G., Ajay Balan, "*JAIIB-Work Book,* Paper-1: *Principles of Banking,* Paper-2: *Accounting & Finance for Bankers,* Paper-3: *Legal Aspects of Banking,* Taxmann Publications Private Limited, 2006.

Alice Amsden, "*Asia Next Giant*" *South Korea and Late Industrialisation,* Oxford University Press, New York, 1989.

Anand Chandavaarkar, "*Central Banking in Developing Countries*", St. Martin's Press, New York, 1996.

Arondekar, A.M., Agarwal, O.P., Onkar Nath, P.S., Khandelwal, "*Principles of Banking",* Macmillan India Limited, 2005.

Basu, K. "*Some Macro Economics of Indian Reform Experience*", "*Indians' Emerging Economy*", MIT Press, Cambridge, Massachusells, 2004.

Basu, K. and Jindak (eds.), "*Microfinance - Emerging Challenges*", Tata McGraw Hill Publishing Company, New Delhi, 2002.

Basu, S.K., "*Commercial Banks and Agricultural Credit - A Study in Regional Disparity in India,* Allied Publishers (P) Ltd., Bombay, 1979.

Birla Institute of Scientific Research, "*Banks since Nationalisation*", Allied Publishers Pvt. Ltd., New Delhi, dt.1-9-1981, pp.58-62.

Cameron, R. "*Banking and Economic Development*", Some Lessons of History, Oxford University Press, New York, 1972.

Canals, J. "*Universal Banking–International Comparison and Theoretical Perspectives*", Oxford University Press, U.S., 1997.

Caruana, Jaime. "*Announcement of BESEL-II*", remarks at the Press Conference announcing the publication of Basel–II, 2004.

Chandgadkar, D.M., Deshpande, J.V., *"Technology, Risk Management & Supervision in Co-operative Banks"*, Macmillan India Limited, 2007.

Chandrasekhar, C.P. and Sujit Jumar Roy, "*Financial Sector Reforms and the Transformation of Banking*", Some implication for Indian development in V.K, Ramachandram and Madhura Swaminathasn (ed)., Agrarian Studies & Financial Liberalisation and Rural Credit in India, Tulika Books, New Delhi, 2005.

Chavan, P. "*Banking Sector Liberalisation and the Growth and Regional Distribution of Rural Banking*" in Ramachandram and Swaminathan (eds.), *Financial Liberalisation and Rural Credit in India*, Tulika Books, New Delhi, 2005.

Chitra Andrade, "*Banking Products & Services*", 2nd edn., Taxmann Publications Private Limited, 2007.

Dale, Richard, "*International Banking De-regulation*", "*The Great Banking Experiment*" Black Well Publishers, London, 1992.

Di Vanna, Joseph, A. "*The Future of Retail Banking*", Palgrave Macmillan, New York, 2004.

Dreze, J. and Amartya Sen. "*Indian Economic Development and Social opportunity*", Oxford University Press, New Delhi, 1997.

Dutta, S.K., Prasad, P.S.R., Bhorkar, A.D., Bargir, S.D. "*Accounting & Finance for Bankers*", Macmillan India Limited, 2005.

Elmus Wicker, "*The Banking Panics of the Great Depression*", Cambridge University Press, 1996.

Gangadhar Khan, "*Nationalised Banking and Economic Development*", Vora & Co. Pub. Pvt. Ltd., Bombay, 1978, pp.138-158..

Gaurang Vasavada, Sharad Kumar, Upendra Rao, S., Satish Pai, "*General Bank Management*", Macmillan India Limited, 2005.

Ghosh, "*Reducing Rural Poverty and Accelerating Indian Economic Growth*", Salt Lake, Calcutta, India, 1992.

Gopal Saxena, "*Marketing in Commercial Banks: A Study of S.B.I.*", Unpublished Ph.D. Thesis, Manipur University, Manipur, 1992.

Gupta, C.B. "*Business Management for Bankers*", Sultan Chand & Sons, 2002.

Hayward, Peter, "*The Financial Sector – The Responsibilities of the Public Agencies*" in Charles Enoch, David Marston and Michacl Taylor, "*Building Strong Banks Through Survillance and Resolution*", IMF Publication, Washington, DC, 2002.

Home Loans (Know Your Banking-IV), Taxmann Publications Private Limited, 2007.

Indian Institution of Banking & Finance, "*Information System for Banks*", Taxmann Publication (P) Ltd., New Delhi, 2005.

Indian Institution of Banking & Finance, "*Legal Aspects of Banking Operations*", Macmillan, 2005.

Jadhav, Narendra, "*Evolution of Financial Markets in India*", *Monetary Policy, Financial Stability and Central Banking in India*, Macmillan India Limited, New Delhi, 2006

Jain, G.L. "*Principals of Banking*", Arvind Vivek Prakashan, Agra, 2005.

Kabra, K.N. and Suresh, R.R. "*Public Sector Banking*", Peoples' Publishing House, New Delhi, 1970.

Khandelwal, B.N. "*Exchange Banking in India*", Jhalani Publications, Delhi, 1965.

Khubchandani, B.S., "*Practice and Law of Banking*", Macmillan India Limited, 2000.

Kiran Chopra, "*Managing Profits, Profitability and Productivity in Public Sector Banking*" ABS publications, Jalandhar, 1987.

Kulkarni, P.R., "*Laws of Co-operative Banking*", Macmillan India Limited, 2007.

Lakshmi, B., Ahmed Mod, S.J., Gopal, P.V., Saha, A.K. "*Security in Electronic Banking*", 2nd edition, Macmillan India Limited, 2007.

Maheswari, S.N. & Paul, P.R. "*Banking Theory and Practice*", Kalyani Publishers, New Delhi, 1994.

Mathur, O.P. "*Public Sector Banks in India in Indian survey – A case study of S.B.I.*" Sterling Pub. Pvt. Ltd., New Delhi, 1978, pp. 128-132.

Mishkin, Frederic, S. "*The Next Great Globalisation: How Disadvantaged Nations Can Harness Their Financial Systems to Get Rich*", Princeton University Press, New Jersey, 2006.

Mithani, D.M. and Gordon, E. "*Banking and Financial System*", Himalaya Publication House, 2002.

Mohan Rao, P., Trilok Kumar Jain, "*Management of Banking and Financial Institutions*", Deep & Deep Publications Pvt. Ltd., New Delhi, 2002.

Nagaraj, "*Problems of Rural Artisans*", *Khadi Gramodyog*, May 1988, pp. 52-53.

Narayana, M.S. "*A Study of the Attitude of Customers*", An Unpublished M.Phil. Dissertation, submitted to Nagarjuna University, 1988, pp.208-209.

Nayyar, S.K., "*HRD in State Bank of India*", Vinsro Publications, New Delhi, 2000.

Pain, P.K., Pethe, P.M., "*International Banking Operations*", Macmillan India Limited, 2007.

Parandhikar, S.G. "*Banking in India*", Orient Longman, Delhi, 1975.

Parikh, Kirith, S. and Radhakrishna, R. (ed.), "*Indian Development Report 2004-05*", Oxford University Press, New Delhi, 2004.

Philip Kotler, "*Marketing Management*", 10th ed., Prentice Hall of India, New Delhi, 2000, p. 49.

Rajiv Upadhyaya, "*Management of Commercial Banks in India: Public Relations and Customer Services*, Deep & Deep Publications, New Delhi, 1985, p. 78.

Ramesh, "*Changing Role of Commercial Banks: A Study of Andhra Bank*", Ph.D. Thesis submitted to Nagarjuna University, 1989.

Rangarajan, C. "*Innovation in Banking: The Indian Experience impact on Deposits and Credit*, Oxford & IBH Publishers Co., New Delhi, pp.32-38.

Ravi Kumar Bhola. "*Financing Agricultural by Commercial Banks*", Report of the Seminar held in 1968, RBI Publications, Bombay, 1983.

Renu Sobti, "*Banking and Financial Services in India: Marketing Redefined by **2003***", New Century Publications, 4800/24, Bharat Ram Road, Ansari Road, Daryaganj, New Delhi, 2003.

Prasad, P.S.R., Saroja, S., Mallya, K.G., "*CAIIB-Work Book*", Paper-1: *Risk Management*, Paper-2: *Financial Management*, Paper-3: *General Bank Management*, Taxmann Publications Private Limited, 2006.

Ramesh, V., Kang, K.S., Singh, U.P., Jagannathan, P., Sudha Venkat Ram. "*Information Technology, Data Communications & Electronic Banking*, 2nd edition, Macmillan India Limited, 2007.

Ranganadha Chary, A.V. and Paul, R.R. "*Banking & Financial System*", Kalyani Publications, 2003.

Rangarajan, C. "*Innovations in Banking – The Indian Experiences: Impact on Deposits and Credit*", Oxford and IBH Publishing Co., New Delhi, 1982.

Rao, C.H.H. "Policy issues relating to Irrigation and Rural Credit In India", in G.S. Bhalla (ed.), Economic Liberalization and Indian Agriculture Institute for Studies in Industrial Development, New Delhi, 1994.

Reddy Y., Venugopal, "*Lecture on Economic and financial Lecturer on Economic and Financial Sector Reforms in India*", Oxford University Press, India, 2002.

Reddy, Y.V., "*Future of Rural Banking*", Prof. G. Ram Reddy Third Endowment Lecture in Hyderabad, 1996.

Ruma, R. "*Training Policy and Program in the State Bank of Hyderabad – An Evaluation Study*", Osmania University, Hyderabad, 1996.

Sanathnanakrishnan, S. "*Information System for Banks*", Taxmann Publications Private Limited, 2005.

Sawaikar, S.N. Madhwan, E., Trivedi, A.K., Ashok Kumar Gulla, "*Bank Financial Management*", Taxmann Publications Private Limited, 2004.

Sharma, B.P. "*The Role of Commercial Bank in Indians Developing Economy*", S. Chand & Co., (P) Ltd., New Delhi, 1974.

Sharma, Harish, C. "*Nationalisation of Banks in India*", Sahitya Bhavan, Agra, 1970.

Shaw, E.S. "*Financial Developing in Economic Development*", Oxford Press, New York, 1973.

Shekar, K.C. & Shekar, Lekshmy. "*Banking Theory and Practice*", Vikas Publishing House Pvt. Ltd., New Delhi, 1998.

Sheth, N.J., Mittal, B. and Newman, J.B. "*Customer Behaviour–Consumer Behabiour*" New York, The Dryden Press, 1999.

Simha, S.L.M. (Ed.), "*Reforms of the Banking System*", Institute for Financial Management Research, 1973.

Simha, S.L.N. "*Fifth Years of Bretton Twins (IMF and World Banks)*", Institute for Financial for Management and Research, Chennai, India, 1996.

Singh, S. "*Performance Budgeting for Commercial Banks in India*", The Macmillan Co., of India Ltd., 1977.

Srinvasa Rao, K. "*Public Sector Banks in India and the Productivity Question*", Ashish Publishing House, New Delhi, 1989.

Srinvasan, R. "*Priority Sector Lending - A Study on Indian Experiment*, Himalaya Publishing House, 1995.

Srivastava, T.N., "An Introduction to Computers and Their Applications to Banking", MacMillan India Limited, 2000.

Subramanian, K. and Velayudham, T.K. "*Banking Reforms in India: Managing Change*", Tata McGraw Hill Publishing Co. Ltd., New Delhi, 1997.

Sudhir M. Joshi, Ashish Parthasarthy, Mundra, S.S., Vasant Godse. "*Theory and Practice of Treasury & Risk Management in Banks*", Taxmann Publications Private Limited, 2006.

Sundar, S. "*Anti-Money Laundering & Know Your Customer* (*Know Your Banking-III*)", Macmillan India Limited, 2006.

Sundharm, K.P.M. "*Money Banking–Trade and Finance*", Sultan Chand & Sons Publishers, New Delhi, 1998.

Suryakant, B. "*The Indian Banking*", Palak Publications, Mumbai, 2004.

Tandon, Prasash, "*Banking Century*", Penguin Books (India) Ltd., Himalaya Publishing House, 23, Kasturba Marge, New Delhi, 1989.

Vasant Desai, "*Banks and Institutional Management*", Himalaya Publications, 2006.

Vashisht, A. "*Public Sector Banks in India*", H.K. Publishers, Delhi.

Vasudevan, A. "*Central Banking for Emerging Market Economics*", Academic Foundation, New Delhi and "*Money & Banking*", 2003.

Vasudevan, T.M.C., Shyamji Mehrotra, Chandgadkar, D.M. "Co-operative Banking Operations", Macmillan India Limited, 2007.

Vogel, R.C. "*The Effect of Subsidised Agriculture Income on Income Distribution in Costa Rica*", West View Press, 1997.

Von Pischke, J.D., Wadams, D. and Gordon Donald (ed.), "*Rural Financial Markets in Developing Countries*", John Hopkims University Press, Baltimore, 1983.

Wood, G.D. and Sharif, T.A. (eds.), "*Who Needs Credit? Poverty and Finance in Bangladesh*", Zed Books, London, 1997.

Zacharias, K.D., Ravindranath, C.P., Kulkarni, P.R., Gopalakrishnan, B. "*Legal Aspects of Banking Operations*", Macmillan India Limited, 2005.

Zeihaml Valerie, A., Parasuraman, A., Bery Leonard, L. "*Delivering Quality Service*", The Free Press, A Division of Macmillan, Inc., New York, 1990.

Journals/Magazines

Anju Das, "Financial Inclusion an Economic Growth Driver", *Professional Banker,* The ICFAI University Press, February 2007.

Arindam Gupta and Joydeep Biswas, "Financial Liberalization and Indian Capital Market", *The Indian Journal of Commerce,* Vol. 59, No.2, April-June 2006.

Arun, T.G. and Turner, J.D., "Financial Sector Reforms in Developing Countries - The Indian Experience", *The World Economy,* 25(3), 2002, pp. 29-45.

Bhattacharyya, I., and Sensarma, R. "Signalling Instruments of Monetary Policy: The Indian Experience", *Journal of Quantitative Economics,* 2005, 3(2).

Dave, G.L. "Issues regarding measurement and reporting of corporation social performance", *The Indian Journal of Commerce*, Vol. XLIV, Part-II, No.167, 1991, pp. 92-96.

Dhanjagan, R.S. and Selvarajan, V. "Profitability of 14 Nationalised Banks: Examination of Recent Trends", *South Economist, October 15,*1983, pp. 9-13.

Guruswamy, "Corporation Social Responsibility particular in India", *The Indian Journal of Commerce*, Vol. XLVI, Part-II, No. 167, 1991, pp. 78-84..

Haranath, G. and Sathish, A.S. "The Impact of the Internet on Competition in the Banking Industry" by Porters' five force model': *The Journal of Banking information Technology and Management,* Vol. 4, No. 1, January–June 2007.

Jain, C.M., Shurveer S. Bhanawat Dharmalingam Venugopal, "Technology in Banks: Some Thoughts for the Future", "*Professional Banker*, The ICFAI University Press, August, 2004.

Jain, C.M., Shurveer S. Bhanawat, "Productivity of Human Resources in Banking Industry" *Indian Journal of Accounting,* Vol. XXXVI (1), December 2005.

Kaveri, V.S. "Performance Evaluation of Bank Branches", *The Journal of Indian Institute of Bankers*, October-December, 1982, 178-183.

Levine, Ross, 1997. "Financial Development and Economic Growth: Views and Agenda", *Journal of Economic Literature*, 35(2).

Mahendra, K, Goyath Shahadat Khan, "A Comparative Study of Corporate Disclosure issue in Emerging Economies", *The Journal of Accounting and Finance*, Vol. 21, Oct 2006–March 2007.

Matthias Gouthier, Catholic University of Eichstätt-Ingolstadt, Germany Stefan Schmid ESCP-EAP European School of Management, Germany Marketing Theory, Sage Publications Customers and Customer Relationships in Service Firms: The Perspective of the Resource-Based View, Vol. 3, No.1, 2003, pp. 19-43.

Mei Xue Patrick T. Harker, "Customer Efficiency Concept and Its Impact on e-Business Management", *Journal of Service Research*, University of Pennsylvania, Sage Publications, Vol. 4, No. 4, 2002, pp. 53-67.

Mellow, L.D. "Bank Credit for Weaker Sections: Performance and Prospects", *A Journal of Indian Institute of Banks*, April-June, 1980, pp. 87-95.

Mukherjee, K.P. "Nationalised Banks and Agricultural in Bihar", *Journal of Indian Institute of Bankers*, July-September, 1976, pp. 143-147.

Panda, N.M. "Uniformity in Social Reporting: A pragmatic approach for public sector enterprise in India", *The Indian Journal of Commerce*, Vol. XLVI, Part-II, No. 175, 1993, pp. 1-11.

Panda, Tapan Kumar, "Service Quality Value Alignment through Internal Customer Orientation in Financial Service – An Exploratory study in Indian Banks", Publisher "*Scholarly Article*", 2001.

Ramani, D. "The E-Payment System", *E-Business ICFAI journal,* May, 2007

Ranade, A. and Kapur, G. "Appreciating Rupee: Changing Paradigm?", *Economic and Political Weekly*, February 2003.

Rao & Pallavi, "Bankable Banks", *Business Standard*, New Delhi, August, 2004.

Samiuddin and Hifzur-Rehman, Survey of Social Reporting Practices in Indian Companies, *The Indian Journal of Commerce*, Part-II, 1991, pp. 34-38.

Satish Jayachandran, University of South Carolina; Kelly Hewlett, University of South Carolina; Peter Kaufman, Illinois State University; Journal of the Academy of Marketing Science, *Customer Response Capability in a Sense-and-Respond Era: The Role of Customer Knowledge Process, Vol. 32, No.3, 2004, pp. 19-33.*

Satyabhusan Dash, Ed. Bruning, Kalyan Ku Guin, "The moderating effect of power distance on perceived interdependence and relationship quality in commercial banking: a cross cultural comparison", *Journal of International Bank Marketing*", 2006, Vol. 24, Issue 5.

Shesunoff, A. "The wait is over for Internet Banking", *ABA Banking Journal*, New York, Vol.1, 91, 1999.

Srinvasan, R. and Sriram, M.S. "Micro Finance and Introduction", *IIMB Management Review*, June 2005.

Sharma, "A Case study for public interest reporting in India", *The Indian Journal of Commerce*, Vol. XLIV, Part-II, No. 167, 1991, pp. 70-72.

Shun Yin Lam Nanyang, Technological University; Venkatesh Shankar, University of Maryland; Krishna Erramilli, M. and Bysan Murthy, Nanyang Technological University; Customer Value, Satisfaction, Loyalty, and Switching Costs: An Illustration From a Business-to-Business Service Context, *Journal of the Academy of Marketing Science*, Vol. 32, No.3, 2004, pp. 29-31.

Varughese, A.G., "Retail Banking in India", *Professional Banker,* The ICFAI University Press, April 2005.

Voice of the People on the Lending Practices of Micro Finance Institutes in Krishna District of Andhra Pradesh mimeo APMAS.

Vinod Kumar. "*Profitability of Private Sector Banks in India-1969,* An unpublished Ph.D. Thesis submitted to Meerut University, Meerut, 1984.

Reports

Banking Sector Reforms: Rationale and Relevance (Rangarajan), 1998.

Government of India, 1998. "Report of the Committee on Banking Sector Reforms" (Chairman: M. Narasimham).

Indian Banks Association Bulletin, June 2005.

Mohanty, M.S., Gert Schnabel and Pablo Gracia-Luna, "Banks and Aggregate Credit: What New?" *BIS Papers*, No.28, August, 2006.

RBI "Agriculture Advances of Public Sector Banks - An Analysis", Vol. 28 (1994) Issue 4.p. 641 RBI Bulletin, Vol.(9) (1955).

RBI Bulletin, "Coping with Liquidity Management: A Practitioner's View", January, 2006a & June 2006c.

RBI Bulletin, "Economic Growth, Financial Deepening and Financial Inclusion", November 2007. "Development of Financial Markets in India".

RBI Bulletin, "Transforming Indian Banks: In Search for a Better Tomorrow," 2003.

____ , "Some Apparent Puzzles for Contemporary Monetary Policy", January 2005.

_______ , "Financial Sector Reforms and Monetary Policy: The Indian Experience", December 2006a.

_______, "Economic Growth, Financial Deepening and Financial Inclusion," July 2006b, 1305-1320 November.

——. "Reforms, Productivity and Efficiency in Banking: The Indian Experience", 279-293. March, 2006c.

Reddy, Y.V. "Credit Policy, Systems and Culture." RBI Bulletin, March, 2004.

——. "Credit Counseling: An Indian Perspective." RBI Bulletin, 1117-1120. October, 2006a.

——. "The Role of Financial Education: The Indian Case." RBI Bulletin, 1131-1135. October 2006b, 2006c, 2006d. "Rural Banking: Review and Prospects", RBI Bulletin, January.

——. Report of the Working Group on Introduction of Credit Derivatives in India (Convenor: B Mahapatra), Mumbai, March, 2003.

——. Report of the Working Group on Flow of Credit to the SSI sector (Chairman: A.S. Ganguly), Mumbai, September, 2004.

____ "Evolution of Central Banking in India." RBI Bulletin, June, 2006b.

—— 2006. Handbook of Statistics on the Indian Economy, 2005-06.

——. "Financial Stability: Indian Experience." RBI Bulletin, July, 2004.

____ "Monetary Policy and Exchange Rate Frameworks: The Indian Experience", April 2006b.

Report of Advisory Committee on Flow of Credit to Agriculture and Related Activities from Banking System (V.S. Vyas), RBI, Bombay, June 2004.

Report of the Committee on Banking Sector Reforms (Chairman: M. Narasimham), 1998.

Report of the Committee on Fuller Capital Account Convertibility, Tarapore Committee, 2006.

Report of the Committee on the Financial System. (Chairman: M. Narasimham), 1991.

Reserve Bank of India, Report on Trend and Progress of Banking in India, 1990-91.

Reserve Bank of India. "Report of the Committee on Fuller Capital Account Convertibility" (Chairman: S.S. Tarapore), July 2006.

Reserve Bank of India, Report of the Working Group on Call Money Market, 2003a.

——. Report of the Working Group on Instruments of Sterilisation (Chairperson: Usha Thorat), 2003b.

——. 2004a. Report on Currency and Finance, 2003-04.

——. 2004b. Annual Report, 2003-04.

——. 2005. Report of the Technical Group on Money Market, May.

——. 2006. Report of the Committee on Fuller Capital Account Convertibility (Chairman: S.S. Tarapore).

Talwar, R.K. "Government of India, Report of the Customer Services in Banks", 1997, pp. 9-46.

Unpublished Ph.D./M.Phil. Theses

Anil Kumar, "*Performance Evaluation of the 14 Nationalised Banks in India with special reference to priority sector-1970-80*", Ph.D. Thesis submitted to Nagarjuna University, 1985.

Ashok Kumar Bohra, "*An Analytical Study of the Role of Lead Banks in Rural Financing Rajasthan: A Case Study*", Ph.D. thesis submitted to Jodhpur University, Jodhpur, 1987.

Brahmanandam, G.N. "*Financing Small Scale Industries by Commercial Banks in Guntur District*", Ph.D. Thesis submitted to Nagarjuna University, Guntur, 1983.

Daniel, "*Role of Commercial Banks in Financing, the Schemes for Poverty, Self Employment Schemes to educate unemployed youth – Regional Study of Hubli, Dharwad Corporation Area in Karnakata State*", Ph.D. Thesis submitted to Karnataka University, 1987.

Kannaji Rao, "*Marketing of Services in Commercial Banks: A Study of Marketing operations of Andhra Bank*," Unpublished Ph.D. Thesis, Andhra University, Visakhapatnam, 1994.

Karunagrana, A. "*Performance Differentials of Foreign and Domestic Banks of India*", unpublished M.Phil. dissertation at C.D.S., submitted to Jawaharlal Nehru University, New Delhi, 1993.

Katilya Perumal, "*Deposits Mobilisation by Private Sector Banks*", An Unpublished Ph.D. Thesis submitted to Annamalai University, Annamalainagar, India, 1982.

Mamata, Ray. "*Regional Financial Institutions–Lending Behaviour and Path –Dependence, Madras 1921-1969*", Ph.D. Thesis, University of Calcutta, 2003.

Narayana, M.S. "*Social Banking*", Nagarjuna University, Guntur District, Ph.D. Thesis, 2002.

Radha, T. "*Impact of Banking sector reforms in Commercial Banks in India*", Andhra University, Visakhapatnam. Ph.D. Thesis, 2002.

Rajendra Bail, R. "*Deposit Mobilisation by Commercial Banks – A Study*", University Post-Graduate Centre, Khammam, Kakatiya University, 1986.

Rama Jyothsna Ratna Kumari, V. "*Priority Sector Lending by Commercial Banks – A Study of the Vysya Bank Ltd, Guntur District.*", Ph.D. Thesis submitted to Nagarjuna University, 1990, pp.193-194.

Rama Krishna, "Finances for Small Scale Industries in India", *Published Thesis of Bombay University, Aisa Pub. House, 1962, pp. 182-190.*

Robert, M. "*Profitability of Private Sector Banks in India since 1969*", An unpublished Ph.D. Thesis submitted to Madras University, Madras, 1992.

Satish Bahadur Mathur, "*Sickness in Small Scale Sector causes and cure with special reference to role of Commercial Banks*", Ph.D. Thesis submitted to Osmania University, Hyderabad, 1992.

Satyam Murthy, B. "*Profitability Trends in Scheduled Commercial Banks in India Changing the period 1970-82 – An Analytical Approaches,* An unpublished thesis submitted to the University of Bombay, Bombay, 1991.

Vinod Kumar. "*Profitability of Private Sector Banks in India-1969,* An unpublished Ph.D. Thesis submitted to Meerut University, Meerut, 1984.

News Papers

Brahmanad, P.R. "*Freeing Banks to Lend More*", The Hindu Business Line, October, 30, 1994.

Mritiunjoy Mohanty, "*Micro-credit, NGOs and Poverty Alleviation*", The Hindu, November 15th, 2006.

Subhasish Roy, "*New Challenges for Banks*", The Hindu Business Line, March 13, 2007.

Sundeep Sigh, "*Banks will increase not just your tenure but EMI too*" Indian Express, March 2007.

Sundaram, R. The Hindu - A Seminar on Customer Relationship Management held at the PKR Arts College for Women in Gobichettipalayam, focused on the need to develop customer banker relationship and improving Service Quality in the Banking Industry, dt. 09-01-2005.

Conference Papers

Balamohandas, V. "*Indian Banking: Yesterday, Today and Tomorrow*", Andhra Bank Endowment Lecture in Andhra University, Visakhapatnam, 19th July, 2005.

Mohan, Rakesh, Small-Scale Industry Policy in India, A Critical Evaluation, National Council of Applied Economic Research, New Delhi, 2004.

RBI Bulletin, "Monetary Policy Transmission in India", Paper presented at the BIS' Deputy Governor's Meeting on "Transmission Mechanisms for Monetary Policy in Emerging Market Economies – What is New?" *RBI Bulletin,* April 2007b.

Reddy, Y.V. "Development of Money Market in India", Address at the Fifth J.V. Somayajulu Memorial Lecture at Madras, February, 1999.

Reddy, Y.V. Economy: Challenges for Policy Makers", Speech at the Colegio de Economistas Madrid, Spain, November 23, 2000. Monetary and Financial Sector Reforms in India: A Central Banker's Perspective.

The 7th Bank Economic conference of India hosted by Central Bank of India, 1983 at Bombay.

Internet

www.rbi.org.in

www rbihist @vsnl.net

www:H:/icicibankltd.htm

www.andhra bank.com.

www.state bank of India.htm,

www.ingvysyabankltd.in.org.

Index

S

T

U

V

W